CISI

CW01424659

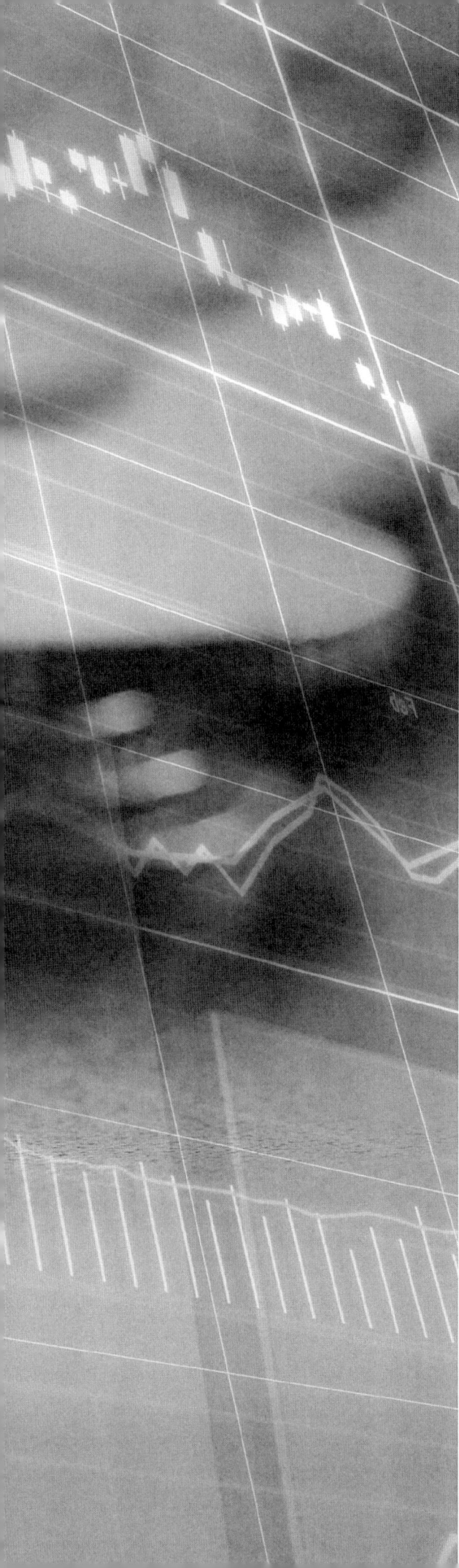

Capital Markets Programme

Securities

Edition 10, September 2014

This learning manual relates to syllabus
version 14.0 and will cover examinations from
11 December 2014 to 10 December 2015

Welcome to the Chartered Institute for Securities & Investment's Securities study material.

This workbook has been written to prepare you for the Chartered Institute for Securities & Investment's Securities examination.

Published by:
Chartered Institute for Securities & Investment
© Chartered Institute for Securities & Investment 2014
8 Eastcheap
London
EC3M 1AE
Tel: +44 20 7645 0600
Fax: +44 20 7645 0601

Email: customersupport@cisi.org
www.cisi.org/qualifications

Author:
Martin Mitchell FCSI

Reviewers:
Julie Harnum, MBA (FS)
Jon Beckett, Chartered MCSI

This is an educational manual only and Chartered Institute for Securities & Investment accepts no responsibility for persons undertaking trading or investments in whatever form.

While every effort has been made to ensure its accuracy, no responsibility for loss occasioned to any person acting or refraining from action as a result of any material in this publication can be accepted by the publisher or authors.

A learning map, which contains the full syllabus, appears at the end of this manual. The syllabus can also be viewed on cisi.org and is also available by contacting the Customer Support Centre on +44 20 7645 0777. Please note that the examination is based upon the syllabus. Candidates are reminded to check the Candidate Update area details (cisi.org/candidateupdate) on a regular basis for updates as a result of industry change(s) that could affect their examination.

The questions contained in this manual are designed as an aid to revision of different areas of the syllabus and to help you consolidate your learning chapter by chapter.

Learning manual version: 10.1 (September 2014)

Learning and Professional Development with the CISI

The Chartered Institute for Securities & Investment is the leading professional body for those who work in, or aspire to work in, the investment sector, and we are passionately committed to enhancing knowledge, skills and integrity – the three pillars of professionalism at the heart of our Chartered body.

CISI examinations are used extensively by firms to meet the requirements of government regulators. Besides the regulators in the UK, where the CISI head office is based, CISI examinations are recognised by a wide range of governments and their regulators, from Singapore to Dubai and the US. Around 40,000 CISI examinations are taken each year, and it is compulsory for candidates to use CISI learning manuals to prepare for CISI examinations so that they have the best chance of success. CISI learning manuals are normally revised every year by experts who themselves work in the industry and also by our Accredited Training partners, who offer training and elearning to help prepare candidates for the examinations. Information for candidates is also posted on a special area of our website: cisi.org/candidateupdate.

This learning manual not only provides a thorough preparation for the CISI examination it refers to, it is also a valuable desktop reference for practitioners, and studying from it counts towards your Continuing Professional Development.

CISI examination candidates are automatically registered, without additional charge, as student members for one year (should they not be members of the CISI already), and this enables you to use a vast range of online resources, including CISI TV, free of any additional charge. The CISI has more than 40,000 members, and nearly half of them have already completed relevant qualifications and transferred to a core membership grade. You will find more information about the next steps for this at the end of this manual.

With best wishes for your studies.

Ruth Martin, Managing Director

It is estimated that this manual will require approximately 100 hours of study time.

What next?
See the back of this book for details of CISI membership.

Need more support to pass your exam?
See our section on Accredited Training Providers.

Want to leave feedback?
Please email your comments to learningresources@cisi.org

Chapter One
Asset Classes

This syllabus area will provide approximately 28 of the 100 examination questions

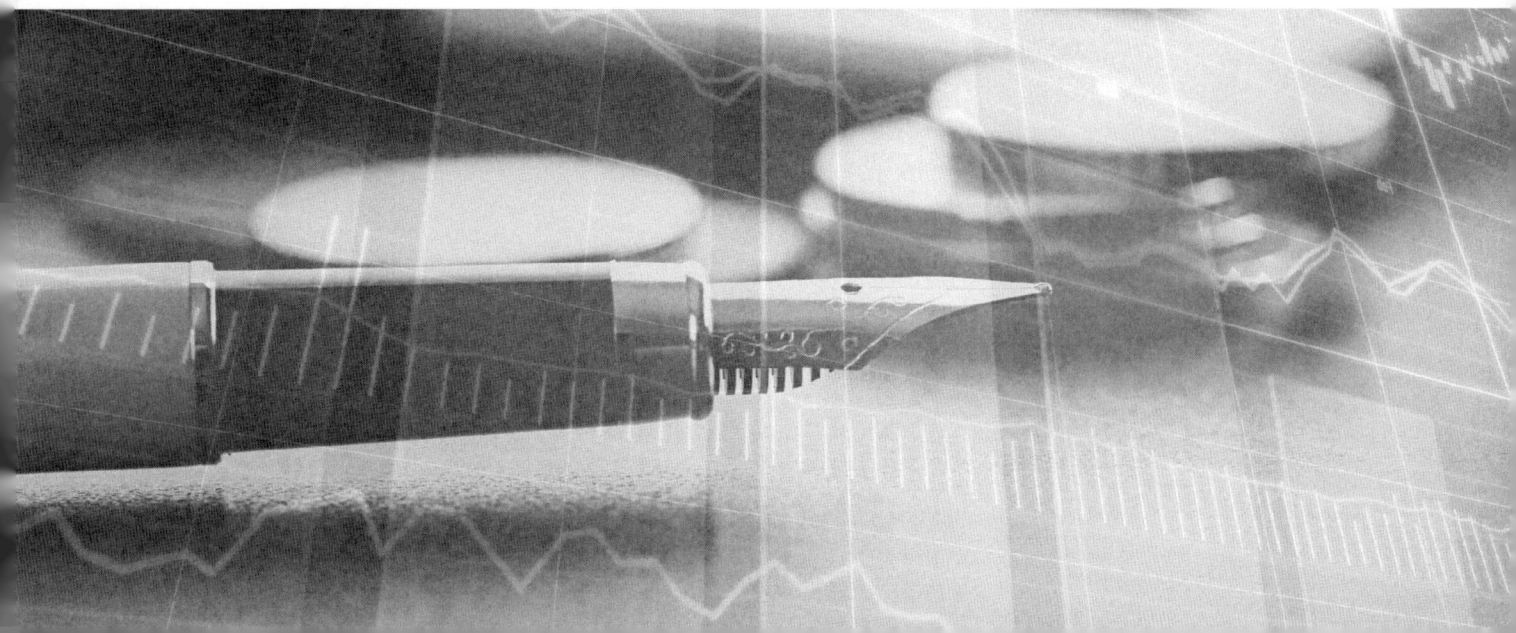

Introduction: Shares and Bonds

As a broad introduction to this chapter, it is useful to provide a reminder of the essential differences between the two major types of securities: shares (or equities) and bonds.

Investors in **bonds** essentially hold an IOU (I owe you) from another organisation, such as a company. Bond investors:

- loan money to an organisation in return for an **agreed rate of interest**;
- have an **agreed date** on which they get their money back;
- may have **legal recourse** against the issuer of the bond if the interest on the bond is not paid;
- may have **legal recourse** against the issuer of the bond if repayment does not occur.

Investors in **equities** hold a stake in the company. Equity investors:

- purchase a small piece, or **share**, of a company;
- cannot be certain that they will receive **dividend payments**;
- cannot be certain of the **amount of dividend** that they will receive;
- are liable to the **total amount** invested in fully paid shares.

Securities like shares and bonds take one of two main forms: registered and bearer. The form determines how an investor proves ownership of a particular investment. Bearer certificates, as their name suggests, means that the person that 'bears' (or holds) them, has title to them, like banknotes. Registered certificates, on the other hand, require that the holder be registered as an owner (on title) to the investment. The certificate itself is less important.

Example

Mr X owns 100 shares in Marks and Spencer plc. If a burglar breaks into Mr X's house and steals his share certificates, can he pretend that he owns the Marks and Spencer shares and sell them?

Fortunately, the answer is no.

The answer to the above example is no because most shares in the UK are held in **registered** form. This means that the certificate is simply evidence of ownership. The proof that counts is the name and address held on the company's share register.

Some securities come in **bearer** form. Unlike registered securities, the **physical possession** of the certificate is the proof of ownership. Bearer securities are easier to transfer since there is no register. They can simply be handed over. However, this does raise a few problems.

- It is difficult for the authorities to monitor ownership, making them attractive investments for **money launderers**.
- The issuing company has difficulty knowing to whom **dividends** or **interest payments** are to be sent.
- **Physical security** of the certificates is of greater importance and can increase the cost of holding the investment.

Examples of securities that are usually held in bearer form, which will be encountered later in this chapter, are **eurobonds** and **American depositary receipts (ADRs)**.

1. Shares

Learning Objective

1.1.1   Know the principal features and characteristics of ordinary shares and non-voting shares: 'A' ordinary shares; redeemable shares; partly paid shares and calls; ranking for dividends; ranking in a liquidation; voting rights; purpose of non-voting shares

Shares can be divided into two categories: ordinary shares and preference shares. Every company has ordinary shares in issue. In addition to the ordinary shares, some companies issue preference shares.

The performance of **ordinary shares** is closely tied to the fortunes of the company. Holders of ordinary shares have the right to **vote** on key decisions and receive **dividends**. Some companies issue more than one class of ordinary shares (perhaps distinguished as **A** ordinary shares and **B** ordinary shares) and one class may have more voting rights than the other. Occasionally one class of shares may not have any voting rights at all; these shares are described as non-voting shares.

Redeemable shares are shares offered by a company to shareholders that may be bought back by the company at its election. Companies are permitted to issue ordinary shares that can be redeemed, as long as conventional non-redeemable ordinary shares are also in issue.

Preference shares are less risky than ordinary shares and potentially less profitable. Holders generally do not have the right to vote on company affairs, but they are entitled to receive a **fixed dividend** each year (as long as the company feels they have sufficient profits). These dividends must be paid before any dividends are paid to ordinary shareholders, hence the term preference. Although preference shares tend to be non-voting, it is common for preference shareholders to become entitled to vote in the event of no dividend being paid for a **substantial** period of time. Precisely how long substantial is will be detailed in the company's constitution.

As just stated, companies have an obligation to pay dividends to preference shareholders before they pay a dividend, if any, to the ordinary shareholders. The **ranking of dividend payments** to the different kinds of preference shareholders is addressed in Section 1.2.

In the case of a winding-up or liquidation of a company, the priority and manner in which the owners of different tiers of the capital structure of that company are dealt with is referred to as the **liquidation ranking**.

The first and simple rule is that all shareholders or equity participants are subordinate to debt-holders. There are separate provisions for the priority of debt-holders, based upon the seniority of the debt, whether there is a fixed charge associated with the debt or a floating charge, and other covenants that were granted at the time of debt issuance.

Once the obligations to the debt-holders have been discharged, preference shareholders will take priority over the ordinary shareholders in the case of liquidation. From the proceeds following a liquidation event (which may be defined to include events other than a winding-up of the company), the preference shareholders will receive the par value of their shares before there is any distribution to the ordinary shareholders.

There is one further consideration which relates to the issuance of preference shares as part of early-stage or venture funding of a start-up company, and this is often referred to as **liquidation preference**.

The liquidation preference is the amount that must be paid to the preference shareholders, such as venture capital or **angel** investors, before distributions may be made to common stockholders. The liquidation preference is payable on either the liquidation of a company, asset sale, merger, consolidation or any other reorganisation resulting in the change of control of the start-up. It is usually expressed as a percentage of the original purchase price of the preferred, such as **2x**. Thus, if the purchase price of the preferred is £2 per share, a liquidation preference of 2x will be £4 per share. In effect, the preference shareholders will receive twice the nominal value of their shares upon liquidation before the proceeds (if any) are distributed to the ordinary shareholders.

1.1   Features of Ordinary Shares

The ordinary shareholders of a company take the greatest risk. If the company is liquidated, they will only receive any pay-out if there is money remaining after satisfying all of the other claims from creditors, bondholders and preference shareholders.

If the company is sufficiently profitable, the ordinary shareholders may receive dividends. Dividends for ordinary shareholders are proposed by the directors and generally ratified by the shareholders at the annual general meeting (AGM). However, the ordinary shareholders will only receive a dividend after any preference dividends have been paid.

Each ordinary share is typically given the **right to vote** at AGMs and extraordinary general meetings (EGMs), although sometimes voting rights are restricted to certain classes of ordinary shares. Such different classes of shares (often called **A** and **B** ordinary shares), are created to separate ownership and control, as illustrated in the following example:

Example ───

ABC plc is a small, successful, privately owned company with two founding directors, each holding 500 of its total issue of 1,000 ordinary shares. ABC needs more investment for expansion and the company agrees to issue 200 new shares to venture capitalists. However, the venture capitalists require control over the company as a condition of their investment.

This is achieved by creating a second class of ordinary shares. The founding directors' shares become non-voting A shares and the venture capitalists hold voting B shares. The result is that, although the founding directors hold non-voting A shares, they still own most of the company (1,000 shares of the total 1,200 shares), but control is now exercised by the venture capitalists since it is their B shares that have votes.

If they do have voting shares, each shareholder may, if they so wish, appoint a third party, or **proxy**, to vote on their behalf. A proxy may be an individual or group of individuals appointed by the board of directors of the company to represent the shareholders formally who send in proxy requests, to vote the represented shares in accordance with the shareholders' instructions.

Each ordinary share has a **nominal value**, which represents the minimum amount that the company must receive from subscribers on the issue of the shares. Occasionally, the company may not demand all of the nominal value at issue, with the shares then referred to as being **partly paid**. At some later date, the company will call on the shareholders to pay the remaining nominal value and make the shares fully paid.

Most ordinary shares are registered, meaning that the issuing company maintains a register of who holds the shares. This contrasts with bearer instruments when the issuer does not maintain a register – they can be transferred to other investors by simply handing over the certificate. For registered shares, a transfer requires a change of entry in the shareholders' register.

1.2   Types of Preference Share

Learning Objective

1.1.2   Understand the differences and principal characteristics of the following classes of preference shares: cumulative; participating; redeemable; convertible

Preference shares can come in a variety of forms.

- **Cumulative** – a cumulative preference shareholder will not only be paid this year's dividend before any ordinary shareholders' dividends, but also any unpaid dividends from previous years.
- **Participating** – one drawback of preference shares when compared to ordinary shares is that, if the company starts to generate large profits, the ordinary shareholders will often see their dividends rise, whereas the preference shareholders still get a fixed level of dividend. To counter this, some preference shares offer the opportunity to participate in higher distributions.
- **Redeemable** – these are preference shares that enable the company to buy back the shares from the shareholder at an agreed price in the future. The shares, from the company's perspective, are similar to debt. The money provided by the preference shareholders can be repaid, removing any obligation the firm has to them.
- **Convertible** – in this case, the preference shareholder has the right, but not the obligation, to convert the preference shares into a predetermined number of ordinary shares, eg, perhaps one preference share may be converted into two ordinary shares. This is another method of avoiding the lack of upside potential in the preference shares, compared to ordinary shares.

Note that a particular preference share may exhibit more than one of these features.

1.3   Tax Credits on UK Dividends

Learning Objective

1.1.3   Understand the purpose and use of dividends from the point of view of the investor and the treatment of the tax credit

1.3.1   The Purpose of Dividends for Investors

The payment of dividends represents a share in the profits made by a company; they are paid to a shareholder as a return for providing its risk capital.

For large, listed UK companies, dividends are usually paid twice a year and are expressed in pence per share. **Interim dividends** are paid in the second half of a company's accounting period while **final dividends**, usually the larger of the two payments, are paid after the end of the company's accounting year.

It is up to the company's directors to determine the amount of any dividend to be paid, if any, and their decision needs to be ratified by the shareholders at the AGM. Although shareholders can vote for the final dividend to be paid at or below its proposed rate, they cannot vote for it to be increased above this level.

The principal benefit of dividend payments from an investor's perspective is that there is a recurring income stream paid, which constitutes an integral part of the total return to an investor for allocating capital to that particular asset. Rather than having to realise the return by selling the asset and receiving a one-time capital gain, the investor has the opportunity at any time to do this, but in the interim there is a periodic return, paid as a dividend, which contributes to the investor's cash flow. For many classes of investors, who desire a regular income from their investments, the receipt of dividends is a vital part of the reward which is obtainable from taking the risk in making the investment.

However, there is no guarantee that the dividend will always be paid. An interesting example is BP, the UK-listed oil company, which had become very popular with pension fund investors due to its regular dividends. Following the Gulf of Mexico oil spill, the dividends ceased. Many long-established companies, which have a reliable history of paying dividends, and even of consistent growth in the dividends paid out, become relatively attractive to certain investors. There is a trade-off between the kinds of new enterprises, which may grow quickly and do not pay dividends, but where the capital gains can be considerable (as also is the possibility of losses), and more mature businesses. For holders of shares in such mature companies, there may be less scope for large capital gains, but the total return to an investor is much enhanced by the regular dividend income that can be obtained from the holding.

1.3.2   Dividend Taxation

If a UK resident receives dividends on shares held, they will probably be subject to UK income tax. However, dividends received are deemed to have already suffered tax at 10% before they are received. This is called the **tax credit** on the dividends.

The effect of this credit under the applicable rules is that no income tax is payable by any recipient of dividends whose total income is below the higher-rate tax level, after adding in the grossed-up value of those dividends. This means that the investor only has to pay further income tax if they are a higher-rate taxpayer (40%) or an additional-rate (45%) taxpayer.

It is not a proper credit, however, because a non-taxpayer cannot recover it.

When the dividends are received by higher-rate payers, additional tax of 25% of the amount received becomes payable, equivalent to 32.5% of the grossed-up value, minus the tax credit. Note that it is not 40%, as dividends are taxed differently from other income. For additional-rate taxpayers, additional tax of approximately 30.5% of the amount received becomes payable, equivalent to 37.5% of the grossed-up value, minus the tax credit.

This concept is illustrated in the following example.

Example

Mr X Ample is a higher-rate taxpayer (40%) and has 100 shares in ABC plc. ABC pays a dividend of 90p on each share. Mr Ample will receive £90 (90p x 100 shares) and, as far as the tax authority is concerned, he will be considered as having received £100 and having paid tax of £10 already. The £100 is referred to as the gross dividend and the £90 received is the net dividend.

Since he is a higher-rate taxpayer, Mr Ample will have to pay a further 25% of the net dividend to complete his tax due and payable.

In summary, Mr X Ample:

Received 90p x 100 shares the net dividend	=	£90
Tax credit = 10/100 of the net dividend	=	£10
Gross dividend entitlement	=	£100
Tax due = 32.5% (10% tax credit + 25% of net dividend payment received) x £100	=	£32.50
Deemed paid by way of the tax credit	=	(£10)
Remaining to be paid	=	£22.50

1.4   Stock Indices

Learning Objective

1.1.4   Understand how different indices are created and their purpose: types of index; purpose of weighted indices; purpose of unweighted indices; sector versus national indices; price return, total return and net total return indices

1.4.1   Stock Market Indices

A stock market index is a method of measuring the performance of a section of the stock market. Many indices are cited by news or financial services firms and are used as benchmarks to measure the performance of portfolios and to provide the general public with an easy overview of the state of equity investments. Their methods of construction may vary according to whether they are capitalisation weighted or not. Capitalisation weighted refers to market capitalisation which is the number of shares in issue multiplied by the price per share.

There are various organisations that have become specialists in constructing and maintaining equity indices. This includes managing their composition, making periodic adjustments and making index data public in real time and on an historical basis. For example, Standard & Poor's (S&P), a well-known credit ratings agency in the US, is the manager of the S&P 500 index. This index represents 500 companies that trade on the US markets that are said to be representative of the US market as a whole. The index is weighted according to the market share of each company in the markets and the index is used as benchmark; a basis for comparison to other markets or individual investments within the US markets. The Dow Jones Industrial Average (DJIA), also known as 'the Dow', is another example of a US index. The DJIA, however, is made up of only 30 companies that trade on US exchanges: either the NYSE or NASDAQ. The Dow is one of the oldest and most-referenced stock market indices in the world; companies in the DJIA include Disney, General Electric and Microsoft. In addition, the Russell organisation in the US is well known for maintaining several indices of US stocks, including the Russell 2000, which represents the smallest capitalisation issues trading in US markets.

In the UK, the best-known index is the FTSE 100 index, which consists of the 100 largest companies traded on the London Stock Exchange (LSE) as measured by market capitalisation. FTSE 100 companies represent about 81% of the market capitalisation of the whole LSE. The index is maintained by the FTSE Group, a company which originated as a joint venture between the *Financial Times* and the LSE. It is calculated in real time while the LSE is open for trading, and published every 15 seconds.

The FTSE 100 started at a base level of 1000 points in January 1984, meaning that the value of the 100 constituent companies at that time equated to 1000 index points. As the value of the constituent companies increases (or decreases), the FTSE 100 increases (or decreases). So, if the value of the constituents grew by 10% in the first nine months following the index publication date, the index would have risen to 1100 index points. At the time of writing, the FTSE 100 stood at 6,855 index points.

The following table provides information on the composition and geographical scope of many of the largest and best-known global equity indices.

Index name	Composition	Geographical scope
FTSE 100	Largest 100 UK companies listed on the LSE as measured by market capitalisation	UK and multinationals
DJIA	30 large US companies selected by a committee that includes the managing editor of the Wall Street Journal	US-domiciled multinationals
Nikkei Stock 225	225 large and regularly traded Japanese companies traded on the Tokyo Stock Exchange (TSE)	Japanese corporations
Hang Seng	50 companies listed on the Hong Kong Stock Exchange selected on the basis of market value, turnover and financial performance	Hong Kong/China
STOXX	A family of indices, based around the STOXX Global 1800 index that consists of 600 of the largest capitalisation companies from each of three regions – Europe, the Americas and Asia/Pacific	Global developed markets
MSCI World	A market capitalisation-based index including companies from 23 countries, totalling approximately 1,700 companies	Global developed markets
FTSE Eurofirst 300	The 300 largest listed companies by market capitalisation from across Europe	European-domiciled corporations
Cotation Assistée en Continu (CAC) 40 (CAC quarante)	A capitalisation-weighted measure of the 40 most significant values among the 100 highest market caps on Euronext Paris	French-domiciled companies; approximately 45% of its listed shares are owned by foreign investors, more than any other main European index
Deutscher Aktien IndeX (DAX)	The DAX includes the 30 major German companies trading on the Frankfurt Stock Exchange	The base date for the DAX is 30 December 1987 and it was started from a base value of 1,000. The Xetra system calculates the index
S&P 500	Standard & Poor's manages the composition of the index. The 500 constituents are selected by S&P from the largest cap stocks traded in the US	US-traded stocks which are multinational companies operating in global markets
FTSE All Share	The FTSE All Share index, originally known as the FTSE Actuaries All Share index, is a capitalisation-weighted index, comprising around 600 of more than 2,000 companies traded on the LSE	To qualify, companies must have a full listing on the LSE with a sterling or euro-dominated price on the Stock Exchange Electronic Trading Service (SETS)

Index name	Composition	Geographical scope
NASDAQ Composite	Covers issues listed on the NASDAQ stock market, with over 3,200 components, of which around 300 are non-US stocks. It is an indicator of the performance of stocks of technology companies and growth companies	Since both US and non-US companies are listed on the NASDAQ stock market, the index is not exclusively a US index
NASDAQ 100	Consists of the largest non-financial companies listed on the NASDAQ. It is a modified market value-weighted index	Does not contain financial companies, and includes companies incorporated outside the US

1.4.2   National and Sector Indices

A **national index** represents the performance of the stock market of a given nation and reflects investor sentiment on the state of its economy.

The most regularly quoted market indices are national indices, composed of the stocks of large companies listed on a nation's largest stock exchanges. The concept may be extended well beyond an exchange.

For example, the **Wilshire 5000 index**, the original total market index, represents the stocks of nearly every publicly traded company in the US, including all US stocks traded on the NYSE (but not ADRs or limited partnerships) and NASDAQ.

More specialised indices exist, tracking the performance of specific **sectors** of the market. Some examples include the **Wilshire US REIT**, which tracks more than 80 American real estate investment trusts, and the **Morgan Stanley Biotech index**, which consists of 36 American firms in the biotechnology industry.

1.4.3   Construction of Indices and Weighting

The construction of an index usually involves the **total market capitalisation of the companies weighted by their effect on the index**, so the larger stocks make a greater difference to the index than the smaller market cap companies.

However, the one major exception to this method of construction and calculation is the DJIA which is price-weighted rather than market capitalisation-weighted. Since it is such a widely quoted index, it is worth considering the method of calculation.

The sum of the prices of all 30 DJIA stocks is divided by the **Dow divisor**. The divisor is adjusted in case of stock splits, spin-offs or similar structural changes, to ensure that such events do not alter the numerical value of the DJIA. Early on, the initial divisor was composed of the original number of component companies, which made the DJIA at first a simple arithmetic average. The present divisor, after many adjustments, is less than one, meaning the index is larger than the sum of the prices of the components.

That is:

$$DJIA = \frac{\Sigma p}{d}$$

where:

p = the prices of the component stocks; and

d = the Dow divisor.

Events such as stock splits or changes in the list of companies composing the index, alter the sum of the component prices. In these cases, in order to avoid discontinuity in the index, the Dow divisor is updated so that the quotations right before and after the event coincide:

$$DJIA = \frac{\Sigma p_{old}}{d_{old}} = \frac{\Sigma p_{new}}{d_{new}}$$

The Dow divisor is currently 0.15571590501117.

The DJIA is often criticised for being a price-weighted average, which gives higher-priced stocks more influence over the average than their lower-priced counterparts, but takes no account of the relative industry size or market capitalisation of the components. For example, a $1 increase in a lower-priced stock can be negated by a $1 decrease in a much higher-priced stock, even though the lower-priced stock experienced a larger percentage change. In addition, a $1 move in the smallest component of the DJIA has the same effect as a $1 move in the largest component of the average. IBM and Visa are among the highest-priced stocks in the average and therefore have the greatest influence on it. Alternatively, General Electric and Pfizer are among the lowest-priced stocks in the average and have the least amount of sway in the price movement. Many critics of the DJIA therefore recommend the float-adjusted market-value-weighted S&P 500 or the Wilshire 5000 as better indicators of the US stock market.

All FTSE equity index constituents are fully free-float-adjusted, in accordance with FTSE's index rules, to reflect the actual availability of stock in the market for public investment. Each FTSE constituent weighting is adjusted to reflect restricted shareholdings and foreign ownership, so as to ensure an accurate representation of investable market capitalisation.

1.4.4 Total Return Index

A total return index is one that calculates the performance of a group of stocks, assuming that dividends are reinvested into the index constituents. For the purposes of index calculation, the value of the dividends is reinvested in the index on the ex-dividend date. Total return index data is not available at the stock level.

Some indices, such as the S&P 500, have multiple versions. These versions can differ, based on how the index components are weighted and on how dividends are accounted for. For example, there are three versions of the S&P 500 index:

*   **price return**, which measures the price performance and, therefore, disregards income from dividends;
*   **total return**, which measures the performance of both price return and dividend reinvestment; and

- **net total return**, which accounts for dividend reinvestment after the deduction of a withholding tax.

1.5 Free-Float and Market Capitalisation

Learning Objective

1.1.5 Know the implications of free-float on market capitalisation

The free-float of a public company is an estimate of the proportion of shares that are not held by large owners and that are not stock with sales restrictions (restricted stock that cannot be sold until it becomes unrestricted stock).

The free-float or a public float is usually defined as being all shares held by investors other than:

- shares held by owners owning more than 5% of all shares (those could be institutional investors, strategic shareholders, founders, executives, and other insiders' holdings);
- restricted stocks (granted to executives who can be, but don't have to be, registered insiders);
- insider holdings (it is assumed that insiders hold stock for the very long term).

1.5.1 Free-Float Factor

Under market capitalisation-weighted indices, the total market capitalisation of a company is included, irrespective of who is actually holding the shares and whether they are freely available for trading.

The free-float factor represents the proportion of shares that is free-floated as a percentage of issued shares and is then rounded to the nearest multiple of 5% for calculation purposes. To find the free-float capitalisation of a company, first find its market cap (number of outstanding shares x share price) then multiply by its free-float factor.

A free-float adjustment factor is introduced in the calculations of most of the major global equity indices.

For example, the following press release from STOXX ltd, which maintains the various Euro Stoxx indices, reflects the adjustment to the free-float factor for Volkswagen in 2008, and the changes that this had on various indices.

Example

ZURICH (October 28, 2008) – STOXX ltd, the leading provider of European equity indices, today announced it was to change Volkswagen's free-float factor to 0.3732 from 0.4963. This decision reflects the changes in the shareholder structure of Volkswagen and results in a lower weighting of Volkswagen in the respective indices.

Indices affected are the Dow Jones EURO STOXX 50, Dow Jones STOXX 600 Large, Dow Jones STOXX Total Market Large, Dow Jones STOXX Sustainability and its respective sub- and sector-indices. The adjustment will be effective as of the opening of trading on Friday, 31 October, 2008.

In essence, **free-float market cap** equates to the total value of buying all the shares of a particular company which are traded in the open market.

The free-float method is seen as a better way of calculating market capitalisation, because it provides a more accurate reflection of market movements and is more representative of the investable universe. When using a free-float methodology, the resulting market capitalisation is smaller than what would result from a full market capitalisation method. This is useful for performance measurement, as it provides a benchmark more closely related to what money managers can actually buy.

2. Debt Instruments

2.1 Features and Characteristics

Learning Objective

1.2.1 Know the principal features and characteristics of debt instruments

As outlined at the start of this chapter, a bond is essentially an I owe you (IOU) issued by an organisation (the borrower, or issuer), in return for money lent to it.

The **nominal value** (or **par value**) of a bond is the amount that the borrower will pay back to the holder of the bond on maturity.

The **issuer** of a bond is important. If a company issuing a bond is considered high-risk, it will need to offer a high rate of interest on the bond to attract investors. Some of the most significant issuers of bonds are governments; the bonds issued by the UK government are generally referred to as **gilts**.

The **redemption date** of a bond is the date on which the borrower agrees to pay back the nominal value of the bond. It is also referred to as the date on which the bond matures, ie, the **maturity date**.

A bond's **coupon** is the interest rate that the borrower pays to the bondholder, expressed as a percentage of the nominal value. In diagrammatic form:

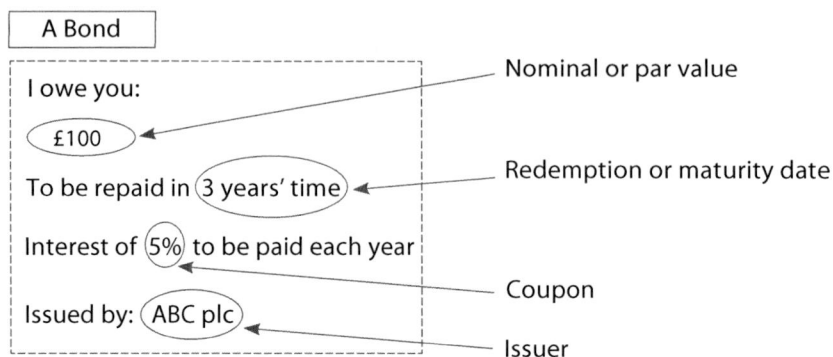

2.2   Yields

Learning Objective

1.2.2   Understand the uses and limitations of the following: flat yield; gross redemption yield (using internal rate of return); net redemption yield; modified duration in the calculation of price change

The yield is a measure of the percentage return that an investment provides. For a bond, there are three potential ways yields can be calculated: the flat yield (also known as the interest or running yield), the gross redemption yield (GRY) and the net redemption yield (NRY).

2.2.1   Flat Yield

The flat yield only considers the coupon and ignores the existence of any capital gain (or loss) if the bond is held through to redemption. As such, it is best suited to short-term investors, rather than those investors who might hold the bond through to its maturity and benefit from the gain (or suffer from the loss) at maturity.

The calculation of the flat yield is as follows:

$$\text{Flat yield} = (\text{annual coupon/price}) \times 100$$

For example, the flat yield on a 5% gilt, redeeming in six years and priced at £104.40, is:

$$(5\%/104.40) \times 100 = 4.79\%$$

Exercise 1

a.   Calculate the flat yield on a 4% gilt, redeeming in eight years and priced at £98.90
b.   Calculate the flat yield on a 7% gilt, redeeming in three years and priced at £108.60

The answers can be found at the end of this chapter.

Using the flat yield, it is simple to see how a change in interest rates will impact bond prices. If interest rates increase, investors will want an equivalent increase in the yield on their bonds. However, because the coupon is fixed for most bonds, the only way that the yield can increase is for the price to fall. This causes the inverse relationship between interest rates and bond prices. **When interest rates rise, bond prices fall and vice versa**.

2.2.2   Gross Redemption Yield (GRY)

The GRY is a fuller measure of yield than the flat yield, because it takes both the coupons and any gain (or loss) through to maturity into account. As such, it is more appropriate for long-term investors than the flat yield. In particular, because it ignores the impact of any taxation (hence GRY), this measure of return is especially useful for non-tax-paying long-term investors such as pension funds and charities.

The calculation of the GRY utilises the approach covered in Section 2.6 of this chapter to arrive at the present value of a bond. It is the **internal rate of return** (IRR) of the bond. The IRR is simply the discount rate that, when applied to the future cash flows of the bond, produces the current price of that bond.

Example

Assume that there is a US government bond known as 5% Treasury Note and that it will be repaid in exactly five years' time. Its current price is $115, and so if an investor buys $10,000 nominal of the bond today, it will cost $11,500, excluding brokers' costs. The annual interest payments will amount to $500, and its flat yield, using the formula in Section 2.2.1, will be 4.35%.

In five years' time, however, the investor is only going to receive $10,000 when the bond is redeemed, and so will make a loss of $1,500 over the period. If an investor were simply to look at the flat yield, it would give a misleading indication of the true return that they were earning. The true yield needs to take account of this loss to redemption and this is the purpose of the redemption yield.

Very simply, the investor needs to write off that loss over the five-year period of the bond, let us say at the rate of $300 per annum, so the annual return that the investor is receiving is actually $200 – the annual interest of $500 less the $300 written off. If you recalculate the flat yield, the return reduces to 1.74%.

The GRY, then, gives a more accurate indication of the return that the investor receives, and can be used to compare the yields from different bonds to identify which is offering the best return.

Example

The following data gives the prices of two US government stocks that are both due to be repaid in 2025. Consider the data and identify which is producing the best overall return assuming that the investor will hold the stock until redemption.

Stock Name	Redemption	Price	Flat Yield	GRY
7.625% Treasury	2025	148.72	5.127%	3.356%
6.875% Treasury	2025	140.44	4.895%	3.410%

As can be clearly seen, although the first stock appears to be the more attractive on the face of it, it will in fact produce a poorer overall return to the investor. An investor concerned with maximising their overall return will clearly pick the second.

2.2.3 Net Redemption Yield (NRY)

The NRY is similar to the GRY, in that it takes both the annual coupons and the profit (or loss) made through to maturity into account. However, it looks at the after-tax cash flows rather than the gross cash flows. As a result it is a useful measure for tax-paying, long-term investors.

The coupon received from UK government bonds (gilts) is generally taxable, but any gain made on redemption (or subsequent sale) is not taxable. This makes gilts with a low coupon attractive to higher-rate taxpayers, as the price will be lower than par, resulting in a substantial part of the return coming in the form of a tax-free capital gain.

2.2.4 Modified Duration

It is clear that, if interest rates rise, the price of fixed-rate debt instruments (eg, most gilts and many corporate debt issues) falls, and vice versa.

If an investor thinks that interest rates are going to fall in the future, then investing in fixed-interest securities is a good idea because, if the investor is correct, their price will rise.

However, some fixed-interest securities will be more responsive to a movement in interest rates than others. They will all rise in value when interest rates fall, but some will probably rise by more than others. The ones that rise the most are the more **volatile** securities.

All other things being equal, a lower-coupon bond will be more volatile to a change in interest rates than a higher-coupon bond. Similarly, all other things being equal, a longer-dated bond will be more responsive than a shorter-dated bond.

To identify which bonds are more volatile, **volatility measures** can be used.

The one measure of volatility required for this examination is **modified duration**.

The modified duration of a particular debt instrument shows the **expected change in its price**, given a **specified change in interest rates**. The higher the modified duration, the more the price of that instrument will move. The modified duration is the **approximate percentage change in the price of a bond brought about by a 1% change in the interest rate**.

Example _____

If a bond is priced at £95.84 and its modified duration is 1.02, what is the effect on the price after an increase in interest rates by one percentage point?

If interest rates rise by one percentage point, the bond's price will fall by 1.02/100 x £95.84 = £0.98.

If interest rates rise by one half of a percentage point, the bond's price will fall by 1.02/100 x £95.84 x 0.5 = £0.49.

_____

2.3 Interest and Conversion Premium Calculations

Learning Objective

1.2.3 Be able to calculate: simple interest income on corporate debt; conversion premiums on convertible bonds; flat yield; accrued interest (given details of the day count conventions)

2.3.1 Interest on Corporate Debt

Corporate debt (see Section 4) requires servicing by making regular interest payments. Interest on bonds is calculated by reference to the coupon rate, coupon frequency and nominal value. As seen in Section 2.2.1, the flat yield is calculated using the coupon rate and the bond's price.

Example

For example, XYZ plc has issued bonds paying an annual 8% coupon and maturing in 2020. The bonds are currently priced at 106, meaning investors have to pay £106 for each £100 of nominal value.

If an investor buys £5,000 nominal value, the bonds will cost £5,300 (£5,000 x 106/100).

The interest income for the investor each year will be the nominal value multiplied by the coupon rate – £5,000 x 8% = £400. If the interest was paid semi-annually, then the annual payment would be split into two portions.

The flat yield for the investor will be the coupon divided by the price expressed as a percentage, ie, (8%/106) x 100 = 7.55%.

2.3.2 Convertible Bonds

Some corporates issue bonds with conversion rights, known as **convertible** bonds. Convertible bonds give the holder of the bond the right, but not the obligation, to convert the bond into a predetermined number of ordinary shares of the issuer. Given this choice, the holder will choose to convert into shares if, at maturity, the value of the shares they can convert into exceeds the redemption value of the bond.

Because there is this potential advantage to the value of a convertible bond if the share price rises, and the downside protection of the redemption value if the shares do not perform well, convertible bonds generally trade at a **premium** to their share value. The calculation of the premium is shown by the following example.

Example

A convertible bond issued by XYZ plc is trading at £114. It offers the holder the option of converting £100 nominal into 25 shares. The shares of XYZ are currently trading at £3.90.

To calculate the premium, first work out the share value of the conversion choice.

For £100 nominal value, that is £3.90 x 25 shares = £97.50.

The bond is trading at £114, so the premium in absolute terms is £114 – £97.50 = £16.50.

It is more usual to express it as a percentage of the conversion value:

(£16.50/£97.50) x 100 = 16.9%

Exercise 2

The convertible bonds issued by ABC plc are trading at £110. Each £100 nominal value offers the holder the option of converting into 15 ordinary ABC shares. The ordinary shares of ABC are currently trading at £6.40. What is the conversion premium, expressed in percentage terms?

The answer can be found at the end of this chapter.

Convertible bonds enable the holder to exploit the growth potential in the equity, while retaining the safety net of the bond. It is for this reason that convertible bonds trade at a premium to the value of the shares they can convert into. If there were no premium, there would be an arbitrage opportunity for investors to buy the shares more cheaply via the convertible than in the equity market.

Usually, convertible bonds are issued where the price of each share is set at the outset, and that price will be adjusted to take into account any subsequent bonus or rights issues. Given the share price, it is simple to calculate the **conversion ratio** – the number of shares that each £100 of nominal value of the bonds can convert into.

$$\text{Conversion ratio} = \frac{\text{Nominal value}}{\text{Conversion price of shares}}$$

Example

£100 nominal value of a convertible bond is able to convert into shares at £4.46 each.

The conversion ratio is £100/£4.46 = 22.42 shares

If the issuing company had a 1 for 1 bonus issue, then the conversion price would halve and the conversion ratio would double.

2.3.3 Flat Yield

As already seen in Section 2.2.1, the simplest measure of the return used in the market is the flat (interest or running) yield. You will recall that the flat yield looks at the annual cash return (coupon) generated by an investment as a percentage of the cash price. In simple terms, what is the regular annual return that you generate on the money that you invest?

The calculation of the flat or running yield is provided by the formula:

$$\text{Flat Yield} = \frac{\text{Annual Coupon Rate}}{\text{Market Price}}$$

As already explained in Section 2.2.1, the flat yield only considers the coupon and ignores the existence of any capital gain (or loss) through to redemption. As such, it is best suited to short-term investors in the bond, rather than those investors that might hold the bond through to its maturity and benefit from the gain (or suffer from the loss) at maturity.

Limitations of Flat Yield

There are three key drawbacks for using flat yield as a robust measure in assessing bond returns.

- Since it only measures the coupon flows and ignores the redemption flows, when applicable, it is giving an incomplete perspective on the actual returns from the bond. A bond that has been purchased at a price away from redemption will be significantly undervalued when the par value is excluded from the calculation.
- The calculation completely ignores the timing of any cash flows and, because there is no discounted cash flow analysis, the time value of money (see Section 2.6) is completely overlooked.
- With floating rate notes (see Section 4.2), the return in any one period will vary with interest rates. If the coupon is not a constant, using a flat-yield basis for measuring returns becomes an arbitrary matter of selecting which coupon amount among many possible values to use for the calculation.

2.3.4 Accrued Interest

Listed bond prices are **flat prices**, which do not include accrued interest. The flat price is alternatively referred to as the **clean price**. Most bonds pay interest semi-annually. For settlement dates when interest is paid, the bond price is equal to the flat price. Between payment dates, however, the price of the bond will be the flat price plus the accrued interest.

Accrued interest is the interest that has been earned, but not paid, and is calculated by the following formula:

$$\text{Accrued interest} = \text{Coupon payment} \times \frac{\text{Number of days since last payment}}{\text{Number of days between payments}}$$

The following graphic shows how the **dirty price** (ie, the clean price plus accrued interest) of a bond fluctuates over the lifetime of the bond, in this case two years. The assumption made is that the flat price remains constant over the two years, but will actually fluctuate with interest rates and because of other factors. The flat price is what is listed in bond tables for prices. The accrued interest must be calculated according to the formula above. Note that the bond price steadily increases each day until reaching a peak the day before an interest payment, then drops to minimum immediately following the payment.

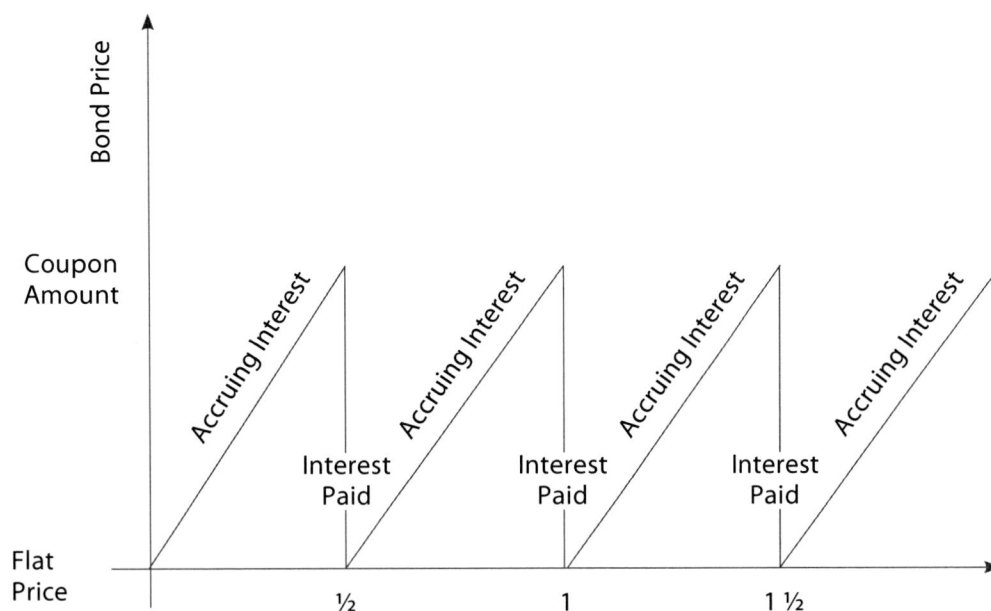

Calculating the Purchase Price for a Bond with Accrued Interest

Example

An investor purchases a corporate bond with a settlement date on 15 September with a face value of £1,000 and a nominal yield of 8%, which has a listed price of 100.25, and which pays interest semi-annually on 15 February and 15 August. How much should the investor pay for the bond, or in other words what is its dirty price?

The semi-annual interest payment is £40 and there were 31 days since the last interest payment on 15 August. Assuming the settlement date fell on an interest payment date, the bond price would equal the listed price: 100.25 x £1,000.00 = £1,002.50.

Since the settlement date was 31 days after the last payment date, accrued interest must be added. Using the above formula, with 184 days between coupon payments, we find that:

$$\text{Accrued Interest} = £40 \times \frac{31}{184} = £6.74$$

Therefore, the actual purchase price for the bond will be £1,002.50 + £6.74 = £1,009.24.

Day Count Conventions

Historically, different day count conventions have evolved in calculating accrued interest to take into account the fact that fixed-income securities have different coupon payment date characteristics, and to address issues related to the vagaries of the calendar system. The Julian calendar has uneven-length months and also has leap years, when once every four years there are 366 days to a year rather than 365. This has given rise to a number of different ways of counting the intervals between payments and even the length in days of the year assumed in the calculations.

There is no central authority defining day count conventions, so there is no standard terminology. Certain terms, such as **30/360**, **actual/actual** (ACT/ACT), and **money market basis** must be understood in the context of the particular market. There has also been a move towards convergence in the marketplace, which has resulted in the number of conventions in use being reduced.

In the example just cited, the day count is what can be called actual/actual, since the exact number of days between coupons and the actual days since the last payment have been used.

Common day count conventions that affect the accrued interest calculation are:

- **ACT/360 (days per month, days per year)** – each month is treated normally and the year is assumed to be 360 days, eg, in a period from 1 February 2011 to 1 April 2011 T is considered to be 59 days divided by 360.
- **30/360** – each month is treated as having 30 days, so a period from 1 February 2011 to 1 April 2011 is considered to be 60 days. The year is considered to have 360 days. This convention is frequently chosen for ease of calculation: the payments tend to be regular and at predictable amounts.
- **ACT/365** – each month is treated normally, and the year is assumed to have 365 days, regardless of leap year status, eg, a period from 1 February 2011 to 1 April 2011 is considered to be 59 days. This convention results in periods having slightly different lengths.
- **ACT/ACT – (1)** – each month is treated normally, and the year has the usual number of days, eg, a period from 1 February 2011 to 1 April 2011 is considered to be 59 days. In this convention leap years do affect the final result.
- **ACT/ACT – (2)** – each month is treated normally, and the year is the number of days in the current coupon period multiplied by the number of coupons in a year, eg, if the coupon is payable 1 February and August then on 1 April 2011 the number of days in the year is 362, ie, 181 (the number of days between 1 February and 1 August 2011) x 2 (semi-annual).

2.4 Spreads and Pricing Benchmarks

Learning Objective

1.2.4 Understand the concept of spreads: be able to convert spread over a government benchmark to a LIBOR-based spread; spread over government bond benchmark; spread over/under LIBOR; spread over/under swap

Commentators often refer to **spreads** in the bond markets. A spread is simply the difference between the yield available on one instrument and the yield available elsewhere. It is usually expressed in **basis points**, with each basis point representing 1/100 of 1%.

Spreads are commonly expressed as spreads over government bonds. For example, if a ten-year corporate bond is yielding 6% and the equivalent ten-year gilt is yielding 4.2%, the spread over the government bond is 6% − 4.2% = 1.8% or 180 basis points. This spread will vary, mainly as a result of the relative risk of the corporate bond compared to the gilt, so for a more risky corporate issuer the spread will be greater.

Spreads are also calculated against other benchmarks, such as the published interest rates represented by LIBOR (the London inter-bank offered rate). Because the government is less likely to default on its borrowings than the major banks (which provide the LIBOR rates), the spread of instruments versus LIBOR will generally be less than the spread against government bonds. If the equivalent LIBOR rate was 4.5%, the spread over LIBOR would be 6% − 4.5% = 1.5% or 150 basis points, compared to the 180 basis point spread over government bonds.

The use of a particular pricing benchmark is generally determined by the type of debt asset class. Also, specific features of a bond can mean that pricing off a benchmark security/rate becomes more difficult eg, a ten-year corporate bond, with a put/call feature, is unlikely to price off the ten-year gilt but rather a benchmark curve, as the estimate of the maturity of the corporate bond is unlikely to coincide with the specific maturity of the given gilt because of the put/call feature. (The term **pricing off** simply means the price/value of one thing – here a bond – being determined from the price/value of something else – here another bond.)

The comparison tends to be against one of three yields:

1. **Government bond yields** – benchmarks for corporate bonds are generally selected according to market convention; typically, the most recently issued government bond closest to the maturity of the corporate bond is selected as a benchmark. Gilts, bunds and US treasuries are the reference securities in the UK, Europe and US, respectively.
2. **LIBOR** (the London Inter-Bank Offered Rate) – the rate at which funds in a particular currency and for a particular maturity are available to one bank from other banks. LIBORs are gathered and published on a daily basis. At times of financial stress, such as during the banking crisis in the autumn of 2008, the spread between LIBOR and the applicable base rates can widen dramatically, which, in that instance, reflected the incapacity or unwillingness of banks to engage in normal money market activities.
3. **Swap rates** – there is a very active market in exchanging floating rates for fixed rates in the so-called **swaps market**. The rates available on swaps are also used as benchmarks against which to judge yields.

The spreads on a particular instrument could be above or below benchmarks as shown in the following example:

Example

UBX Inc is a well-established and highly rated company. It has bonds in issue that expire in approximately ten-years' time and are currently yielding 5.40%. Comparative government bonds (based on the ten-year T-Bond) are yielding 5.15%, and the ten-year swaps rate is 5.20%. Three month LIBOR is 5.54%.

The spreads can be summarised as follows:

- UBX bonds spread above government bonds = 25 basis points (5.40%–5.15%).
- UBX spread under LIBOR = 14 basis points (5.40%–5.54%).
- UBX bonds spread over swap rates = 20 basis points (5.40%–5.20%).

2.5 The Yield Curve

Learning Objective

1.2.5 Understand the role of the yield curve and the relationship between price and yield with reference to the yield curve (normal and inverted)

In the UK government bond market, there is a range of gilts available with various periods until maturity. By plotting the GRYs of these gilts on a graph, with yields on the **Y** axis and time to maturity on the **X** axis, a pattern emerges. The line of best fit across these points is the **yield curve**. It shows the yields available to investors in gilts over different time horizons. The yield curve is a visual representation of what is known as the **term structure of interest rates** – the relationship between yields on financial instruments from the same issuer, but with different periods (terms) to maturity.

The yield curve provides a useful tool for comparison – eg, if ten-year gilts yield 4%, then a ten-year corporate bond should provide a higher yield to compensate investors for the additional default risk they face.

2.5.1 The Normal Yield Curve

Typically, the shape of the yield curve is upward sloping to the right, as shown in the following diagram:

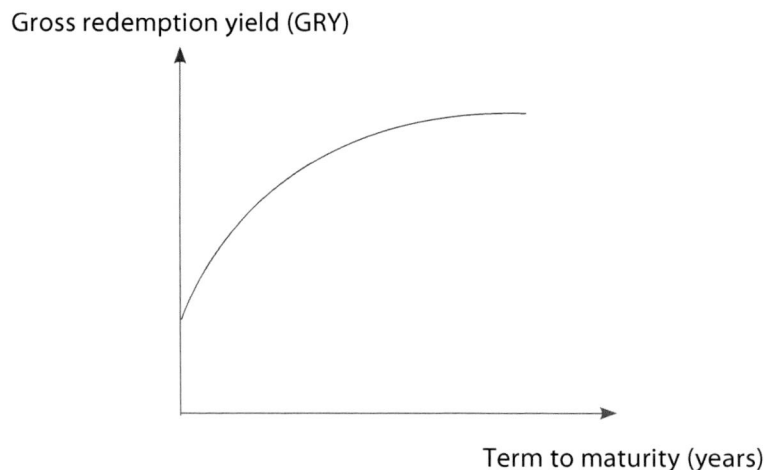

Gross redemption yield (GRY)

Term to maturity (years)

This is known as the normal yield curve, and its shape captures the fact that investors have a **liquidity preference**: they prefer more rather than less liquidity. As a result of this, they are willing to accept a lower yield on more liquid, short-dated gilts, and demand a higher yield on less liquid, longer-dated gilts. In other words, given the same coupon rate, the price of a short-dated gilt will be higher than a longer-dated gilt, resulting in a higher yield for the longer-dated gilt than the equivalent shorter-dated gilt.

2.5.2 The Inverted Yield Curve

Occasionally, the yield curve may not exhibit its normal, upward sloping to the right shape. Instead, it might be downward sloping to the right, known as the inverted yield curve.

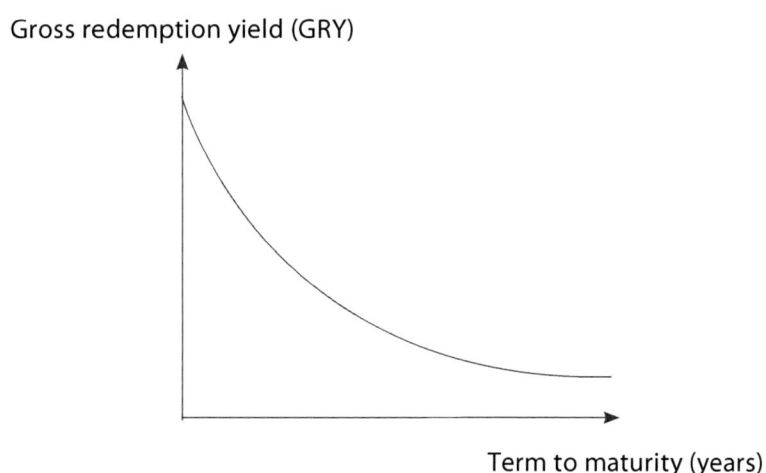

Gross redemption yield (GRY)

Term to maturity (years)

Clearly, in an inverted yield curve scenario, yields available on short-term gilts exceed those available on long-term gilts. This occurs when there is an expectation of a significant **reduction in interest rates** at some stage in the future. The consequence of this is that, when investing in longer-term gilts that will be outstanding when the interest rates fall, the investor is willing to accept a lower yield. For shorter-term gilts that will not be outstanding when the interest rate falls, the investor is demanding a higher yield.

The existence of an inverted yield curve does not remove any liquidity preference, but the impact of the anticipated interest rate fall outweighs the effect of the liquidity preference.

2.5.3 Inflation and the Yield Curve

Nominal yields are drawn from conventional debt instruments and include investors' anticipation of inflation. However, in addition to nominal yield curves, real yield curves can be observed from the yields on instruments that already include an uplift for inflation within their returns, such as the UK's index-linked gilts and the US Treasury Inflation Protected Securities (TIPS). More detail is provided on these instruments in Section 3.3 of this chapter. The difference between nominal yields and real yields reveals the term structure of inflation – the expectations for inflation in the future that is currently captured within bond prices.

Generally, if inflation is expected to increase, then the yields demanded by investors need to reward them for the anticipated inflation – so yields and the yield curve would be expected to rise. However, when the Bank of England (BoE) or another central bank, such as the US Federal Reserve, is concerned about inflationary pressures and increases short-term interest rates to counter the danger, the impact on medium- and long-dated bonds can be that the yields fall. This is because the investors have confidence that, in the medium term, inflationary pressures will be removed by the pre-emptive actions of the central bank.

2.6 The Present Value of a Bond

Learning Objective

1.2.6 Be able to calculate the present value of a bond (maximum two years) with annual coupon and interest income

Money has a **time value**. That is, money deposited today will attract a rate of interest over the term it is invested. £100 invested today at an annual rate of interest of 5% becomes £105 in one year's time. The addition of this interest to the original sum invested acts as compensation to the depositor for forgoing £100 of consumption for one year.

The time value of money can also be illustrated by expressing the value of a sum receivable in the future in terms of its value today, again by taking account of the prevailing rate of interest. This is known as the sum's **present value**. So, £100 receivable in one year's time, given an interest rate of 5%, will be worth £100/1.05 = £95.24 today, in present value terms. This process of establishing present values is known as **discounting**, the interest rate in the calculation acting as the discount rate.

In other words, the value today, or the present value, of a lump sum due to be received on a specified future date can be established by discounting this amount by the prevailing rate of interest.

To arrive at the present value of a single sum, receivable after n years, when the prevailing rate of interest is r, simply multiply the lump sum by the following:

$$1/(1 + r)^n$$

Referring back to the earlier example, £100 receivable in one year's time, given an interest rate of 5%, will have a present value of:

$$£100 \times 1/(1+r)^n = £100 \times 1/(1+0.05)^1 = £100 \times 1/1.05 = £100 \times 0.9524 = £95.24$$

If £100 were due to be received in two years' time, then the present value will be:

$$£100 \times 1/(1+r)^2 = £100 \times 1/(1.05)^2 = £100 \times 1/1.1025 = £100 \times 0.907 = £90.70$$

Present value calculations can also be used to derive the price of a bond, given the appropriate rate of interest and the cash flows.

Example

Imagine £100 nominal of a two-year bond paying annual coupons of 10%. Given an appropriate rate of interest, the sum of the present values will provide the logical price for the bond.

Using an interest rate of 5% per annum, the following present values emerge:

Time	Cash flow	Discount factor	Present value
End of year one	£10	$1/1.05$	9.52
End of year two	£110	$1/1.05^2$	99.77
Sum of the individual present values = price of the bond			£109.29

Exercise 3

What is the price of the same two-year 10% coupon paying bond if interest rates are:

a. 6%?

b. 4%?

The answers can be found at the end of this chapter.

3.   Government Debt

Most developed countries have active markets for bonds issued by their government, eg, 'gilts' are bonds issued by the UK government. They are issued to cover the government's borrowing needs, and the UK Treasury has created an executive agency called the Debt Management Office (DMO) to issue, service and manage gilts on its behalf.

As with other bonds, gilts are issued with a given nominal value that will be repaid at the bond's redemption date, and a coupon rate representing the percentage of the nominal value that will be paid to the holder of the bond each year. Obviously different gilts can have different redemption dates, and the coupon is payable at different points of the year (generally at semi-annual intervals).

Example

Gilts are denoted by their coupon rate and their redemption date, for example 6% Treasury Stock 2028. The coupon indicates the cash payment per £100 nominal value that the holder will receive each year. This payment is made in two equal semi-annual payments on fixed dates, six months apart. An investor holding £1,000 nominal of 6% Treasury Stock 2028 will receive two coupon payments of £30 each, on 7 June and 7 December each year, until the repayment of the £1,000 on 7 December 2028.

3.1 Classes of Government Debt

Learning Objective

1.3.1 Know the principal features and characteristics of the following classes of government debt: short-, medium-, long-dated; dual-dated; undated

Government debt, such as UK gilts, can be divided into three classes:

- Short-, medium- and long-dated;
- Dual-dated;
- Undated.

UK gilts include Treasury stocks and Exchequer stocks.

3.1.1 Short-, Medium- and Long-Dated Gilts

These are the simplest form of UK government bonds and constitute the largest proportion of the gilts in issue. They are fixed coupon gilts with fixed redemption dates and are subdivided by the DMO into three, based on the period of time that remains until the gilt matures:

- Short – less than seven years to redemption;
- Medium – between seven and 15 years to redemption;
- Long – over 15 years to redemption.

For example, 4.25% Treasury Gilt 2039 would be classified as a long-dated gilt because more than 15 years remain until it reaches its redemption date of 7 September 2039.

3.1.2 Dual-Dated Gilts

These gilts have two specified redemption dates and the DMO can choose to repay the gilt at any point between the two dates. The maturity classification applied to dual-dated gilts is short-, medium- or long-dated depending upon the time remaining to the later of the two dates.

Example

For example, 5% Treasury 2020–24 would enable the DMO to choose to redeem the gilt at the earliest in 2020, and at any time up to the later date of 2024.

What would make the government redeem early or late?

The answer is dependent upon the interest rates at the time. If in 2020 the interest rate that the DMO would have to pay to provide the funds for redemption were only 4%, then it would redeem at the earliest point – saving 1% per annum. By contrast, if the interest rate were greater than 5%, the DMO would not redeem, potentially, until it was forced to in 2024.

3.1.3   Undated Gilts

There are a small number of gilts for which the redemption is at the discretion of the government. Examples include 3.5% War Loan and 2.5% Consolidated Loan Stock (commonly referred to as 2.5% Consols). They are some of the oldest gilts outstanding and, because they all have comparatively low coupons, there is little incentive for the government to redeem them. On issue, these gilts did have a date attached to them, but it was followed by **aft**, meaning that it is the date on, or after, which the government can choose to redeem. If the government issued a gilt with a date of 2022 aft, it could choose to redeem the gilt at any stage after 2022, effectively making the gilt undated.

3.2   Interest Rates and Accrued Interest

Learning Objective

1.3.2   Understand the following features and characteristics of government debt: redemption price; interest payable; accrued interest; effect of changes in interest rates

Government bonds such as UK gilts specify a redemption value (the nominal value of the bond) that will be repaid at the end of the bond's life and a coupon. The coupon is the amount of interest paid to the holder of the bond each year.

Gilts are quoted on the basis of the price a buyer would pay for £100 nominal value.

Example

For example, 6% Treasury 2028 might be trading at 108, so a buyer will have to pay £108 for each £100 nominal value. Why would the buyer be willing to pay more than £100? The answer lies in the available interest rate across the financial markets. If the interest rate available on deposited funds is lower than the coupon rate on the gilt, then that gilt will be a relatively attractive investment and its price will be pushed upwards until the return it offers is in line with other investments.

This is an example of the inverse relationship between interest rates and bond pricing.

As interest rates across the financial markets decrease, the quoted price of gilts will increase. Conversely, if interest rates increase, the quoted price of gilts will decrease. In summary, there is an **inverse relationship** between gilts prices and interest rates.

Bonds' quoted prices are **clean prices**, ie, they are exclusive of interest. If a gilt is purchased between interest payments, an adjustment is made to arrive at the amount of cash required to cover the interest element as well. This is known as the **accrued interest** and it is the amount of interest earned by the bond's seller since the last coupon payment. The price including the accrued interest is the **dirty price**.

Accrued interest is paid to compensate the seller for the period during which the seller has held the gilt, but for which they receive no interest from the bond's issuer. Having only held the gilt for part of the interest-earning period, the seller receives a pro-rata share of the next coupon from the purchaser.

Example

If the £5,000 nominal of 6% Treasury 2028 mentioned above were sold by the original owner exactly halfway between the semi-annual coupon payments at a clean price of £126.46, the settlement would involve the following sum:

Clean price: £126.46 x £5,000/£100 = £6,323

Accrued interest: £5,000 x 6% x 6/12 x 0.5 = £75

Dirty price paid by the buyer to the seller = £6,398

Accrued interest in the gilts market is calculated using the **actual/actual day count convention**. In other words, the seller is compensated for the interest on the basis of the actual number of days that have elapsed since the last coupon was paid, divided by the total number of days in the actual period.

The DMO will pay the coupons to the registered holder of the gilt at each coupon payment date. However, because of the possibility of ownership changes just before the coupon payment date, there is a period prior to each coupon payment date when a gilt is dealt without entitlement to the impending coupon payment. This is known as the **ex-dividend** period. For most gilts this period is **seven working days** prior to the coupon payment date. For the remainder of the year the gilt is described as trading **cum-dividend.**

3.3   Index-Linked Debt

Learning Objective

1.3.3   Understand the following features and characteristics of index-linked debt: inflation – effects and measurement – RPI and CPI; index-linking; effect of the index on price, interest and redemption; return during a period of zero inflation

3.3.1   Inflation

Inflation can be one of the most significant obstacles to successful investing because the **real** value of the income flow from investments such as bonds and equities, as well as the long-term value of capital, is eroded by the effects of inflation and the decline in the purchasing power of the wealth that is created.

Controlling inflation is the prime focus of economic policy in most countries, as the economic costs inflation imposes on society are far-reaching. While there are many negative consequences, the two which are most pertinent for the typical investor are that:

*   inflation reduces the spending power of those dependent on fixed incomes, ie, pensions or fixed coupon investments such as a typical corporate bond (inflation-linked bonds are discussed in Section 3.3.3);
*   individuals are not rewarded for saving. This occurs when the inflation rate exceeds the nominal interest rate; that is, the real interest rate is negative.

Real interest rates are calculated as follows:

$$\text{Real interest rate} = [(1 + \text{nominal interest rate}) / (1 + \text{inflation rate})] - 1$$

So, the real return takes into account the inflation rate and in times of excessive inflation the real returns available may well become negative.

In addition to the specific impact of inflation on returns mentioned, the broader macro-economic problems associated with periods of high inflation are well illustrated by the difficulties faced by investors during the 1970s. This was a period of extremely high inflation, fuelled by surging commodity prices, especially crude oil, which led to demands from organised labour for higher wages. This pushed up the costs to producers of goods and services who, in turn, pushed on these additional costs to end-consumers in the form of higher prices. A vicious circle was created which required very drastic increases in short-term interest rates at the end of the 1970s – the base rates in the US and UK were approximately 20% as the 1980s began – and this caused widespread distress for asset prices. The 1970s was one of the worst periods on record for global stock market returns.

Inflation will also have negative implications for holders of bonds and fixed-income instruments. A major driver of bond prices is the prevailing interest rate and expectations of interest rates to come. Yields required by bond investors are a reflection of their interest rate expectations, which, in turn, will be largely influenced by expectations about inflation. For example, if inflation and interest rates are expected to rise, bond prices will fall to bring the yields up to appropriate levels to reflect the interest rate increases. To remain competitive, equities prices would also suffer.

3.3.2   Consumer Price Indices

Index-linked bonds are ones where the coupon and the redemption amount are increased by the amount of inflation over the life of the bond. The amount of inflation uplift is determined by changes in the **retail prices index (RPI)**.

The RPI, historically, has been the main inflation index used in the UK. It is calculated by looking at the prices of a basket of over 300 goods. The prices are then weighted to reflect the average household's consumption patterns, so those important items on which a lot of money is spent receive a higher weighting than peripheral items.

The index itself is based on movements in prices since a base period. The markets concentrate on the RPI figure, as it is a good indicator of the level of inflation and, consequently, government reaction to it. It also signals the need for potential increases in the yield paid on bonds in order to compensate for the erosion of real returns.

Two more refined measures introduced in the 1990s were the RPIX, which excludes the impact of mortgages, and the RPIY, which excludes mortgages and indirect VAT and local authority taxes.

Historically, the RPIX was used by the government in specifying its inflation target at a level of 2.5%. In December 2003, the Chancellor of the Exchequer changed the UK inflation target to a new base, the harmonised index of consumer prices (HICP), which was renamed the **consumer prices index (CPI)**.

The level of the new CPI inflation target for the BoE's MPC was set at 2% from 10 December 2003. Note that index-linked gilts continue to be calculated on exactly the same basis as in the past, with reference to the RPI, while pensions and benefits were linked to the CPI as of April 2011.

The CPI is calculated each month by taking a sample of goods and services that a typical household might buy, including food, heating, household goods and travel costs.

HICPs were originally developed in the European Union (EU) to assess whether prospective members of European Monetary Union (EMU) would pass the required inflation convergence criterion, and then to act as the measure of inflation used by the European Central Bank (ECB) to assess price stability in the euro area.

There are significant differences between the CPI and the RPI. The CPI excludes a number of items that are included in RPIX, mainly relating to housing. These include council tax and a range of owner-occupier housing costs such as mortgage interest payments, house depreciation, buildings insurance and estate agents fees.

The CPI covers all private households, whereas RPIX excludes the top 4% by income and pensioner households who derive at least three-quarters of their income from state benefits.

The CPI also includes residents of student hostels and foreign visitors to the UK. This means that it covers some items that are not in the RPI, such as unit trust and stockbrokers' fees, university accommodation fees and foreign students' university tuition fees. Although in most cases the same underlying price data is used to calculate the two indices, there are some specific differences in price measurement. For example, different methods are used in the CPI and RPI to adjust prices for quality improvements in new cars and personal computers.

The two indices are also calculated differently. The CPI uses the geometric mean to combine prices within each expenditure category, whereas the RPI uses arithmetic means. The different techniques used to combine individual prices in the two indices tend to reduce CPI inflation relative to RPIX. This is known as the formula effect. When the Chancellor announced the changeover in target measure, the annual rate of RPIX exceeded the CPI by more than 1%.

Producer prices indices (PPIs) measure inflationary pressures at an earlier stage in the production process. Input prices measure the change in prices going into the production process. This will include raw materials and other inputs. Changes in commodity prices will directly affect this number. Output or **factory gate** prices measure the changes in the price on goods as they leave the production process and enter the retail sector. There is obviously a very strong relationship with input price variation.

Historically, any changes in raw material prices have tended to pass on through the productive process and resulted in higher retail prices. In recent years, the generally low level of inflation, coupled with the more competitive nature of the labour market, has made it increasingly difficult for producers to pass on price increases. Consumers are now used to stable prices and are unable to force their wages up in order to compensate for the higher prices.

Summary of Inflation Measures

The main measures of inflation used in the UK are:

- **CPI** – based on an EU-wide formula allowing direct comparison of the inflation rate in the UK against that in the rest of Europe.
- **RPI** – an average measure of change in the prices of goods and services. Once published, it is never revised.
- **RPIX** – RPI excluding mortgage costs. It was previously the target measure for the MPC with a target of 2.5%
- **RPIY** – this is RPI with both mortgage costs and the impact of changes in taxation removed.
- **PPI** – this is based on measuring inflation further up the supply chain at the wholesale level and is sometimes known as 'factory gate' inflation.

A key advantage of the RPI and RPIX is their familiarity and credibility based on their longer history. It will be some time before the CPI becomes as widely recognised. The CPI's exclusion of most elements of owner-occupier housing costs lessens its relevance for some users, but this must be weighed against the significant difficulties encountered in measuring such costs appropriately, reflected in the absence of any international consensus in this area.

3.3.3   Index-Linked Bonds

Index-linked bonds (such as index-linked gilts) differ from conventional bonds in that the coupon payments and the principal are adjusted in line with a published index of price inflation, such as the RPI. This means that both the coupons and the principal on redemption paid by these bonds are adjusted to take account of inflation since the bond's issue. Assuming inflation is positive, the nominal amount outstanding of an index-linked bond is less than the redemption value the government will pay on maturity.

To calculate the inflation adjustment for a coupon payment, two index figures are required: that applicable to the bond when it was originally issued, and that relating to the point at which interest is paid. For UK gilts, the RPI figures used were originally those applicable eight months before the relevant dates (eg, for a December coupon, the previous April RPI data is used). This indexation lag was shortened for index-linked gilts issued after 2005 to just three months and it is the method for index-linking these gilts that is explained below.

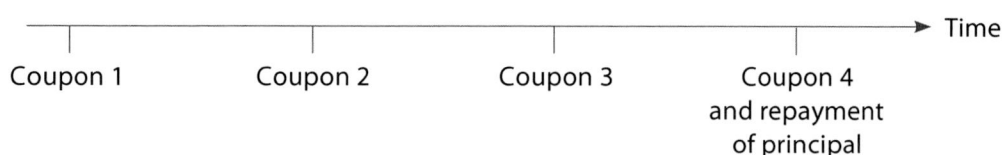

An **index ratio** is used to calculate the coupon payments and the redemption payment. The index ratio for each index-linked gilt measures the growth in the RPI since the gilt was first issued. For a given date, it is the ratio of the reference RPI applicable to that date divided by the reference RPI applicable to the original issue date of the gilt.

The reference RPI for the first calendar day of any month is the RPI for the month three months earlier (so the reference RPI for 1 June is the RPI for March, for the 1 July it is the RPI for April, etc). The reference RPI for any other day in the month is calculated by linear interpolation between the reference RPI applicable to the first calendar day of the month in which the day falls and the reference RPI applicable to the first calendar day of the month immediately following.

The nominal amount of the index-linked gilt is uplifted by the index ratio to give an updated principal. This principal is then used to generate the coupon payable by multiplying by the coupon payable. The coupon payments on an index-linked gilt that pays coupons half-yearly are based on the stated coupon divided by two and multiplied by the nominal value uplifted by the relevant index ratio. The redemption payment is based on the nominal value uplifted by the index ratio that applies at the point of redemption, namely the RPI three months prior to redemption divided by the RPI three months prior to the gilt's issue date.

Example

A 2% index-linked bond 2035 pays semi-annual coupons on 26 January and 26 June each year. An investor holding £20,000 nominal will receive 2% x 6/12 of £20,000 x index ratio each half-year.

At the redemption date in 2035, the investor will receive £20,000 uplifted by the index ratio that captures the RPI increases since issue.

Because these bonds are uplifted by increases in the relevant price index, they are effectively inflation-proof. In times of inflation, they will increase in price and preserve the purchasing power of the investment.

In a period of **zero inflation**, index-linked bonds will pay the nominal coupon rate with no uplift and simply pay back the nominal value at maturity. If there has been deflation rather than inflation over the period between issue and a coupon payment or redemption, index-linked gilts have no deflation floor, so the investor could receive less than the nominal coupon and less than the nominal value at maturity.

3.4 Separate Trading of Registered Interest and Principal of Securities (STRIPS)

Learning Objective

1.3.4 Know the basic purpose and characteristics of the strip market: result of stripping a bond; zero coupon securities

Zero coupon bonds (ZCBs) pay no interest: instead, they promise to pay just the nominal value at redemption. As there is no other possible form of return, investors will pay less than the nominal value when they buy zero coupon bonds, with their return coming in the form of the difference between the price they pay for the bond and the amount they receive when the bond is redeemed. The bond is said to be issued at a discount to its face value, with the discount providing all of the return on a ZCB.

STRIPS is an acronym of Separate Trading of Registered Interest and Principal of Securities. Stripping a bond involves trading the interest (each individual coupon) and the principal (the nominal value) separately. Each strip forms the equivalent of a ZCB. It will trade at a discount to its face value, with the size of the discount being determined by prevailing interest rates and time.

To illustrate how STRIPS work, a ten-year gilt can be stripped to make 21 separate securities: 20 strips based on the coupons, which are entitled to just one of the half-yearly interest payments; and one strip entitled to the redemption payment at the end of the ten years.

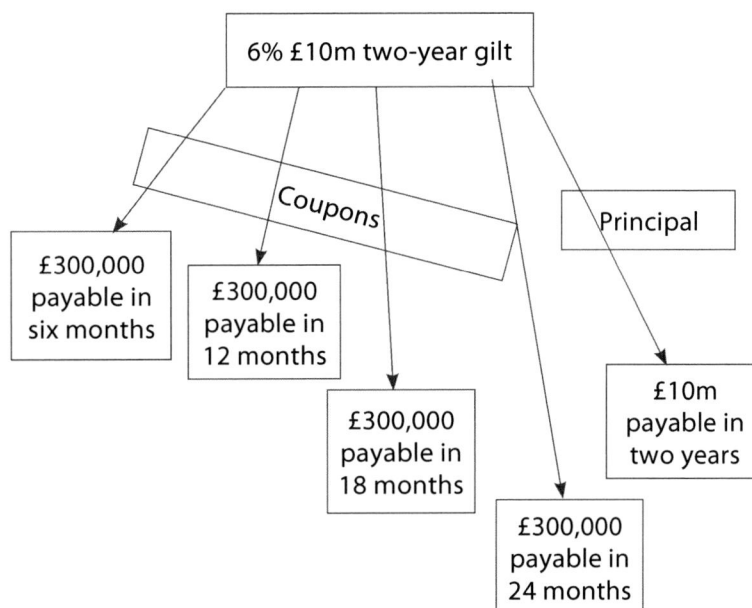

```
                        ┌──────────────────────────┐
                        │  6% £10m two-year gilt    │
                        └──────────────────────────┘

                     Coupons                    Principal

┌───────────┐  ┌───────────┐                         ┌───────────┐
│ £300,000  │  │ £300,000  │                         │ £10m      │
│ payable in│  │ payable in│                         │ payable in│
│ six months│  │ 12 months │                         │ two years │
└───────────┘  └───────────┘  ┌───────────┐          └───────────┘
                              │ £300,000  │
                              │ payable in│
                              │ 18 months │
                              └───────────┘  ┌───────────┐
                                             │ £300,000  │
                                             │ payable in│
                                             │ 24 months │
                                             └───────────┘
```

A STRIPS market has been developed in the UK within the gilts market. Only those gilts that have been designated by the DMO as **strippable** are eligible for the STRIPS market, not all gilts. Those gilts that are stripped have separate registered entries for each of the individual cash flows that enable different owners to hold each individual strip, and facilitates the trading of the individual strips. Only GEMMs (see Chapter 3, Section 4.1.1), the BoE or the Treasury are able to **strip** gilts.

The key benefits of strips are that investors can precisely match their liabilities, removing any reinvestment risk.

Example

An investor wants to fund the repayment of the principal on a £5 million mortgage, due to be paid in five years' time. Using gilts, there are three major choices:

1. The investor could buy a £5 million nominal coupon-paying gilt, but the coupons on this will mean that it will generate more than £5 million.
2. The investor could buy less than £5 million nominal, attempting to arrive at £5 million in five years. However, the investor will have to estimate how the coupons over the life of the bond can be reinvested and what rate of return they will provide – the estimate could well be wrong.
3. The investor could buy a £5 million strip. This would precisely meet their needs.

As seen in the example, strips can meet the liabilities of the investor precisely, removing any **reinvestment risk** that is normally faced when covering liabilities with coupon paying bonds. Furthermore, investors in gilt strips do not need to worry about the risk that the issuer of the bonds will default – gilt-edged securities are considered to be free of any default risk (also known as credit risk).

3.5   International Government Bonds

Learning Objective

1.3.5   Know the features and characteristics of French, German, Japanese and US bonds: settlement periods; coupons; terms and maturities

The following table highlights the way government bonds are referred to and classified across the major economies of the world, and the settlement period for any market transactions that may take place after the bonds are issued.

The coupon payment is the periodic payment that is made by the bond issuer to the bondholder, and the maturity represents the time period during which the coupon payments will be paid, at the conclusion of which the principal amount of the bond will be repaid to the holder.

Country	Name	Coupon Frequency	Maturity	Settlement Period
US	Treasury bonds (T-bonds)	Semi-annual	Over 10 years. The longest maturity is for 30 years and is known as the long bond.	T+1
	Treasury notes (T-notes)	Semi-annual	Two to 10 years	T+1
	Treasury bills (T-bills)	No coupon paid	Less than one year	Trade date
France	OAT	Annual	Seven to 30 years	T+2
	BTAN	Annual	Two to five years	
Germany	Bund	Annual	Over 10 years	T+2
	Bobl	Annual	Five years	
	Schatz	Annual	Up to two years	
Japan	Japanese Government Bond (JGB)	Semi-annual	Long (10 years, most common), super-long (20 years)	T+3*

* Although settlement timetables in global markets are generally moving towards T+2, at the time of writing, no announcement had been made regarding any changes to the settlement periods for Japanese bonds. In view of the uncertainty, these details will not be examined. Candidates should check the Candidate Update section of the CISI's website for further announcements.

4. Corporate Debt

Corporate debt is simply money that is borrowed by a company that has to be repaid. Generally, corporate debt also requires servicing by making regular interest payments. Corporate debt can be subdivided into money borrowed from banks via loans and overdrafts, and money borrowed directly from investors in the form of IOU instruments, typically bonds.

Debt finance is less expensive than equity finance because investing in debt finance is less risky than investing in the equity of the same company. The interest on debt has to be paid before dividends, so there is more certainty. Additionally, if the firm were to go into liquidation, the holders of debt finance would be paid back before the shareholders received anything.

For investors in bonds, firms like Standard & Poor's capture the comparative riskiness of the issuer and the bond in their credit ratings.

However, raising money via debt finance does present dangers to the issuing company. The lenders are often able to claim some or all of the assets of the firm in the event of non-compliance with the terms of the loan – in the same way that a bank providing mortgage finance would be able to claim the property as security against the loan.

4.1 Secured Debt

Learning Objective

1.4.1 Understand the principal features and uses of secured debt: fixed charges and floating charges; asset-backed securities; mortgage-backed securities; covered bonds; securitisation process; role of the trustee

Investors in corporate debt face the risk that the issuer will not be able to pay the interest and/or the principal amount. When this happens, it is known as **default**.

One way for the corporate borrower to lessen the risk of default is to issue secured debt, when the debt offers the company's assets as a guarantee. There are two ways of doing this:

- **fixed charge** – the debt carries a fixed charge over a particular company asset, eg, a building;
- **floating charge** – the debt is secured against a group of the company's assets; in the event of default, a floating charge crystallises over the available assets.

Bonds issued with a fixed charge are generally referred to as **debentures**.

4.1.1 Asset-Backed Securities (ABSs)

Asset-backed securities (ABSs) are bonds that are backed by a particular pool of assets. These assets can take several forms, such as mortgage loans, credit card receivables and car loans. Major banks, such as Citigroup, Bank of America and JP Morgan Chase, commonly securitise the amounts owed by their customers on their credit cards.

The assets provide the bondholders' security, since the cash generated from them is used to service the bonds (pay the interest), and to repay the principal sum at maturity. Such arrangements are often referred to as the **securitisation** of assets. The name 'securitisation' reflects the fact that the resulting financial instruments used to obtain funds from the investors are considered, from a legal and trading point of view, as securities.

Diagrammatically:

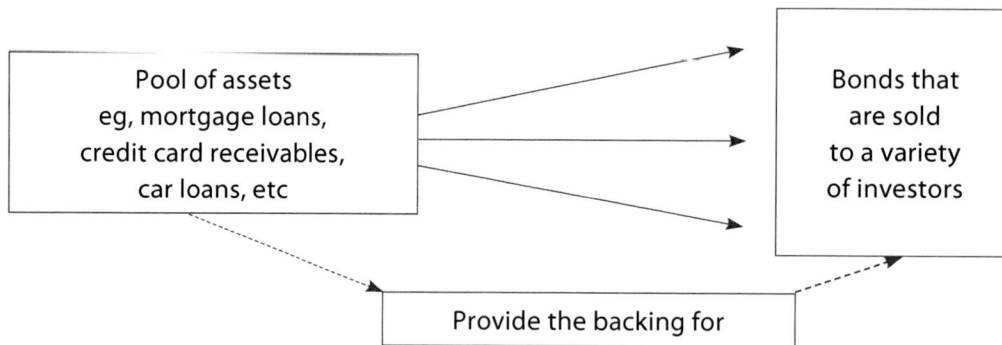

4.1.2   Mortgage-Backed Securities (MBSs)

Mortgage-backed securities (MBSs) are one example of ABSs. They are created from mortgage loans made by financial institutions like banks and building societies. MBSs are bonds that are created when a group of mortgage loans are packaged (or pooled) for sale to investors. As the underlying mortgage loans are paid off by the homeowners, the investors receive payments of interest and principal.

The MBS market began in the US, where the majority of issues are made (or guaranteed) by an agency of the US government. The Government National Mortgage Association (commonly referred to as **Ginnie Mae**), the Federal National Mortgage Association (**Fannie Mae**) and the Federal Home Loan Mortgage Corporation (**Freddie Mac**) are the major issuers. These agencies buy qualifying mortgage loans, or guarantee pools of such loans originated by financial institutions, then they securitise the loans and issue bonds. Some private institutions, such as financial institutions and house builders, issue their own mortgage-backed securities.

As with other ABSs, MBS issues are often subdivided into a variety of classes (or **tranches**), each tranche having a specific priority in relation to interest and principal payments. Typically, as the underlying payments on the mortgage loans are collected, the interest on all tranches of the bonds is paid first. As loans are repaid, the principal is first paid back to the first tranche of bondholders, then the second tranche, third tranche, and so on. Such arrangements will create different risk profiles and repayment schedules for each tranche, enabling the appropriate securities to be held according to the needs of the investor. Traditionally, the investors in such securities have been institutional investors, like insurance companies and pension funds, although some are attracting the more sophisticated individual investor.

4.1.3 Further Details in Relation to Asset-Backed Securities

The investors in ABSs have recourse to the pool of assets, although there may be an order of priority between investors in different tranches of the issue.

The precise payment dates for interest and principal are dependent on the anticipated and actual payment stream generated by the underlying assets and the needs of investors. ABSs based on a pool of mortgage loans are likely to be longer-dated than those based on a pool of credit card receivables. Within these constraints, the issuers of asset-backed securities do create a variety of tranches to appeal to the differing maturity and risk appetites of investors.

ABSs often utilise a **special purpose vehicle** (**SPV**) in order to lessen the default risk that investors face when investing in the securities. This SPV is often a trust, and the originator of the assets, such as the bank granting the mortgage loans, sells the loans to the SPV and the SPV issues the asset-backed bonds. This serves two purposes:

1. The SPV is a separate entity from the originator of the assets, so the assets leave the originator's financial statements to be replaced by the cash from the SPV. This is often described as an **off-balance-sheet** arrangement because the assets have left the originator's balance sheet.
2. The SPV is a stand-alone entity, so, if the originator of the assets suffers bankruptcy, the SPV still remains intact with the pool of assets available to service the bonds. This is often described as **bankruptcy remote** and enhances the creditworthiness of asset-backed securities, potentially giving them a higher rating than the originator of the assets.

Diagrammatically:

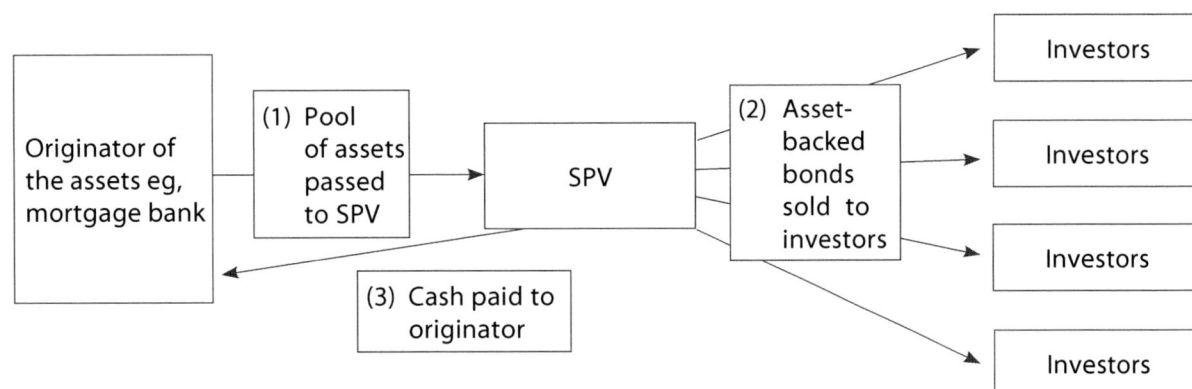

In instances when no SPV is created, the asset-backed bonds are simply referred to as 'covered bonds', referring to the pool of assets that provide the 'cover' to the bondholder. So, with covered bonds, the assets are retained on the balance sheet of the issuing entity, such as a bank, rather than transferred to an SPV. Indeed, when an SPV is used and the assets become distressed, or if there is no market for determining the value of the assets held in the SPV, as was the case during the sub-prime crisis of 2007–08, the originator of the securitisation instruments may decide to transfer the troubled assets fully on to its primary balance sheet to become covered bonds.

4.1.4 The Role of the Trustee in Secured Debt

Trustee for Secured Debt Issues

In the UK a secured debt transaction is called a debenture, whereas the term is not so widely used in the US; the term ABS is more commonly used.

When a corporation either in the UK or US issues a secured debt, it is invariably the case that a trustee will be appointed when debenture stock is issued to a large number of persons.

The mechanics of the process are that, under the terms of the trust deed, the property of the company is mortgaged to the debenture holders to secure payment of the money owing under the debenture(s). However, there is a contract or deed of trust put in place between the company and the trustees. The trustee holds the benefit of the covenant by the company to repay the monies on trust for the holders of the debenture stock.

Under English law, the trustee has wide discretionary powers, whereas under US law its responsibilities are usually clearly defined. The main trustee roles for a UK debenture trustee are:

- **Note Trustee** – is appointed to represent the interests of holders of issues of securities, while providing guidance to the issuer.
- **Security Trustee** – for issues secured by a pledge of securities or other properties, the security is charged in favour of the trustee for the benefit of the various secured parties. The governing documents dictate the order of priority of payments among the entitled parties.
- **Share Trustee** – holds the shares in an issuing SPV in order to ensure off-balance-sheet treatment for the originator of the transaction. Sometimes these SPVs are domiciled in offshore jurisdictions.
- **Successor Trustee** – this role played by a trustee is provided for banks which need to resign because of conflicts of interest (especially in connection with defaulted or bankrupt issues) or when work requirements exceed the bank's capacity.

Benefits of a Trust Deed

The security and all enforcement powers in respect of the trust deed are vested in the trustee as a single entity acting on behalf of all the debenture holders. This enables a coherent enforcement procedure, rather than a series of disparate actions by different debenture holders. This is an advantage to the individual holders as it ensures organised action and parity of treatment. The trust deed would usually provide that all holders are paid proportionately, and a single action by the trustee prevents some holders recovering and not others. It is also an advantage to the company as it means it does not have to defend a series of actions for what might be a trifling breach of any one provision.

Costs

Administration and enforcement by the trustee will be less costly than numerous parties dealing with the company.

Representation of the Interests of the Bondholders

To make bonds a marketable security, a trustee is assigned to represent the interests of the bondholders. The corporate trustee is usually a bank or a trust company, and, although the trustee is paid by the issuing corporation, it represents the interests of the bondholders.

Before marketing a debenture the issuer, often using the corporate trustee as its agent, will engage the services of a **credit rating agency** to assess the creditworthiness of the issuer and the likelihood that all of the terms of the debenture offering are likely to be fulfilled. This engagement is to represent the interest of the bondholders as just stated above, but in this instance there is more cause for a potential conflict of interest, as the credit rating agency will be paid by the issuer, while its ratings are provided to advise the bondholders of the security risk of the offering. Credit ratings agencies will never specifically recommend any particular offering, but the ratings which are provided (these are discussed in Section 4.4) are relied upon by many investors.

The corporate trustee must keep track of all bonds sold, verifying that the amount issued is not greater than what is stated in the indenture and making sure that the corporation complies with all covenants – which are the terms of the indenture – while the bond issue is outstanding.

For instance, the indenture may stipulate that the corporation maintains a certain percentage of assets over liabilities, or that the corporation does not take on too much debt. Adherence to the covenants of the indenture is one of the principal roles of the trustee.

The trustee may either provide services for the payment of dividends and the cash management function, or it may appoint a separate custodian for the purpose.

4.2 Unsecured Debt

Learning Objective

1.4.2 Understand the principal features and uses of unsecured debt: subordinated; guaranteed; convertible bonds

Unsecured debt is not secured against any of the company's assets, so the holder has no special protection against default. To compensate the holder for the additional risk, the coupon on an unsecured bond, or the interest on unsecured bank borrowing, will be higher than on equivalent secured borrowings.

Subordinated debt is not secured and the lenders have agreed that, if the company fails, they will only be repaid once other creditors have been repaid if there is enough money left over. Unsecured debtholders, however, would still be repaid prior to shareholders, as 'lenders' are always repaid before 'owners' in an insolvency. Interest payments on subordinated borrowings will be higher than those on equivalent unsecured borrowings that are not subordinated. This is simply because of the additional default risk faced by subordinated lenders.

Guaranteed debt is when a guarantee is provided by someone other than the issuer. The guarantor is typically the parent company, or another company in the same group of companies as the issuer.

Convertible bonds give the holder of the bond the right, but not the obligation, to convert into a predetermined number of ordinary shares of the issuer.

The following table summarises the characteristics of subordinated, guaranteed and convertible bonds as compared to an unsecured bond issued by the same company.

	Subordinated bond	Guaranteed bond	Convertible bond
Normal life	No difference: typically seven to 30 years to maturity		
Ranking in a liquidation	Below unsecured bonds	Alongside other unsecured bonds	Alongside other unsecured bonds
Risk and rating	Greater risk of default, so a lower credit rating	Risk dependent upon the guarantor's own financial standing, so a higher credit rating	No difference from unsecured bonds
Coupon	Likely to be higher than unsecured bonds	Likely to be lower due to the guarantee	Potentially lower due to the upside potential of the share price
Benefits to the issuer	Attractive regulatory treatment for financial institution issuers	Guarantor is lowering the cost of the debt finance	Upside potential of the shares restricts the cost of the debt and the possibility of conversion lowers the risk of eventual repayment

Fixed-coupon bonds are issued with a fixed rate of coupon. If interest rates rise, the fixed coupon becomes less attractive and the price of the bond falls. The opposite is true of an interest rate fall. As for government bonds, the interest is always calculated by reference to the nominal value of the bond, so a £1,000 nominal 5% ABC corporate bond will pay £50 per annum to the holder.

Floating rate bonds or **notes** are bonds when the coupon rate varies. The rate is adjusted in line with published, market interest rates. The published interest rates that are normally used are based on the London InterBank Offered Rate (LIBOR). There are a number of LIBORs published each day for different currencies and different periods, such as three-month US dollar LIBOR and six-month sterling LIBOR. LIBORs reflect the average rates at which banks in London offer loans to other banks. Until recently, LIBORs were published by the British Bankers' Association (BBA), using quotes provided by a panel of banks; however, after regulatory investigations discovered that LIBORs were being manipulated by a number of those banks, the UK regulator, the Financial Conduct Authority (FCA), concluded that the administrator of LIBOR required regulatory authorisation. LIBORs are now calculated by Intercontinental Exchange Benchmark Administration ltd, an entity owned by exchange operator Intercontinental Exchange Inc, and regulated by the FCA.

Floating rate notes typically add a margin to the LIBOR rate, measured in basis points, with each basis point representing one hundredth of 1%. A corporate issuer may offer floating rate bonds to investors at three-month sterling LIBOR plus 75 basis points. If LIBOR is at 4%, the coupon paid will be 4.75%, with the additional 75 basis points compensating the investor for the higher risk of payment default.

4.3   Debt Seniority

Learning Objective

1.4.4   Understand the seniority of debt and how they rank in default: senior; subordinated; mezzanine; payment in kind notes (PIK)

Debt issued by companies can come in a variety of forms including bonds and bank borrowing. When there are multiple forms of debt, the issuer will have to establish some sort of order as to which debt will be serviced and repaid first, in the event of the company's encountering financial difficulties. In broad terms the seniority of the debt falls into three main headings:

- **Senior** – senior debt or bonds have a claim that is above that of the more junior forms of borrowing and the equity of the issuer in the event of liquidation.
- **Subordinated** – subordinated debt- or bondholders have accepted that their claim to the issuer's assets ranks below that of the senior debt in the event of a liquidation. As a result of accepting a greater risk than the senior debt, the subordinated borrowing will be entitled to a greater rate of interest than that available on the senior debt.
- **Mezzanine and payment in kind (PIK)** – the mezzanine level of debt, if it exists at all, will be even more risky than the subordinated debt. It will rank below other forms of debt but above the equity in a liquidation. As the most risky debt, the mezzanine debt will offer a greater rate of interest than the subordinated and senior levels of debt. Mezzanine borrowing can be raised in a variety of ways – one example is the issue of **PIK notes**. PIK notes are simply ZCBs that are issued at a substantial discount to their face value. When they are repaid, the difference between the redemption value and the purchase cost provides the investor's return.

It should be noted that each of the three main categories can themselves contain sub-categories such as **senior secured**, **senior unsecured**, **senior subordinated** and **junior subordinated**. In practice, the various rating agencies look at debt structures in these narrower terms. Seniority can be contractual as the result of the terms of the issue, or based on the corporate structure of the issuer.

4.4 Credit Ratings

Learning Objective

1.4.3 Understand the principal features and uses of credit ratings: rating agencies; impact on price; uses and risks of credit enhancements; difference between investment grade and sub-investment grade bonds

Bondholders face the risk that the issuer of the bond might default on their obligation to pay interest and the principal amount at redemption. This so-called **credit risk** or **default risk** – the probability of an issuer defaulting on their payment obligations and the extent of the resulting loss – can be assessed by reference to the independent credit ratings given to most bond issues.

There are a significant number of credit ratings agencies around the world, some of whom specialise in particular regions or particular types of company. However, the three most prominent agencies that provide these ratings are Standard and Poor's (S&P), Moody's and Fitch Ratings. Bond issues subject to credit ratings can be divided into two distinct categories: those accorded an investment grade rating and those categorised as non-investment grade or speculative. The latter are also known as **high-yield** or **junk** bonds. Investment grade issues offer the greatest liquidity. The table following provides a comprehensive survey of the credit ratings available from the three agencies.

Although the three rating agencies use similar methods to rate issuers and individual bond issues, essentially by assessing whether the cash flow likely to be generated by the borrower will comfortably service, and ultimately repay, its debts, the rating each gives sometimes differs, though not usually significantly so.

Moody's	S&P	Fitch Ratings	Description
Investment Grade			
Aaa	AAA	AAA	Prime
Aa1	AA+	AA+	High grade
Aa2	AA	AA	
Aa3	AA–	AA–	
A1	A+	A+	Upper-medium grade
A2	A	A	
A3	A–	A–	
Baa1	BBB+	BBB+	Lower-medium grade
Baa2	BBB	BBB	
Baa3	BBB–	BBB–	

Non-Investment Grade			
Ba1	BB+	BB+	
Ba2	BB	BB	Speculative
Ba3	BB−	BB−	
B1	B+	B+	
B2	B	B	Highly speculative
B3	B−	B−	
Caa1	CCC+		Substantial risks
Caa2	CCC		Extremely speculative
Caa3	CCC−	CCC	In default with little prospect for recovery
Ca	CC		
	C		
C	D	D	In default

Occasionally, issues such as ABSs are credit-enhanced in some way to gain a higher credit rating. The simplest method of achieving this is through some form of insurance scheme that will pay out should the pool of assets be insufficient to service or repay the debt.

In 2007–08, a financial crisis arose from ABSs such as MBSs. The credit rating agencies were criticised for the generous ratings they had attached to some of these securities. As a result, it is likely that there will be increased regulatory oversight of the credit rating process in the future.

4.5 Commercial Paper (CP)

Learning Objective

1.4.5   Know the principal features and uses of commercial paper: issuers, including CP programmes; investors; discount security; unsecured; asset-backed; rating; normal life, method of issuance; role of dealer

As mentioned in Section 3.4, ZCBs pay no interest: instead, they promise to pay just the nominal value at redemption. As there is no other possible form of return, investors will pay less than the nominal value when they buy these instruments, with their return coming in the form of the difference between the price they pay for the bond and the amount they receive when the bond is redeemed. The bond is said to be issued at a **discount** to its face value, with the discount providing all of the return.

Discount securities, such as ZCBs, are attractive investments for an investor looking for a fixed sum at some set date in the future. Because the investor is looking for a set, single sum, he does not want to worry about reinvesting regular interest payments.

Commercial paper (CP) is a money market instrument, issued by a company. The money market is the term for the market involving cash deposits and short-term instruments that are issued with less than one year to their maturity. CP is the corporate equivalent of a government's Treasury bill (see Section 5.1). CP is issued at a **discount** to its nominal value and can have a maturity of up to one year in Europe and 270 days in the US; however, it is common to find in both territories that CP will be issued for three months.

Large companies issue CP to assist in the management of their liquidity. Rather than borrowing directly from banks, these large entities run CP programmes that are placed with institutional investors.

The various companies' CP is differentiated by credit ratings – when the large credit rating agencies assess the stability of the issuer.

Asset-backed CP is a short-term investment vehicle with a maturity that is typically between 90 and 180 days. The security itself will be issued by a bank or other financial institution, and the notes are backed by physical assets such as **trade receivables**. Finance companies will typically provide consumers with home loans, unsecured personal loans and retail automobile loans. These receivables are then used by the finance company as collateral for raising money in the CP market. Some finance companies are specialist firms that provide financing for purchases of another firm's products. For example, the major activity of Ally Financial Inc (formerly the General Motors Acceptance Corporation (GMAC)) is the financing of purchases and leases of General Motors' vehicles by dealers and consumers.

It is perhaps important to mention that a missed payment by an issuer of a CP for as little as one day can lead to bankruptcy proceedings. Issuers take great care to repay the principal on the due day.

4.5.1   Commercial Paper (CP) Issuance and the Role of Dealers

There are two methods of issuing CP. The issuer can market the securities directly to a buy-and-hold investor as with most money market funds. Alternatively, it can sell the paper to a dealer, who then sells the paper in the market. The dealer market for CP involves large investment banks and other financial services firms such as gilts dealers and other participants in the money markets.

Unlike bonds or other forms of long-term indebtedness, a CP issuance is not all brought to market at once. Instead, an issuer will maintain an ongoing CP programme. It advertises the rates at which it is willing to issue paper for various terms, so buyers can purchase the paper whenever they have funds to invest. Programmes may be promoted by dealers, in which case the paper is called **dealer paper**. Larger issuers, especially finance companies, have the market presence to issue their paper directly to investors. Their paper is called **direct paper**.

Direct issuers of CP are usually financial companies that have frequent and sizeable borrowing needs and find it more economical to sell paper without the use of an intermediary. In the US, direct issuers save a dealer fee of approximately five basis points, or 0.05% annualised, which translates to $50,000 on every $100 million outstanding. This saving compensates for the cost of maintaining a permanent sales staff to market the paper. Dealer fees tend to be lower outside the US.

CP entails credit risk, and programmes are rated by the major rating agencies. Because CP is a rolling form of debt, with new issues generally funding the retirement of old issues, the main risk is that the issuer will not be able to issue new CP. This is called **rollover risk**. Many issuers obtain credit enhancements for their programmes. These may include a line of credit or other alternative source of financing.

Since the banking crisis of 2008, the primary issuance of CP and the secondary market for CP have been severely curtailed, and it has been difficult to persuade dealers to **make a market** in it.

5.   Money Markets

As well as issuing bonds to fund the government's long-term borrowing needs, developed countries also manage the liquidity needs of the government. This is done primarily through issuing short-term IOUs known as **Treasury bills** (T-bills).

5.1   Definition, Uses and Principal Features

Learning Objective

1.5.1   Understand the features and characteristics of Treasury bills: issuer; purpose of issue; minimum denomination; normal life; no coupon and redemption at par

Treasury bills (T-bills) are short-term loan instruments, guaranteed by the government, with a maturity date that is generally between one and 12 months later. For example, the UK's DMO can issue T-bills with maturities of one month (approximately 28 days), three months (approximately 91 days), six months (approximately 182 days) or 12 months (up to 364 days). They pay no coupon and, consequently, are issued at a **discount** to their nominal value, with the discount representing the return available to the investor.

In the UK, T-bills are issued at weekly **auctions**, known as **tenders**, held by the DMO on the last business day of the week (usually a Friday). These tenders are open to bids from a group of eligible bidders which include all of the major banks. The bids are tendered competitively – only those bidding a high enough price will be allocated any T-bills and they will pay the price that they bid. The bids must be for a minimum of £500,000 nominal of the T-bills, and above this level bids must be made in multiples of £50,000. In subsequent trading, the minimum denomination of T-bills is £25,000.

Since they are guaranteed by the government, T-bills provide a very secure investment for market participants with short-term investment horizons. The return on a T-bill is wholly dependent upon the price paid.

For example, if a purchaser paid £990,000 for £1,000,000 nominal of a three-month T-bill, the return will be the gain made of £10,000. As a percentage of invested funds the return is: £10,000/£990,000 x 100 = 1.01% over three months.

5.2 Repo Markets

Learning Objective

1.5.2 Understand the basic purpose and characteristics of the repo markets: repo; reverse repo; documentation; benefits of the repo market

A repo is a **sale and repurchase agreement**. It is legally binding for both buyer and seller. For example, a gilt repo is a contract in which the seller of gilts agrees to buy them back at a future specified time and price. In effect, a gilt repo is a means of borrowing using the gilt as security, as illustrated in the following diagram:

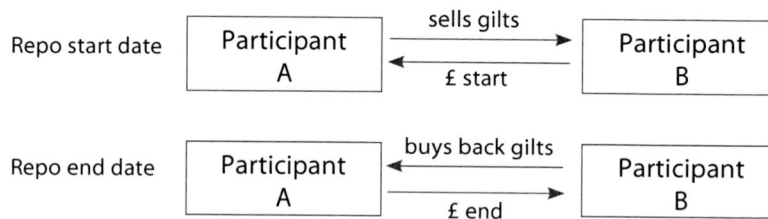

In the above diagram, both parts of the repo transaction are agreed between the participants at the outset: Participant A has entered into a repo transaction, Participant B has entered into a **reverse repo** agreement.

The amount of cash paid over by Participant B at the start of the repo will be less than the amount paid over to Participant B at the end of the repo period. The difference between the two amounts, expressed as a percentage, is the effective interest rate on the repo transaction. It is usually referred to as the **repo rate**.

The obvious benefit to Participant A is that they are able to raise finance against the security of the gilts that they hold – potentially a relatively cheap source of short-term finance. If Participant B is considered a conventional bank simply providing finance, then the benefit of using the repo is the security gained by holding the gilts. However, Participant B may be a gilt-edged market maker (GEMM) that has sold gilts that it does not hold. The repo transaction enables the GEMM to access the gilts that it requires to meet its settlement obligations. In this way, gilt repo facilitates the smooth running of the secondary market in gilts.

The smooth running of the gilts market is further assisted by the DMO's **standing repo facility**. This enables any GEMM, or other DMO counterparty, to enter into a reverse repo arrangement with the DMO, perhaps to cover a short position in gilts. They must first sign the relevant documentation provided by the DMO and then are able to request any amount of a gilt above £5 million nominal. This facility is for next-day settlement, and the facility can be rolled forwards for up to two weeks. The DMO does charge a slightly higher than normal repo rate for firms accessing the standing repo facility.

Although the gilts market has been used as an example, it should be noted that the use of repos is an important liquidity provider for the debt markets as a whole.

6. Eurobonds

Learning Objective

1.6.1 Understand the principal features and uses of eurobonds: issued through syndicates of international banks; immobilised in depositories; accrued interest; ex-interest date; interest payments

Essentially, eurobonds are international bond issues. They are a way for an organisation to issue debt without being restricted to their own domestic market. The currency of issue does not need to be the euro,; eurobonds can be issued in any currency as long as it is different to the currency of the place from which they are issued. So, if a eurobond was issued out of London, it would need to be in a currency other than £ sterling, such as the euro or the US dollar. If a eurobond was issued out of Frankfurt, it would need to be in a currency other than the euro, such as the US dollar or Japanese yen. They are generally issued via a syndicate of international banks. Generally, eurobond issuers do not keep a record of the holders of their bonds; the certificates themselves are all that is needed to prove ownership. This is the concept of bearer documents, when the holder of the certificates (the bearer) has all the rights attached to ownership. Eurobonds are issued in bearer form and, because they are issued internationally, they are largely free of national regulation. Eurobonds have been innovative in their structure to accommodate the needs of issuers and investors. There are **plain vanilla**, fixed-coupon bonds that normally pay the coupons once a year. Additionally, there are ZCBs and other forms of eurobond such as floating rate bonds and bonds with coupons that increase over time (**stepped bonds**).

An absence of national regulation means that eurobonds can pay interest gross, making the buyer responsible for paying their own tax and avoiding **withholding tax** (WHT) (tax being withheld in the country of origin). Initially, eurobonds were aimed at wealthy individuals, but as the market has grown they have increasingly become investments held by institutional investors.

As bearer documents, it is important that eurobonds are kept safe, and this is often achieved by holding the bonds in depositaries, particularly those maintained by Euroclear and Clearstream. When the bonds are deposited in these organisations they are described as being **immobilised**. Immobilisation does not mean that the bonds cannot be transferred in secondary market transactions, it simply means that the bonds are safely held within a reputable depositary and a buyer is likely to retain the bonds in their immobilised form.

As the eurobond market has grown, a self-regulatory organisation has been formed that oversees the market and its participants – the International Capital Market Association (ICMA).

Settlement and accrued interest conventions have been established for the secondary market. Settlement is on a T+2 basis and accrued interest is calculated on the basis of 30 days per month and 360 days per year (30/360 basis).

The following table highlights the major features of eurobonds:

Feature	Detail
Form	Bearer
Interest payments	Gross
Tax	Taxable but untaxed at source
Trades matched through	TRAX system
Trades settled through	Euroclear or Clearstream
Settlement period	Trade day plus two (T+2)
Trading mechanism	Over-the-counter (OTC)

7. Other Securities

7.1 Depositary Receipts (DRs)

Learning Objective

1.7.1 Know the principal features and characteristics of depositary receipts: American depositary receipts; global depositary receipts; means of creation including pre-release facility; registration; rights attached; dividends; transfer to underlying shares

Depositary receipts (DRs) come in two broad forms – **American depositary receipts (ADRs)** and **global depositary receipts (GDRs)**.

The US is a huge pool of potential investment. Therefore, substantial non-US companies may want to attract US investors to raise funds. ADRs facilitate this process; indeed, they were created to make it easier for Americans to invest in overseas companies. GDRs are depositary receipts that are identical to ADRs, except that they are marketed to appeal to a broader base of investors, some of whom may be based outside America.

Both ADRs and GDRs are negotiable certificates evidencing ownership of shares in a corporation from a country outside the US. Each DR has a particular number of underlying shares, or is represented by a fraction of an underlying share.

Example

Volkswagen AG (the motor vehicle manufacturer) is listed in Frankfurt. It has two classes of shares listed – ordinary shares and preference shares. There are separate ADRs in existence for the ordinary shares and preference shares. Each ADR represents 0.2 individual Volkswagen shares.

DRs are typically created (or **sponsored**) by the foreign corporation (Volkswagen in the above example). They will liaise with an investment bank regarding the precise structure of the DR, such as the number or fraction of shares represented by each DR. A **depository** bank will then accept a certain number of underlying shares from the issuer, create the DRs to represent the shares and make these DRs available to US, and potentially other, investors, probably via local brokers. This creation process for an ADR is illustrated by the following diagram:

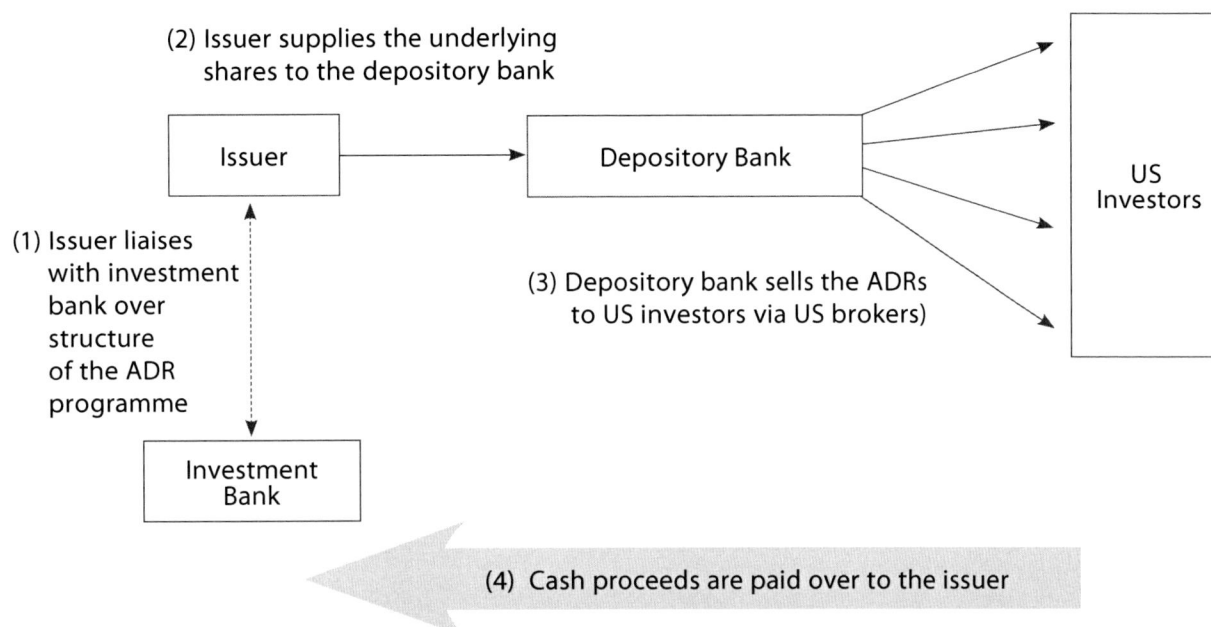

(2) Issuer supplies the underlying
shares to the depository bank

| Issuer | → | Depository Bank | → | US Investors |

(1) Issuer liaises
with investment
bank over
structure
of the ADR
programme

(3) Depository bank sells the ADRs
to US investors via US brokers)

Investment
Bank

(4) Cash proceeds are paid over to the issuer

One characteristic of DRs that must also be considered is **pre-release** or **grey market trading**. When a DR is being created, the depository bank receives notification that, in the future, the shares will be placed on deposit. As long as it holds cash collateral, even though the shares are not yet on deposit, the depository bank can create and sell the receipt (the DR) at this time. Effectively, investors are buying a receipt that entitles them to all the benefits of a share that will, in the future, be held on deposit for them. The DR can be treated in this way for up to three months before the actual purchase of the underlying shares.

The shares underlying the DR are registered in the name of the depository bank, with the DRs themselves transferable as bearer securities. The DRs are typically quoted and traded in US dollars and are governed by the trading and settlement procedures of the market on which they are traded.

The depository bank acts as a go-between for the investor and the company. When the company pays a dividend, it is paid in the company's domestic currency to the bank, which then converts the dividend into dollars and passes it on to the DR holders. The US investors therefore need not concern themselves with currency movements. Furthermore, when a DR holder decides to sell, the DRs will be sold on in dollars. This removal of the need for any currency transactions for the US investor is a key attraction of the DR.

DR holders are entitled to vote, just like ordinary shareholders, only the votes will be exercised via the depository bank.

If the DR represents a UK company's shares, there are tax ramifications. The UK tax authority, Her Majesty's Revenue & Customs (HMRC) levies a tax known as **stamp duty** on share purchases, at 0.5% of the price paid to purchase shares.

However, because DRs may trade outside the UK, ie, in the US, **no stamp duty is charged on the purchase of a DR**. Instead, HMRC charges a **one-off fee for stamp duty of 1.5%**, when the DR is created.

If an investor wants to sell his DRs, he can do so either by selling them to another investor as a DR, or by selling the underlying shares in the home market of the company concerned. The latter route will involve cancelling the DR by delivering the certificates to the depository bank. The depository bank will then release the appropriate number of shares in accordance with the instructions received.

7.2   Warrants

Learning Objective

1.7.2   Know the rights, uses and differences between warrants and covered warrants: benefit to the issuing company and purpose; issuer; right to subscribe for capital; effect on price of maturity and the underlying security; detachability; exercise and expiry; the calculation of the conversion premium (discount) on a warrant (warrant price plus exercise price minus the share price)

Traditionally, a warrant is an instrument issued by a company that allows the holder to subscribe for shares in that company at a fixed price over a fixed period. A typical warrant may have a life of several years.

Warrants are listed and traded on stock exchanges. If the holder decides to exercise, the company will issue new shares.

Example

Warrants are available in a (fictional) investment company, Cambridge Investment Trust plc. Cambridge Investment Trust shares are currently trading at 77p each, and warrants are available, giving the warrant owner the right, but not the obligation, to buy shares at £1 each, up until 2020. The warrants are trading at 4p each.

In the above example, the warrant's **expiry** date is in 2020 and its **exercise price** is 100p.

What are the advantages to a company, such as the one encountered above, that persuade it to issue warrants? Clearly, the sale of warrants for cash will raise money for the company, and, if the warrants are exercised, then further capital will be raised by the company. Similarly to call options, holding the warrant does not entitle the investor to receive dividends or to vote at company meetings, so the capital raised until the warrant is exercised could be considered as free.

Obviously warrants offer a highly geared investment opportunity for the investor, and they are often issued alongside other investments, rather than sold in their own right.

Example

CBC plc is attempting to raise finance by issuing bonds. Their advisers inform them that they could issue bonds paying a coupon of 6% pa, or lower it to 5% pa if they give away a single warrant with each £100 nominal of the bonds. The warrants are detachable from the bonds – in other words, the investors could decide to sell their warrants or keep them, regardless of whether they retain the bonds.

Another type of warrant is a **covered warrant**. These are warrants issued by firms (usually investment banks), rather than the company whose shares the warrant enables the investor to buy. They are offered in the form of **call warrants** (giving the investor the right to buy), or **put warrants** (giving the investor the right to sell). In the UK, covered warrants are traded on the LSE.

7.2.1 Warrant Price Behaviour

Warrants (including covered warrants) are highly geared investments. A modest outlay can result in a large gain, but the investor can lose the value of their entire stake in the warrant. Their value is driven by the length of time for which they are valid (their **maturity** or period until expiry) and the value of the underlying security.

There is a relatively simple method of looking at the price of one warrant relative to other warrants – using the **conversion premium**. This is the price of the warrant plus the exercise price required to buy the underlying share, less the prevailing share price.

Example

For example, calculating the conversion premium for the Cambridge Investment Trust warrants in the example above involves the:

Warrant price	=	4p
Plus exercise price	=	100p
Less share price	=	77p
Conversion premium	=	27p

Note that if the resultant figure were a negative, the warrant would be trading at a **conversion discount**.

8. Foreign Exchange (FX)

8.1 Introduction

Learning Objective

1.8.1   Know the principal features and uses of spot, forward and cross rates: quotation as bid-offer spreads; forwards quoted as bid-offer margins against the spot; quotation of cross rates

The foreign exchange ('forex' or 'FX') market is the collective way of describing all the transactions in which one currency is exchanged for another, anywhere in the world. There is no physical exchange for the currency market in London; it is purely **over-the-counter (OTC)** and dominated by the banks.

There are two types of transaction conducted on the FX market:

1. **Spot transactions** are immediate currency deals that are settled within two working days.
2. **Forward transactions** involve currency deals that are agreed for a future date at a rate of exchange fixed now.

As we will see in Section 8.2, both spot and forward rates are quoted by dealers in the form of a buying rate (the **bid**) and a selling rate (the **offer**). The **spread** between these two prices enables the FX dealer to make a profit.

The users of the FX market fall into two broad camps.

First, FX transactions are driven by international trade. If a Japanese company sells goods to a US customer, they might invoice the transaction in US dollars. These dollars will need to be exchanged for Japanese yen by the Japanese company and this is the FX transaction. The Japanese company may not be expecting to receive the dollars for a month after submission of the invoice. This gives them two choices:

1. They can wait until they receive the dollars and then execute a **spot** transaction.
2. They can enter into a forward transaction to sell the dollars for yen in a month's time. This will provide them with certainty as to the amount of yen they will receive and assist in their budgeting efforts.

The second reason for FX transactions is speculation. If an investor feels that the US dollar is likely to weaken against the euro, he can buy euros in either the spot or forward market to profit if he is right.

Trading of foreign currencies is always done in pairs. These are currency pairs when one currency is bought and the other is sold, and the prices at which these take place make up the exchange rate. When the exchange rate is being quoted, the name of the currency is abbreviated to a three-character reference; so, for example, sterling is abbreviated to GBP.

The most commonly quoted currency pairs are:

- US dollar and Japanese yen (USD/JPY);
- Euro and US dollar (EUR/USD);
- US dollar and Swiss franc (USD/CHF);
- British pound and US dollar (GBP/USD).

When currencies are quoted, the first currency is the base currency and the second is the counter or quote currency. The base currency is always equal to one unit of that currency, in other words, one pound, one dollar or one euro. For example, at the time of writing, the EUR:USD exchange rate is 1:1.3693 which means that €1 is worth $1.3693.

When currency pairs are quoted, a market maker or foreign exchange trader will quote a **bid** and an **ask price**. Staying with the example of the EUR/USD, the quote might be 1.3692/94. So if you want to **buy** €100,000 then you will need to pay the higher of the two prices and deliver $136,940; if you want to **sell** €100,000 then you get the lower of the two prices and receive $136,920.

Generally, exchange rates around the world are quoted against the US dollar. A **cross rate** is any foreign currency rate that does not include the US dollar, eg, GBP/JPY is a cross rate. Obviously a cross rate will be of particular interest to companies doing international business between the constituent countries, eg, a UK company selling goods or services to Japanese consumers, and receiving payment in yen.

8.2 Spot and Forward Transactions

Learning Objective

1.8.2   Be able to calculate spot and forward settlement prices using: adding or subtracting forward adjustments; interest rate parity

A typical sterling/dollar spot quote might look something like this:

GBP/USD spot rate 1.8055–1.8145

- Buyer's rate: £1 buys $1.8055.
- Seller's rate: $1.8145 buys £1.

The buyer's rate and seller's rate refer to buying and selling dollars respectively. The difference between the buyer's and seller's rates is generally referred to as the **bid-offer spread**. It enables the bank offering the deals to make money.

How much will an investor get if the above spot rate is applied? If the investor wants to sell $50,000 for pounds sterling, he will get £27,556. This is based on the seller's rate of $1.8145:£1.

The forward market is almost exactly the same as the spot market, except that currency deals are agreed for a future date, but at a rate of exchange fixed now. These rates of exchange are not directly quoted. Instead, quotes on the forward market state how much must be added to, or subtracted from, the present spot rate.

For example, the three month GBP/USD quote might be:

spot $1.8055–$1.8145

three-month forward 1.00–0.97c pm

pm stands for **premium**. It is used when the dollar is going to be more expensive relative to sterling in the future. It is deducted from the quoted spot rate in order to arrive at the forward rate. £1 will buy fewer dollars in three months' time and, if you have dollars in three months' time, the bank will sell you more sterling per dollar than they will now. The premium is quoted in cents, unlike the spot rate, which is quoted in dollars. So 1.00 pm is a premium of 1 cent or 0.01 dollars. And 0.97 pm is a premium of 0.97 cents or 0.0097 dollars.

The three-month forward quote is, therefore: $1.7955–$1.8048.

Alternatively the three-month forward rate might exhibit a discount, rather than a premium, for example:

spot   1.8055–1.8145

three-month forward   0.79–0.82c dis

dis stands for **discount**. The discount is used when the dollar is going to be cheaper relative to sterling in the future. It needs to be added to the quoted spot rate to arrive at the forward rate. £1 will buy more dollars in three months' time and, if you have dollars in three months' time, the bank will sell you less sterling per dollar than they will now. The three-month forward quote is therefore:

three-month forward $1.8134–$1.8227

The logic is that the forward rate will always exhibit a wider spread than the spot rate.

8.2.1   Interest Rate Parity

The concept of interest rate parity in determining the exchange rate between currencies arises from one of the cornerstone ideas in financial theory, which is that of **rational pricing** and the notion of **arbitrage**.

Rational pricing is the assumption in financial economics that asset prices will reflect the arbitrage-free price of the asset as any deviation from this price will be 'arbitraged away'.

Arbitrage is the practice of taking advantage of a pricing anomaly between securities that are trading in two (or possibly more) markets. One market can be the physical or underlying market; the other can often be a derivative market.

When a mismatch or anomaly can be exploited (ie, after transaction costs, storage costs, transport costs and dividends), the arbitrageur 'locks in' a risk-free profit. In general terms, arbitrage ensures that the **law of one price** will prevail.

Interest rate parity results from recognising a possible arbitrage condition and arbitraging it away.

Consider the returns from borrowing in one currency, exchanging that currency for another currency and investing in interest-bearing instruments of the second currency, while simultaneously purchasing futures contracts to convert the currency back at the end of the investment period. Under the assumption of arbitrage, the returns available should be equal to the returns from purchasing and holding similar interest-bearing instruments of the first currency.

If the returns are different, investors could theoretically arbitrage and make risk-free returns.

Interest rate parity says that the spot and future prices for currency trades incorporate any interest rate differentials between the two currencies.

A forward exchange contract is an agreement between two parties to either buy or sell foreign currency at a fixed exchange rate for settlement at a future date. The forward exchange rate is the exchange rate set today even though the transaction will not settle until some agreed point in the future, such as in three months' time.

The relationship between the spot exchange rate and forward exchange rate for two currencies is simply given by the differential between their respective nominal interest rates over the term being considered. The relationship is purely mathematical and has nothing to do with market expectations.

The idea behind this relationship is embodied in the principle of interest rate parity and is expressed as follows:

$$\text{Forward rate for GBP/USD} = \text{£ Spot rate} \times \left[\frac{(1+\text{US \$ Short-term interest rate})}{(1+\text{UK £ Short-term interest rate})} \right]$$

Example

The GBP/USD spot exchange rate = 1.5220. If the three-month interest rate for the UK is 4.88% and for the US, 3.20%, what will the three-month forward exchange rate be?

As the three-month interest rates are quoted on a per annum basis, they must be divided by four to obtain the rate of interest that will be payable (%) over three months:

Sterling: 4.88%/4 = 1.22%
Dollar: 3.20%/4 = 0.8%

Applying the interest rate parity formula:

$$\text{Forward rate for GBP/USD} = \$1.5220 \times \left[\frac{(1+0.008)}{(1+0.0122)} \right] = \$1.5157$$

The forward exchange rate in the example of $1.5157 is lower than the spot exchange rate of $1.5220. That is, in three months' time, £1 will buy $1.5157 or $0.0063 fewer dollars than is available at the spot rate (ie, the difference is 63 pips).

If this relationship did not exist, then an arbitrage opportunity would arise between the spot and forward rates.

It is important to realise that the forward rate calculated under the notion of arbitrage and interest rate parity is not a forecast of what the rate of exchange will actually be in three months. The actual rate will vary according to all of the factors which influence exchange rates in the forex market. The three-month forward rate in this example is simply a mathematically derived rate resulting from the interest rate differentials prevailing between the two currencies being exchanged.

8.3   Factors Affecting Foreign Exchange (FX) Rates

Learning Objective

1.8.3   Understand the factors that affect foreign exchange rates

Historically, exchange rates were fixed as part of the 1944 Bretton Woods agreement and not subject to market forces. Resetting or changing these exchange rates took place, as it did in the UK in the 1960s, by a formal devaluation whereby the rates which had been set in 1944 were modified. The UK government undertook a devaluation of the pound against the dollar from £1= $2.80 to £1= $2.40 in 1968.

The era of fixed exchange rates came to an end during the 1970s, largely as a result of a currency crisis for the USD and the end of the **official** convertibility of currencies into gold, which was abandoned in August 1971. There have been attempts by governments to reintroduce managed exchange rates but these efforts have essentially failed, and the current regime of freely floating exchange rates is now accepted as the only feasible way for the FX market to function effectively.

There are exceptions to floating currencies; for example, some Middle Eastern countries, such as Saudi Arabia and the UAE, peg their currencies to the US dollar.

Questions regarding the determination of the FX rates by the markets comes down to several related issues concerning the demand and supply for individual currencies, monetary and interest rate policy, issues relating to purchasing power parity, and speculation.

8.3.1   Purchasing Power Parity

In the short term, it appears that the primary factors affecting the manner in which market participants decide on the **appropriate** exchange rates are those of supply and demand and, to a greater or lesser extent, market sentiment.

Purchasing power parity (PPP) theory concerns the rate to which exchange rates should tend to move over the long term. PPP theory predicts that amounts of different currencies (at current exchange rates) should have equal purchasing power.

The concept of PPP can be appreciated by considering an example.

Example

If a basket of goods costs £100 in London and the same basket of goods costs $200 in New York, the PPP theory predicts that the exchange rate between the two countries will be £1 = $2.

If two economies experience differing rates of inflation then, over time, the exchange rate will tend to alter in the direction of restoring PPP.

If, after a number of years, the basket of goods now costs £150 in London due to the impact of inflation on UK prices and yet it only rises to $210 in New York, this suggests that the exchange rate between the two currencies should now be £1 = $1.40: there should have been a decline in the value of sterling.

PPP has some plausibility over the long term and gives an underlying theme to the FX markets. If one economy consistently has an inflation rate in excess of its competitors, then its currency will deteriorate against its trading partners.

Factors Affecting the Demand for Sterling

- Foreigners need sterling to pay for exports of UK goods to overseas markets.
- Overseas investors want to invest capital in the UK.
- Speculation – if sterling is expected to increase relative to one or more other currencies, speculators will buy sterling.
- Currency rate management activities of central banks including the BoE.
- Demand will be downward-sloping with respect to price – less demand for exports and less interest from foreign investors as sterling advances relative to other currencies.

Factors Affecting the Supply of Sterling

- When UK importers purchase foreign currencies to pay for imported goods arriving in the UK they are increasing the supply of sterling into the markets.
- UK residents wishing to invest in overseas assets will have to sell sterling to buy foreign currency.
- Speculation – if sterling is expected to decrease relative to one or more other currencies speculators will sell sterling.
- The BoE may sell the domestic currency to purchase additional foreign currency reserves in order to influence the exchange rate as part of macro-economic policy.
- Supply will be upward-sloping with respect to price.

8.3.2 Foreign Currency Trading and Speculation

While the previous discussion has focused on the underlying economic and fundamental factors which influence exchange rates, there is no question that the FX market is also one where there is a huge amount of speculative trading activity. Much of this trading is conducted by the large banks, which are the dominant players in the OTC market for FX.

The volume of transactions has been estimated by the Bank for International Settlements (BIS) at approximately $4 trillion in nominal amounts traded daily. Just as with derivatives, the nominal amount traded is somewhat misleading since the speculative activity in FX is focused on the amount that is traded at the margin. In other words, if one places an order to sell $1 million to purchase £600,000, but only holds the position for a few hours (minutes), there is a sense in which the nominal amounts are not really exchanged, but, just as in the case of a swap or contract of difference (CFD), it is the marginal difference which is really being traded or at risk.

According to the BIS, the most widely traded currency pair is the USD/EUR. Approximately 30% of overall turnover each year is between these two currencies. USD/YEN was the next most traded currency pair, generating 18% of turnover, followed by USD/GBP with 11%.

The FX market is extremely liquid and, in the case of major currency pairs such as the trade in EUR/USD, there is great depth to trading within the inter-bank market. Some other currency pairs, involving more exotic or less traded currencies such as the Hungarian forint, will obviously be far less liquid, with much wider spreads between the bid and the ask than for EUR/USD or GBP/USD.

FX markets can be extremely volatile at times, especially when the markets in other asset classes are acting in an erratic manner. There is a fascinating correlation between certain currency pairs and equity markets and some of this is explicable by reference to the carry trade. In essence, the carry trade in FX involves the borrowing of funds in a currency where the rate of interest is relatively low – examples are the Japanese yen and the Swiss franc – and then the purchase of securities, often government bonds, which have a relatively high yield such as is the case with short-term instruments available from the Australian government.

The more volatile periods for FX trading are often seen when central bank officials (such as the Federal Reserve chairman) talk to the press or release minutes of meetings. Any hint of a change in central bank policy will tend to impact the FX rates. Another key mover of FX rates is when the US Labour Department issues its monthly employment data, more commonly known as the Non-Farms Payroll (NFP) report, on the first Friday of each month at 8:30 Eastern time.

Other economic events which can strongly impact the FX market are releases of inflation data, gross domestic product (GDP) data, and retail sales data from major government organisations, such as the Office for National Statistics (ONS) in the UK and Eurostat which provides economic data for the EU. Also important to the sudden movements of exchange rates are the results of auctions of government securities and any changes in short-term rates announced by central banks.

9. Prime Brokerage and Equity Finance

9.1 Prime Broker Services

Learning Objective

1.9.1 Know the main services provided by an equity and fixed income prime broker, including: securities lending and borrowing; leverage trade execution; cash management; core settlement; custody; rehypothecation

Prime brokerage is the term given to a collection of services provided by investment banks to their hedge fund clients. **Hedge funds** are investment funds that are typically only open to a limited range of investors. They tend to follow complex investment strategies, often involving derivatives. However, among the more straightforward strategies adopted is the equity long/short strategy. This involves taking both long positions in equities (in other words, buying shares) and, at the same time, committing to sell equities that are not held by the fund (described as selling short). The hope is that the gain in one half of the strategy (the long or the short) will more than cover the loss on the other half of the strategy (the short or the long). Selling short inevitably means that the fund will need to **borrow** the securities it has sold until the position is unwound.

The typical services that are provided by a prime broker include the following:

1. **Securities lending and borrowing** – eg, to cover short positions in a long/short strategy.
2. **Leveraged trade execution** – undertaking trades on the fund's behalf that are partly financed by borrowed funds.
3. **Cash management** – maximising the return that is generated from cash held by the fund.
4. **Core settlement** – taking the necessary steps to make sure that any securities purchased become the property of the fund, and the appropriate cash is received for any sales made of the fund's securities in a timely manner.
5. **Custody** – keeping safe the securities held by the fund, and processing any corporate actions promptly and in accordance with its targets.
6. **Rehypothecation** – in addition to holding collateral and having a charge over the fund's portfolio, the prime broker might also require a right to re-charge, dispose of or otherwise use the customer's assets which are subject to the security, including disposing of them to a third party. This is commonly described as a **right of rehypothecation**. When assets have been rehypothecated, they become the property of the prime broker, as and when the prime broker uses them in this way, for instance by depositing rehypothecated securities with a third-party financier to obtain cheaper funding, or by lending the securities to another client.

9.2 Sources of Equity Finance

Learning Objective

1.9.2 Know the use of the main sources of equity and fixed income financing: stock borrowing and lending; repurchase agreements; collateralised borrowing; tri-party repos; synthetic financing

In order to finance and create positions in equities and bonds required by their hedge fund clients, prime brokers have a number of possibilities:

1. **Stock borrowing and lending** – prime brokers can arrange for the appropriate securities to be borrowed to cover the hedge fund's short positions and also use the fund's long positions to lend to others and provide additional returns to the fund as a result.
2. **Repurchase agreements** – repurchase agreements (repos) are essentially when the prime broker arranges the sale of securities owned by the fund for cash, while agreeing to buy back the equivalent securities later for a slightly inflated price. The increase in price is effectively the borrowing cost of the cash, and is often referred to as the **repo rate**.
3. **Collateralised borrowing** – prime brokers advance cash to the customer against the security of a first fixed charge over the customer's portfolio. In the event of the customer's default, this gives the prime broker a right of recourse against the charged assets for the amounts owing to it. The availability of the portfolio as collateral in this way should enable the bank to provide loans at more competitive rates than would be the case with an unsecured loan.
4. **Tri-Party repos** – in the case of a tri-party repo, a custodian bank or clearing organisation acts as an intermediary between the two parties to the repurchase or repo agreement outlined above. The tri-party agent is responsible for the administration of the transaction including collateral allocation, the marking to market, and, when required, the substitution of collateral. The lender and the borrower of cash both enter into tri-party transactions in order to avoid the administrative burden of the simpler form of bilateral repos. Moreover, there is an added element of security in a tri-party repo because the collateral is being held by an agent and the counterparty risk is reduced.
5. **Synthetic financing** – this is when the prime broker will create exposure to particular securities by using derivatives, like swaps, rather than directly buying and holding the securities themselves. This route is generally substantially cheaper than outright purchases.

9.3 Stock Lending

Learning Objective

1.9.3 Know the uses of, requirements and implications of stock lending: what is stock lending; purpose for the borrower; purpose for the lender; function of market makers and stock borrowing and lending intermediaries; effect on the lender's rights; lender retains the right to sell; collateral

Stock lending is the temporary transfer of securities, by a lender to a borrower, with agreement by the borrower to return equivalent securities to the lender at a pre-agreed time.

There are two main motivations for stock lending: securities-driven, and cash-driven. In securities-driven transactions, borrowing firms seek specific securities (equities or bonds), perhaps to facilitate their trading operations. In the cash-driven trades, the lender is able to increase the returns on an underlying portfolio, by receiving a fee for making its investments available to the borrower. Such transactions may boost overall income returns, enhancing, for example, returns on a pension fund.

The terms of the securities loan will be governed by a **securities lending agreement**, which requires that the borrower provide the lender with collateral, in the form of cash, government securities, or a letter of credit of value equal to or greater than the loaned securities. As payment for the loan, the parties negotiate a fee, quoted as an annualised percentage of the value of the loaned securities. If the agreed form of collateral is cash, then the fee may be quoted as a **rebate**, meaning that the lender will earn all of the interest that accrues on the cash collateral, and will rebate an agreed rate of interest to the borrower.

9.3.1 Benefits of Stock Lending

The initial driver for the securities lending business was to cover **settlement failure**. If one party fails to deliver stock to you, it can mean that you are unable to deliver stock that you have already sold to another party. In order to avoid the costs and penalties that can arise from settlement failure, stock can be borrowed at a fee, and delivered to the second party. When your initial stock finally arrives (or is obtained from another source) the lender will receive back the same number of shares in the security they lent.

The principal reason for borrowing a security, therefore, is to cover a **short position**. As you are obliged to deliver the security, you will have to borrow it. At the end of the agreement you will have to return an equivalent security to the lender. Equivalent in this context means fungible, ie, the securities have to be completely interchangeable. Compare this with lending a ten euro note. You do not expect exactly the same note back, as any ten euro note will do.

Securities lending and borrowing is often required, by matter of law, in order to engage in short selling. In fact, regulations enacted in 2008 in the US, Australia and the UK, among other jurisdictions, required that, before short sales were executed for specific stocks, especially banks and financial services companies, the sellers first pre-borrowed shares in those issues.

There is an ongoing debate among global policymakers and regulators about how to impose new restrictions on short selling and in June 2010, during a period of turbulence for the eurozone, Germany took a unilateral step in banning the naked short selling of credit default swaps (CDSs) (ie, when the short seller had no interest in the underlying security for the credit default swap).

The FCA lists the following positive aspects of stock lending in its guidance to the investment community:

- It can increase the liquidity of the securities market by allowing securities to be borrowed temporarily, thus reducing the potential for failed settlements and the penalties this may incur.
- It can provide extra security to lenders through the collateralisation of a loan.
- It can support many trading and investment strategies that otherwise would be extremely difficult to execute.

- It allows investors to earn income by lending their securities on to third parties.
- It facilitates the hedging and arbitraging of price differentials.

9.3.2   Risks of Stock Lending

Many feel that securities lending can aid market manipulation through short selling, which can potentially influence market prices. Short selling itself is not wrong, but market manipulation certainly is.

The debate about the merits and validity of short selling is sometimes emotion-charged, and features in the rhetoric of politicians in populist attacks on the financial services industry. It is probably fair to say that for most investment professionals, who actually work in the financial markets, the notion that short selling in itself is an abusive practice is not palatable. There may be times when the activity can be disruptive, but markets have a tendency to over-react in either direction and the periodic focus given to short selling when a market is moving down should be counterbalanced by the tendency for markets to become too frothy and for long investors to become exuberant when markets are going up.

At the time of writing, the Financial Conduct Authority (FCA) is conducting a thematic review of the investment management industry that includes assessing whether or not stock lending is undertaken in the best interests of customers. For example, is the lending of assets by a fund manager done for a pension fund client in the best interests of that fund and its existing and potential pensioners? In particular, the FCA is looking at whether there is a danger that the profits generated from stock lending are not appropriately shared with the managers' customers, and whether the risk that loaned assets are not returned is placing unnecessary risk on the fund.

9.3.3   Stock Borrowing and Lending Intermediaries (SBLIs)

Securities lending has increasingly become a volume business which has encouraged the proliferation of various specialist intermediaries to undertake principal and/or agency roles in this field. These SBLIs provide a service in separating out the underlying owners of securities – which are typically large pension funds or insurance companies – from those who would be borrowers of those securities, typically hedge funds and other asset managers, and liaising with both sides. The economy of scale offered by SBLIs in pooling together securities of different clients has also enabled smaller asset-holders to participate in this market.

Asset managers and custodian banks have added securities lending to the other services they offer. Owners and SBLIs will often **split** revenues from securities lending at commercial rates. The split will be determined by many factors, including the service level and provision by the agent of any risk mitigation, such as an indemnity. Securities lending is often part of a much bigger relationship and therefore the split negotiation can become part of a bundled approach to the pricing of a wide range of services.

Custodian Banks

Since custody is a highly competitive business, for many providers it is often run as a loss-making activity. Supplementing their custodian role by acting as an SBLI can add a new level of revenue-generation for custodian banks. Many large custodian banks have therefore added securities lending to their core custody businesses.

From the perspective of the custodian, the advantages of acting as an SBLI are that they already have:

- an existing banking relationship with their customers;
- investment in technology and global coverage of markets arising from their custody businesses;
- the ability to pool assets from many smaller underlying funds, insulating borrowers from the administrative inconvenience of dealing with many small funds;
- experience in local operations in developing as well as developed markets;
- the capability to provide indemnities and manage cash collateral efficiently.

Prime Brokers

In contrast to those SBLIs that act as agent intermediaries, **principal SBLI intermediaries**, such as prime brokers, can assume principal risk, offer credit intermediation and take positions in the securities that they borrow. A beneficial owner may often be reluctant to take on credit exposures to borrowers they are not familiar with, who may not be regulated or who may not have a good credit rating. This could well exclude many hedge funds. In such circumstances, a prime broker, acting as an SBLI, will be providing a **credit intermediation service** in taking a principal position between the lending institution or beneficial owner of the securities and the hedge fund.

A further role of prime brokers is to take on **liquidity risk**. Typically they will borrow on an **open basis**, which gives the beneficial owner the option to recall the underlying securities if they want to sell them or for other reasons. However the SBLI will be lending to clients on a **term basis**, giving them certainty that they will be able to cover their short positions.

One way to mitigate this risk is to use in-house inventory (stock) if available. For example, proprietary trading positions can be a stable source of lending supply if the long position is associated with a long-term derivatives transaction. Efficient inventory management is seen as critical and many securities lending desks act as central clearers of inventory within their organisations. This can require a significant technological investment.

Securities lending is also one of the central components of a prime brokerage operation in regard to its **hedge fund** clients. In particular, two hedge fund strategies that are heavily reliant on securities borrowing are long/short equity and convertible bond arbitrage.

Administration

For SBLIs it is important that there is adequate documentation in place with borrowing counterparties, which sets out the terms and conditions of the service being provided and the risks involved.

If assets are **pooled** within an SBLI, the SBLI must ensure that only assets belonging to customers who have consented to securities lending are lent out. The SBLI should maintain a separate account or be able to demonstrate that it maintains adequate systems to differentiate between the safe custody investments of those customers who have not consented to stock lending activity and those that have consented.

If collateral is required from the borrower, the SBLI must consider whether that collateral should be provided in advance of the lending, given the risks of the transaction and normal practice in the relevant market. The level and type of collateral should take account of the creditworthiness of the borrower and the risks associated with the collateral being offered.

Cash or assets held in favour of a customer for stock lending activity must be held in accordance with the appropriate custody rules. This includes dividends, stock lending fees and any other payments received in relation to stock lending.

9.3.4 Legalities

Securities lending is legal and clearly regulated in most of the world's major securities markets. Most markets mandate that the borrowing of securities be conducted only for specifically permitted purposes, which generally include to:

- facilitate settlement of a trade;
- facilitate delivery of a short sale;
- finance the security; or
- facilitate a loan to another borrower who is motivated by one of these permitted purposes.

In the UK those involved in securities lending will generally be supervised by the FCA. They will be subject to the FCA's Handbook, including the Inter-Professional Conduct Chapter of the Market Conduct Sourcebook; and also subject to the provisions of the Financial Services and Markets Act (FSMA 2000) on, among other things, market abuse.

They will also have regard to the provisions of the Stock Borrowing and Lending Code, produced by the Stock Lending and Borrowing Committee, a committee of market participants, chaired by the BoE, which includes a representative of the FCA.

Effect on a Lender's Rights and Corporate Actions

When a security is loaned, the **title** of the security transfers to the borrower. This means that the borrower has the advantages of holding the security, just as though they owned it. Specifically, the borrower will receive all coupon and/or dividend payments, and any other rights such as voting rights. In most cases, these dividends or coupons must be passed back to the lender in the form of what is referred to as a **manufactured dividend**.

If the lender wants to exercise its right to vote, it should recall the stock in good time so that a proxy voting form can be completed and returned to the registrar by the required deadline. Similar issues are involved in other corporate actions such as capitalisation issues. Technically, the consequences arising from any corporate action by the issuer of a security, such as a capitalisation matter or rights issue, when that security has been lent to another would, *prima facie*, be to the benefit/cost of the borrower. Under the terms of the security agreement it is customary that these costs/benefits flow back to the lender, and the exact manner in which this is implemented should be reflected in the **securities lending agreement**.

The term **securities lending** is sometimes used erroneously as a synonym of **stock loan**. The latter is used in private hedged portfolio stock collateralised loan arrangements, where the underlying securities are hedged so as to convert the variable asset to a relatively stable asset, against which a usually non-recourse or limited-recourse loan can be placed.

The Legal Underpinnings for Stock Lending

Parties to a stock lending transaction generally operate under a legal agreement, which sets out the obligations of the borrower and lender. In securities lending, the lender effectively retains all the benefits of ownership. The borrower can use the securities as required – perhaps by lending them on to another party – but is liable to the lender for all the benefits such as dividends, interest and stock splits.

The **Global Master Securities Lending Agreement (GMSLA)** has been developed as a market standard for securities lending. It was drafted with a view to compliance with English law and covers the matters which a legal agreement ought to cover for securities lending transactions. This agreement is kept under review, and amendments are made from time to time, although parties to an existing agreement will need to agree that any amendments will apply to their agreement.

Stock Lending Versus Repo

While stock lending and sale/repurchase agreements (repos) are similar, the difference is that a stock lender charges a fee to the borrower, whereas a repo counterparty pays (or receives) a rate of interest.

Example

A large pension fund manager with a position in a particular stock agrees that the security can be borrowed by a securities lender. The securities lender, a prime broker or investment bank, will then allow a hedge fund client to borrow the stock and sell it short. The short seller would like to buy the stock back at a lower price and realise a profit when returning the security to the broker from whom it has been borrowed.

Once the shares are borrowed and sold, cash is generated from selling the stock. That cash would become collateral for the borrower. The cash value of the collateral is marked-to-market on a daily basis so that it exceeds the value of the loan by at least 2%. The pension fund manager has access to the cash for overnight investment and this enables the pension fund to maintain a long position in the stock. The pension fund manager is able to earn additional income from lending the stock, and the hedge fund manager is able, providing that their prediction that the price of the security is going to decline is correct, to profit from the short sale. In addition, the prime broker earns a spread from facilitating the transaction and also by providing this prime brokerage service to the hedge fund client.

10. Collective Investment Schemes (CISs)

Learning Objective

1.10.1   Know the key features, risks, charges, valuation and yield characteristics of unit trusts and OEICs/ICVCs

1.10.2   Know the key features, risks, charges, valuation and yield characteristics of investment trusts

1.10.3   Know the key features, risks, charges, valuation and yield characteristics of the main types of exchange-traded products

1.10.4   Know the key features, risks, charges, valuation and yield characteristics of non-mainstream pooled investments (including UCIS)

A collective investment is a way of investing money with other people to participate in a wider range of investments than those feasible for most individual investors, and to share the costs of doing so.

Terminology varies with country, but collective investments are often referred to as investment funds, managed funds, mutual funds or simply funds. Across the world large markets have developed around collective investment, and these account for a substantial portion of all trading on major stock exchanges.

Collective investments are promoted with a wide range of investment aims either targeting specific geographic regions (eg, emerging Europe) or specified themes (eg, technology). Depending on the country, there is normally a bias towards the domestic market to reflect national self-interest as perceived by policy-makers, familiarity, and the lack of currency risk. Funds are often selected on the basis of these specified investment aims, as well as their past investment performance and other factors such as fees.

10.1   Unit Trusts

A unit trust is a professionally managed collective investment fund.

- Investors can buy units, each of which represents a specified fraction of the trust.
- The trust holds a portfolio of securities.
- The assets of the trust are held by **trustees** and are invested by **managers**.
- The investor incurs annual management charges and possibly also an initial charge.

An authorised unit trust (AUT) must be constituted by a **trust deed** made between the manager and the trustee.

The basic principle with AUTs is that there is a single type of undivided unit. This is modified when there are both income units (paying a distribution to unit-holders) and accumulation units (rolling up income into the capital value of the units).

If a fund wishes to market the unit trust in other member states of the EU, it may apply for certification under **UCITS** (Undertakings for Collective Investment in Transferable Securities).

10.1.1 Trustees

1. Trustees of a unit trust must be authorised by the FCA and fully independent of the trust manager.
2. Trustees are required to have capital in excess of £4 million and, for this reason, normally are large financial institutions such as a bank and insurance companies.
3. The primary duty of the trustees is to protect the interests of the unitholders.
4. The investor in a unit trust owns the underlying value of shares based on the proportion of the units held. They are effectively the beneficiary of the trust.
5. The trust deed of each unit trust must clearly state its investment strategy and objectives, so that investors can determine the suitability of each trust.
6. The limits and allowable investment areas for a unit trust fund are also laid out in the trust deed together with the investment objectives.

10.1.2 The Role of the Manager

The manager must also be authorised by the FCA and his role covers:

- Marketing the unit trust.
- Managing the assets in accordance with the trust deed.
- Maintaining a record of units for inspection by the trustees.
- Supplying other information relating to the investments under the unit trust as requested.
- Informing the FCA of any breaches of regulations while he is running the trust.

10.1.3 Buying and Selling Units

Unit trust units can be purchased in a number of ways; for example, via a newspaper advertisement, over the phone or over the internet. These methods will generally require payment with the order, or some form of guarantee of payment. A contract note will be produced and sent to the investor as evidence of the purchase.

Investors can sell their units via the same source that they purchased them, or can contact the fund managers direct, for example by telephone.

10.1.4 Unit Trust Pricing

The calculation of buying and selling prices will take place at the **valuation point,** which is at a particular time each day. The fund is valued on the basis of the net value of the constituent assets and a typical spread between buying and selling prices in the market will be in the range of 5–7%.

Some fund managers use single pricing, in which case there is the same price quoted for buying and selling units, with any charges being separately disclosed.

10.1.5 Charges

The charges on a unit trust can be taken in three ways – an initial charge which is made up front, an annual management charge made periodically and an exit charge levied when the investor sells. Whatever charges are made must be explicitly detailed in the trust deed and documentation. The documents should provide details of both the current charges and the extent to which the manager can change them.

The up-front initial charge is added to the buying price incurred by the investor. Initial charges tend to be higher on actively managed funds, often in the range of 3% to 6.5%. Lower initial charges are typically levied on index trackers. Some managers will discount their initial charges for direct sales including sales made over the internet. It is not unusual for those managers that charge low or zero initial charges to make exit charges when the investor sells units.

When they apply, exit charges are generally only made when the investor sells within a set period of time, such as the first three or five years. Furthermore, these exit charges tend to be made on a sliding scale with a more substantial charge made for those exiting earlier than those exiting later. Both the set period and the sliding scale reflect the fact that, if the investor holds the unit for longer, the manager will benefit from the regular annual management charges that effectively reduces the need for the exit charge.

The annual management charge is generally levied at a rate of 0.5% to 1.5% of the underlying fund. Like the initial charge, the annual management charge will typically be lower for trusts that are cheaper to run, such as index trackers, and higher for more labour intensive actively managed funds.

10.2   Open-Ended Investment Companies (OEICs)

Open-ended investment companies (OEICs) are a type of open-ended collective investment formed as a corporation under the Open-Ended Investment Companies Regulations of the United Kingdom. Pronounced **oiks**, they are also known as ICVCs, which is an acronym for investment companies with variable capital. The terms ICVC and OEIC are used interchangeably, with different investment managers favouring one over the other.

With the implementation of the FSMA 2000, the range of UK-authorised OEICs was extended to be similar to that of unit trusts, including money market funds and property funds, for example.

Both OEICs and unit trusts are types of open-ended collective investments (see Section 10.3.1). However, with a unit trust, the units held provide beneficial ownership of the underlying trust assets. A share in an OEIC entitles the holder to a share in the profits of the OEIC, but the value of the share will be determined by the value of the underlying investments. For example, if the underlying investments are valued at £125,000,000 and there are 100,000,000 shares in issue, the net asset value of each share is £1.25.

The holder of a share in an OEIC can sell back the share to the company in any period specified in the prospectus.

An OEIC may take the form of an **umbrella fund** with a number of separately priced sub-funds, adopting different investment strategies or denominated in different currencies. Each sub-fund will have a separate client register and asset pool.

Classes of shares within an OEIC may include **income shares**, which pay a dividend, and **accumulation shares**, in which income is not paid out and all income received is added to net assets.

OEICs are similar to investment trusts in that both have corporate structures. The objective of the company in each case is to make a profit for shareholders, by investing in the shares of other companies. They differ in that an investment trust is a closed-ended investment and an OEIC is open-ended. The open-ended nature of an OEIC means that it cannot trade at a discount to net asset value (NAV) (see Section 10.3.1).

10.2.1 Buying and Selling OEICs

OEICs are single-priced instruments. Therefore, there is no bid/offer spread with OEICs. The buying price reflects the value of the underlying shares, with any initial charge reflecting dealing costs and management expenses being disclosed separately. The costs of creation of the fund may be met by the fund. When the investor wishes to sell the OEIC, the **authorised corporate director (ACD)** will buy it. The money value on sale will be based on the single price, less a deduction for the dealing charges.

10.3   Investment Trusts

Investment trusts have a long history in the UK. The Foreign and Colonial Investment Trust was the first to be founded in 1868 with the aim of *'giving the investor of moderate means the same advantage as the large capitalist'*. Today, it invests in more than 650 different companies in 36 countries.

In general, investment trusts provide a way for the small investor to have some exposure to investments in very large portfolios of assets, primarily equities, which are impractical for the investor to buy individually. In mid-2009 there were more than 600 investment trusts tracked by Trustnet, with total assets in the region of £60 billion.

Investment trusts are a form of collective investment, pooling the funds of many investors and spreading their investments across a diversified range of securities.

Investment trusts are managed by professional fund managers who select and manage the stocks in the trust's portfolio. Investment trusts are generally accessible to the individual investor, although shares in investment trusts are also widely held by institutional investors, such as pension funds.

Despite their name, investment trusts are not trusts but **public limited companies (plcs)** listed on the LSE. However, whereas other companies may make their profit from providing goods and services, an investment trust makes its profit solely from investments. The investor who buys shares in the investment trust hopes for dividends and capital growth in the value of the shares.

10.3.1 Comparison between Investment Trusts and Unit Trusts/OEICs

Investment trusts have wider **investment freedom** than unit trusts and OEICs/ICVCs. Investment trusts can:

- invest in unquoted private companies as well as quoted companies;
- provide venture capital to new companies or companies requiring new funds for expansion.

The corporate structure of an investment trust gives it a further advantage over unit trusts and OEICs, because it can raise money more freely to help it to achieve its objectives. Unit trusts' and OEICs' powers to borrow are more limited. The ability to borrow allows an investment trust to leverage returns for the investor. Such gearing also increases the volatility of returns.

Unlike unit trusts which are normally open-ended funds, investment funds are **closed-ended**. In the case of an **open-ended fund**, the trust can create new units when new investors subscribe and it can cancel units when investors cash in their holdings. In the case of a closed-ended fund, new investors buy investment trust shares from existing holders of the shares who wish to sell.

Because investment trusts are closed-ended investments, the number of shares in issue is not affected by the day-to-day purchases and sales by investors, which allows the managers to take a long-term view of the investments of the trust. With an open-ended scheme such as a unit trust or an OEIC, if there are more sales of units or shares by investors than purchases, the number of units reduces and the fund must pay out cash. As a result, the managers may need to sell investments even though it may not be the best time to do so from a strategic and long-term viewpoint.

Being closed-ended also means that the price of shares of the investment trust rises and falls according to demand for and supply of the shares of the investment trust, and not directly in line with the values of the underlying investments. In this way, investment trust prices can have greater volatility than unit trusts and OEICs, whose unit prices are directly related to the market values of the underlying investments.

Because prices are dependent on supply and demand, the price of the shares can be lower than the net asset value (NAV) of the share (see Section 10.3.3).

When the prices of the trust's share are below the NAV investors can buy investment trusts at a discount, while the income produced by the portfolio is based on the market value of the underlying investments. The income yield is therefore enhanced.

Charges incurred on investment trust holdings can be compared with the alternatives. Some unit trusts and OEICs have initial charges of around 5%. Initial charges may be much lower than this (at around 0.25%) for some investment trust savings schemes. However, there may be charges on selling investment trust holdings.

An investment trust is also subject to FCA rules.

10.3.2 Buying and Selling Shares in Investment Trusts

Prices

The quotation of the price of investment trust shares is similar to that for equities generally, and a dealer will give two prices.

- The higher price is the offer price, at which an investor can buy the shares.
- The lower price is the bid price, at which a holder of the shares can sell.

In a price quote in the financial media, a single price may be given: this will typically be the mid-market price, between the offer and bid prices.

The difference between the offer price and the bid price is the spread.

Dealing

Shares in investment trusts can be bought through a stockbroker, who is likely to charge the same level of commission as for other equities. If a broker is not providing any advice and is providing an execution only service, then commission may be as low as 0.5%, or £10 per deal.

Stamp duty will be payable at 0.5% of the purchase consideration. If the broker is providing an advisory service, commission will be higher, for example, 1.5% or 2% of the purchase consideration.

Some brokers provide discretionary investment trust management services for individuals with larger sums to invest. The broker will select trusts that meet the investor's investment objectives and will charge an annual management fee in addition to dealing charges.

An investor can usually deal directly through the investment trust managers instead of through a broker, and may incur lower charges by doing so.

Small investors who do not have an account with a broker may prefer to deal through the managers. However, the managers may only deal on a daily basis, while a broker will be able to quote an up-to-the-minute price and a deal can be made instantly by telephone.

10.3.3 Net Asset Value (NAV) and Investment Performance

An investment trust share is similar to any other equity, except that the specific objective of the company is to invest rather than to transact other forms of business. The past performance of the trust can be measured against standard benchmarks of performance, such as market indices most closely covering the market sector in which the trust invests.

Aspects of investment trusts influencing the assessment of performance are:

- dividend growth and gross yield (calculated in the same way as for other shares);
- net asset value (NAV);
- levels of discount/premium to NAV;
- gearing.

The NAV is essentially the net worth of an investment trust company's equity capital, usually expressed in pence per share, and is calculated from adding together the following:

- the value of the trust's listed investments at mid-market prices;
- the value of its unlisted investments at directors' valuation;
- cash and other net current assets.

The company's liabilities are deducted from this figure, including any issued preference capital at nominal value. The resulting figure is the asset value or shareholders' funds of the company. Dividing by the number of shares gives the NAV per share. The valuation may be carried out monthly, weekly or daily.

By way of illustration, the NAV of an investment trust with assets worth £10 million, with liabilities of £4 million and 12 million ordinary shares is 50p per share, ie, (£10 million – £4 million) divided by 12 million shares. However, this figure is an undiluted figure. It does not make any allowances for any warrants in issue (see Section 7.2).

Most investment trusts operate at a discount to NAV. The level of premium or discount relates to the demand for shares, and any factor that influences demand will affect it. For example, if investment in emerging markets becomes unpopular because of a global recession, share prices for investment trusts which focus on that sector may fall and, if the values of the underlying assets have not fallen so much, the level of discount to NAV may increase.

10.3.4 Split Capital Investment Trusts

A split capital investment trust is like other investment trusts, in that it has a single portfolio of investments. A split capital trust, however, involves a number of different classes of share, with holders of the different classes having different entitlements to returns of capital or income from the trust.

A split capital trust has a limited life. The period of time remaining to the planned winding-up of the trust is usually very significant to how the prices of the different classes of share move.

Split capital investment trusts allow trust managers to tailor returns to appeal to different investors with different strategies, circumstances and attitudes. For example, if a low-risk but rising income is required, stepped preference shares may be suitable. If an increasing income is required but high risk is acceptable, an income share may be more appropriate.

The capital value of all classes of share will vary up until the trust is wound up. At that stage, the amount of capital returned will depend on the class of share and the order of priority in which the trust is wound up.

10.4 Exchange-Traded Funds (ETFs)

An exchange-traded fund (ETF), also known as an exchange-traded product (ETP), is an investment fund traded on many global stock exchanges in the same manner as a typical stock for a corporation. An ETF holds assets such as stocks or bonds and trades at approximately the same price as the NAV of its underlying assets over the course of the trading day. Most ETFs track an index, such as the S&P 500 or MSCI EAFE, and European Australasia and Far East ETFs can be attractive as investment vehicles because of their low costs, tax-efficiency, and stock-like features.

Only authorised participants (typically, large institutional investors) actually buy or sell shares of an ETF directly from/to the fund manager, and then only in creation units – large blocks of tens of thousands of ETF shares – which are usually exchanged in kind with baskets of the underlying securities. Authorised participants may wish to invest in the ETF shares long-term, but usually act as market makers on the open market, using their ability to exchange creation units with their underlying securities to provide liquidity of the ETF shares and help ensure that their intra-day market price approximates to the NAV of the underlying assets. Other investors, such as individuals using a retail broker, trade ETF shares via a secondary market such as the NYSE/Arca exchange in the US.

Closed-ended funds are not considered to be ETFs, even though they are funds and are traded on an exchange. ETFs have been available in the US since 1993 and in Europe since 1999. ETFs have traditionally been index funds, but in 2008 the US Securities and Exchange Commission (SEC) began to authorise the creation of actively managed ETFs.

10.4.1 Trading Features of an Exchange-Traded Fund (ETF)

The selection of ETFs available is now very diverse and provides investors with a real alternative to some of the more traditional funds. One of the key features of ETFs is that, since they are listed securities and trade in the same manner as shares, the pricing takes place in real time and the funds can be bought or sold during all times when markets are open. This is unlike the position with many types of collective investment vehicles, such as unit trusts and other investment funds, where the pricing of the fund based on the NAV of the constituents is computed at the end of each day and where the ability to transact is also limited to certain prescribed times. For investors and traders who want to be able to react quickly to market movements and have immediate pricing and settlement for their positions (subject only to the normal settlement period for any listed share), the variety of ETF products is preferable to the more traditional structured investment products.

One can purchase an ETF which has been designed and constructed to track a general stock index, such as the S&P 500 (SPY) or the NASDAQ 100 index (QQQQ), or indices for market sectors (eg, industrials, financials), geographical regions, currencies, commodities such as gold, silver, copper and oil, and even certain managed funds with objectives and management criteria laid out in an offering prospectus.

Another factor which has led to the increasing popularity of ETFs is that many of them are constructed in a manner which enables an investor to buy or take a long position with an ETF with a view to benefiting from a downward movement in a particular sector or index. This feature makes it easier for many investors to take a short position than having to borrow stock from a brokerage. In addition, it is also possible to purchase from a variety of ETFs if leverage is **built in** to the position taken.

For example, if one has a bearish view on the direction of the S&P 500 index, it is possible to purchase an ETF which trades on the NYSE/Arca exchange under the symbol SDS, which is known as UltraShort S&P 500 ProShares fund, and this fund will return twice the inverse return of a long position in the S&P 500 index. In essence, the mechanics for many kinds of inverse ETFs are that one buys (or goes long) the ETF and this will profit as the sector or index goes down.

ETFs are also available to track the performance of various fixed-income instruments such as US Treasury bonds or indices which track high-yield bonds and other corporate bonds. Again, these can be used to take a long position on higher yields, in effect to be short the bond on a price basis. One well-known ETF traded in the US under the symbol TBT tracks the yield on US T-bonds of 20 years plus maturity. The fund moves in line with the real-time yields of the long end of the US Treasury curve, and therefore the fund moves inversely to the price of such US T-bonds.

Charges and Taxation

Many ETF products are managed by large financial intermediaries, including BlackRock and JP Morgan Chase, and the fees and charges are very competitive and often considerably lower than those applied for more traditionally managed funds.

Also, no stamp duty is applied to purchases of ETFs available from UK exchanges.

Tracking Methods

While the operation, marketing and construction of an ETF requires skills on the part of the ETF management company, many funds are in effect tracker funds and therefore have to reflect the composition of a reference index or commodity.

The large amounts of funds invested in tracker funds can have a distorting effect on the market, for example if many tracker funds buy a particular share at the point when it is included in the index. Undoubtedly, inclusion in an index can be beneficial to the price of a share, while exclusion may be a factor causing a share to receive less attention from investors and to fall out of favour.

Physical Versus Synthetic ETFs

When tracking an index, the providers of ETFs can use either physical or synthetic replication to ensure their ETFs mimic their designated indices as accurately as possible.

Physical replication means the ETF will buy and own most or all of an index's constituents in order to replicate the index's performance. Despite being simple and transparent, since physical replication involves buying and selling index components, this strategy is inherently labour intensive and costly. These additional costs are ultimately passed along to investors in the form of higher charges.

In contrast, synthetic replication involves the ETF provider entering into a contract with a counterparty (typically a bank) to deliver the return of the fund's benchmark index in exchange for a fee. This **swap** contract means that, for example, an equity ETF will not actually hold any stocks at all. Instead it will have a contractual relationship with the counterparty bank. This may generally reduce costs and any possibility of tracking error, but it increases risk for investors. This is because there is a danger of the counterparty being unable to honour its obligation under the contract, known as counterparty risk.

10.5 Unregulated Collective Investment Schemes (UCISs) – an Example of Non-Mainstream Pooled Investments

10.5.1 Regulated and Unregulated Collective Investment Schemes

A collective investment scheme, according to the FCA, is any arrangement:

- the purpose or effect of which is to enable those taking part (either by owning the property, or part of it, or otherwise) to participate in or receive profits or income arising from the acquisition, holding, management or disposal of the property;
- when persons taking part do not have day-to-day control over the management of the property; and
- whether either the contributions and profits or income are pooled, or the property is managed as a whole by or on behalf of the operator of the scheme, or both.

The FCA distinguishes two types of CISs:

- Regulated CISs that are either authorised by the FCA, or, if they are from outside the UK, they are recognised by the FCA. Recognition enables overseas CISs to be marketed to the public in the UK and the FCA will only recognise an overseas scheme if certain specified criteria are met.
- Unregulated collective investment schemes (UCISs) are those schemes that are not authorised or recognised by the FCA. UCISs may be established, operated and/or managed in the UK or in a jurisdiction outside the UK.

UCISs are described as unregulated because they are not subject to the same restrictions as a regulated CIS (eg, in terms of their investment powers and how they are run). Although the schemes themselves are not authorised or recognised, persons carrying on certain regulated activities in the UK in relation to UCISs (including providing personal recommendations, arranging deals and establishing, operating and managing schemes) are subject to regulations, particularly from the FCA.

UCISs are deemed to be among a group of investments referred to as 'non-mainstream pooled investments' that cannot be promoted to retail investors unless they meet specific exemptions; for example they can be shown to be sophisticated or high net worth investors. Furthermore, UCISs are generally regarded as being characterised by a high degree of volatility, illiquidity or both – and therefore are usually regarded as speculative investments. This means that in practice they are rarely regarded as suitable for more than a small proportion of an investor's portfolio. The schemes can offer exotic investments – such as golf courses in Mexico or forests in Brazil, off-plan property in Eastern European countries – and some not so exotic, such as wine in France.

10.5.2 The Risks of Unregulated Collective Investment Schemes (UCISs)

As with most other investments, a client investing in a UCIS could lose some or all of their principal investment. However this risk is likely to be particularly relevant to UCISs. UCISs frequently invest in assets that are not available to regulated CISs (for example, because they are riskier or less liquid), or are structured in a way that is different from regulated CISs. Unlike regulated CISs, UCISs are not subject to investment and borrowing restrictions aimed at ensuring a prudent spread of risk. As a result they are generally considered to be a high-risk investment and firms should always ensure that clients fully understand the risks before investing.

Typical risks encountered in an individual UCIS are likely to include the following:

- **Liquidity** – most unregulated investments will not offer daily liquidity. It is normal for investors wishing to redeem their investment to serve notice of their intention and for the redemption to take effect at the next available redemption date – typically at the end of the month in which notice is served. The investment will be sold at the price prevailing at the end of the following month and the realisation value returned to the investor approximately 14 days later. It can be seen, therefore, that the elapsed time from serving notice to receiving the proceeds can be up to two and a half months.

- **Fixed- or long-term commitment** – mainly due to the liquidity constraints set out above, investment must be regarded at outset as long-term.

- **Lack of Financial Services Compensation Scheme (FSCS) cover** – due to the unregulated status, should the provider of the investment become insolvent, cease trading, or suffer an act of fraud or malfeasance in relation to a UCIS, the investor is not eligible to make a claim under the FSCS. As a result, extra care should be taken by the adviser to satisfy him/herself that the investment is commercially and financially viable. Information must be sought from the fund's managers and from other institutions representing the fund, such as auditors, accountants, bankers and legal representatives. Much of this information is available in the fund prospectus and/or memorandum.

- **There is no guarantee of capital or income return** – while this represents a risk, it is not necessarily significantly different to the risk associated with a regulated investment.

- **High charges** – some unregulated investments may have higher administration charges associated with them. This can only be determined on an individual fund basis. Some unregulated investments include a **performance fee** for the manager if they hit a level of performance in excess of (say) 20% p.a. It is usual, in these cases, for there also to be a **high water mark** which means that if the price of the investment falls in a year only to rise again in the next, the manager will not become eligible to receive an additional fee, until the previous maximum fund price is surpassed.

- **Gearing** – this means that the fund can borrow money to enhance the total funds available to it for investment. If the fund goes up in value (and the capital value of the loan remains static) this can lead to a higher multiple of gains (net of interest charges) being available for distribution to the investors. The risk is that in the event of a loss in the value of the fund's assets, this can lead to a higher multiple of loss to the investor, because the loan will still require repayment in its entirety before NAV can be attributed to the investors.

- **Currency/geopolitical** – an offshore investment may have a base currency other than sterling. This means that there is **currency exposure** in the translation of value back into GBP from whatever the base currency is. If, during the period of investment, the base currency strengthens against sterling, this is advantageous to the investor; and vice-versa. Part of the due diligence process is to establish whether fund management **hedges out** the currency risk thereby neutralising its effect on underlying fund performance. Similarly, investing offshore may expose the investor to parts of the world which are less politically stable than the UK. If there is the slightest risk that assets might be sequestrated as a result of political unrest and/or government instability, the due diligence process should establish this and communicate the risk to the investor.

- **Fraud and money laundering** – in the same way as one cannot **regulate away** completely the possibility of fraud, extra care is required to verify the credentials of fund management and the supporting administration team associated with an offshore investment.

- **Conflict of interest** – routine due diligence should establish whether any person associated with the proposal, capital raising, management or administration of the fund has an interest in the fund's success over and above their own role, duty or responsibility. If multiple interests exist, there is no implication of impropriety as long as any potential conflict of interest is disclosed in the fund prospectus and understood by the investor.

- **Single asset** – an unregulated investment may represent a single project, the success of which is dependent upon certain criteria. This may be deemed **high risk**.

Exercise Answers

Exercise 1

a. Calculate the flat yield on a 4% gilt, redeeming in eight years and priced at £98.90.

$$(4\%/98.90) \times 100 = 4.04\%$$

b. Calculate the flat yield on a 7% gilt, redeeming in three years and priced at £108.60.

$$(7\%/108.60) \times 100 = 6.45\%$$

Exercise 2

The share value of the conversion choice is currently 15 x £6.40 = £96.

The bond is trading at £110, so the premium is £14 per £100 nominal value.

Expressed as a percentage: 14/96 x 100 = 14.6%.

Exercise 3

a.

Time	Cash flow	Discount factor	Present value
End of year one	£10	1/1.06	9.43
End of year two	£110	$1/1.06^2$	97.90
Sum of the individual present values = price of the bond			£107.33

b.

Time	Cash flow	Discount factor	Present value
End of year one	£10	1/1.04	9.62
End of year two	£110	$1/1.04^2$	101.70
Sum of the individual present values = price of the bond			£111.32

Chapter Two
Primary and Secondary Markets

This syllabus area will provide approximately 10 of the 100 examination questions

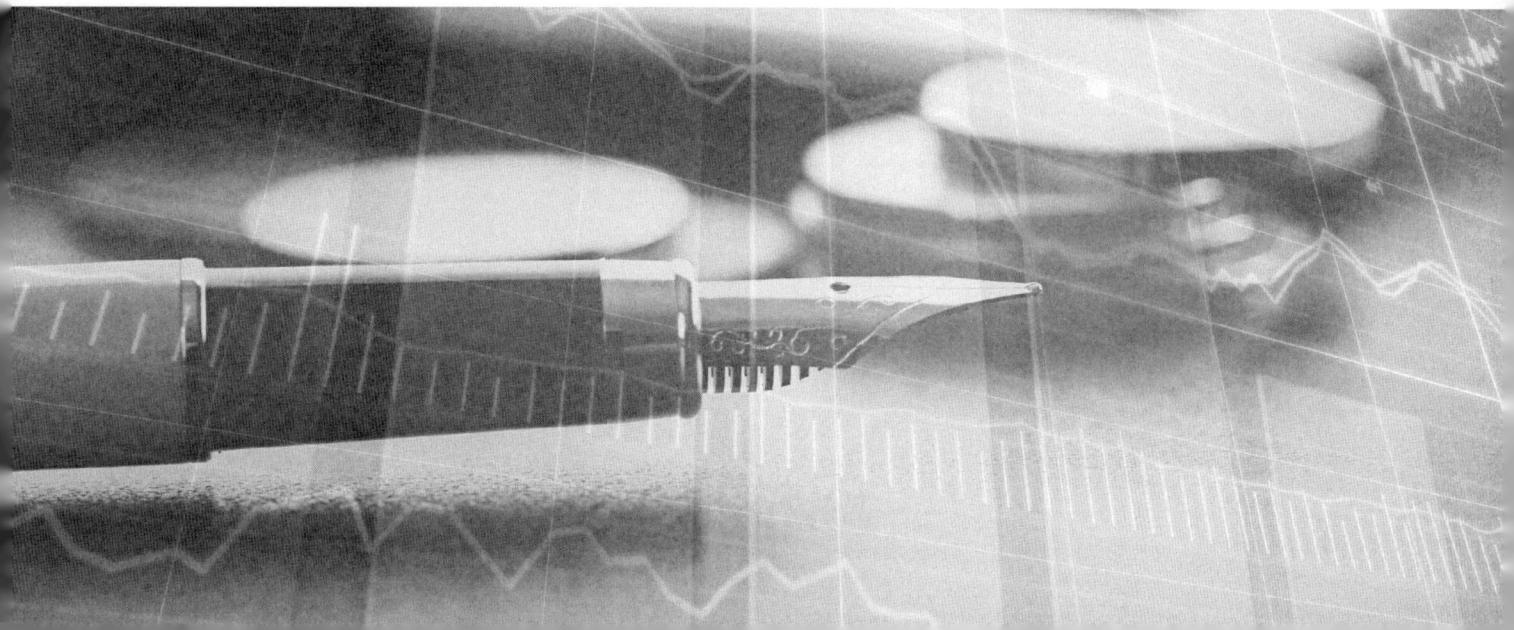

1. The Primary and Secondary Markets

Learning Objective

2.1.1 Know the principal characteristics of, and the differences between, the primary and secondary markets. In particular: the role of the listing authority; users of the primary market; users of the secondary market; uses of primary and secondary markets

Stock exchanges such as the LSE in the UK, and the NYSE in the US, are organised marketplaces for issuing securities and then trading those securities via their members. All stock exchanges provide both a primary and a secondary market.

1. The **primary market**, or the new issues market, is where securities are issued for the first time. The primary markets exist to enable issuers of securities, particularly companies, to raise capital, and to enable the surplus funds held by potential investors to be matched with investment opportunities the issuers offer. It is a crucial source of funding. The terminology often used when companies raise capital on the stock exchange is that they first access the primary market and **float**. The process that the companies go through when they float is often called the **initial public offering (IPO)**. Companies can use a variety of ways to achieve flotation, such as offers for investors to subscribe for their shares (offers for subscription).

2. The **secondary market** is where existing securities are traded between investors, and the stock exchanges provide a variety of systems to assist in this, such as the LSE's SETS that is used to trade the largest companies' shares. These systems provide investors with liquidity, giving them the ability to sell their securities if they wish. Trading activity in the secondary market also results in the ongoing provision of buy and sell prices to investors via the exchange's member firms.

Each jurisdiction has its own rules and regulations for companies seeking a listing, and continuing obligations for those already listed. In the UK, there is the **United Kingdom Listing Authority (UKLA)** which is a division of the FCA. The formal description of the UKLA is that it is the **competent authority for listing** – making the decisions as to which companies' shares and bonds (including gilts) can be admitted to be traded on the LSE. The rules are contained in a rule book called the **Listing Rules**.

The UKLA sets the rules relating to becoming listed on the LSE, including the implementation of any relevant EU directives. The LSE is responsible for the operation of the exchange, including the trading of the securities on the secondary market, although the UKLA can suspend the listing of particular securities and therefore remove their secondary market trading activity on the exchange.

In a similar way in the US, the **Securities and Exchange Commission (SEC)** requires companies seeking a listing on the US exchanges (such as the NYSE and NASDAQ) to register certain details with the SEC first. Once listed, companies are then required to file regular reports with the SEC, particularly in relation to their trading performance and financial situation.

1.1 Users of the Markets

1.1.1 Users of Primary Markets

Issuers of new securities, such as corporations engaging in IPOs or follow-on offerings as well as the issuers of certain kinds of debt instruments, are the main suppliers of new securities in the primary markets.

The main **purchasers** of newly issued securities are large institutional investors such as pension funds, insurance companies and collective investment vehicles, such as unit trusts, which are buying the securities being offered on behalf of their clients, who are primarily members of the general public.

1.1.2 Users of Secondary Markets

In the secondary market, where existing securities are bought and sold throughout the daily trading sessions, there will be a variety of participants. In addition to the previously mentioned institutional investors engaged in the purchase of newly issued securities, these same institutions will, as a result of changes in their asset allocation decision making, be engaged in selling previously owned securities within their portfolio and, in turn, adding other securities which have been available in the secondary market previously. The constant shifting of priorities in portfolio allocation constitutes a large part of the transactional volume which arises each day, for example, in the activities of the LSE and the NYSE.

Also the secondary markets will be used by short-term speculators and traders who may hold securities for very short periods – perhaps even a few minutes or hours – when the motivation is to attempt to make profits from anticipating the direction of short-term price changes in the variety of securities which are available for trade in the secondary markets.

Increasingly the principal users of secondary markets are various funds and trading vehicles which engage in **automated** trading strategies – sometimes characterised as **high frequency trading (HFT)** when the objective is to exploit transitory price discrepancies which may exist in relation to quite complex algorithmic trading strategies.

1.2 Motivations for the Use of Primary and Secondary Markets

The principal use and benefit of **primary markets** is to allow owners of capital to purchase new securities, which are made available from new issuers of securities. The issuers wish to raise capital for a variety of purposes, such as business expansion or acquisitions, and the buyers of the offerings wish to allocate their capital across what they perceive as attractive investment opportunities. In general terms, the holders of these newly issued securities are seeking longer-term investment objectives. However, some activity in the primary market – such as when there is a highly publicised IPO – may be for short-term speculative purposes. The manner in which some buyers of newly issued securities buy a new offering, and then, in the midst of some rather exaggerated market excitement about the new issue, sell the new issue shortly afterwards is known as **flipping**.

The principal use and benefit of **secondary markets** is that they provide a liquid environment within which owners of securities may want to sell a current holding and when a willing buyer wants to purchase existing securities. The larger capitalisation issues are usually bought and sold in substantial amounts during each trading session and the **spread**, ie, the difference between the price that the securities are being offered – or the ask price – and the price that buyers are prepared to buy these securities – the bid price – is narrow. One characteristic of a liquid market is that spreads are narrow. Another feature which provides for more liquidity is the activity of speculators – including HFT activities – when the continuous buying and selling of securities with very short-term holding period horizons provides a depth to the secondary market, which would not be available if the secondary market only existed for institutions seeking longer-term investment reallocations.

2. Stock Exchanges

Learning Objective

2.2.1   Understand the purpose, role and main features of stock exchanges. In particular: scope; provision of liquidity; price formation; brokers versus dealers

2.2.2   Understand the purpose, role and main features of alternative trading venues: off-exchange trades; dark pools; OTC; private transactions; multilateral trading facilities

2.1   Purpose and Role

Stock exchanges offer membership to investment banks and firms of stockbrokers. Becoming a member of an exchange enables these banks and stockbrokers to be involved in secondary market trades.

Stock exchanges provide trading platforms to enable listed securities to be bought and sold in the secondary market. As a consequence of the ongoing activities of the major participants in the secondary market – institutional investors, banks, and speculators – these exchanges provide liquidity to existing and potential investors, enabling existing investors to sell their securities and allowing potential investors to become actual investors by purchasing securities. Furthermore, because these exchanges aggregate and integrate the trading activity on their systems as well as some alternative venues, the prices at which trades are executed is the **market price** at any given time. This is described as the **price formation** process, or sometimes markets are characterised as **price discovery mechanisms**.

Brokers simply arrange deals for their clients, as well as potentially giving advice to their clients as to which securities they should buy, sell or retain. In return for arranging (and potentially advising), the brokers will earn a commission that is typically calculated as a set percentage of the value of the deal. Acting as a broker is often described as **dealing as agent**, and firms of stockbrokers tend to act as brokers on the stock exchanges.

Dealers, in contrast to brokers, actually buy or sell securities. If a client wants to sell shares, a dealer may buy those shares; if another client wants to buy shares, a dealer may sell those shares. Acting as a dealer is often described as **dealing as principal**, because the dealer is taking a principal position by either buying, or selling the securities. It is the investment banks that tend to act as dealers on the stock exchanges.

2.2 Trading Systems

Historically, stock exchanges were physical locations where the members would gather. The brokers would bring orders from their clients and arrange deals with the dealers on the floor of the exchange. This was referred to as 'open outcry' trading. However, stock exchanges have introduced electronic systems to execute deals, and the physical exchange floor is increasingly unusual. Today the majority of the world's major stock exchanges run secondary market trading systems that are solely **electronic**.

2.2.1 Over-the-Counter (OTC)

Over-the-counter (OTC) is the term given to trading which is conducted by networks of dealers and when the trading is not co-ordinated or subject to the formal procedures and standardised formats of an exchange. Many types of trading and investment activities are conducted on OTC platforms, including most in fixed-income markets and derivatives.

The transactions which are conducted in an OTC market result in bilateral contracts, in which two parties agree on how a particular trade or agreement is to be settled in the future. Such transactions are usually between an investment bank and its clients directly. Forwards and swaps are prime examples of such contracts and these deals are mostly done via a computer or telephone. For derivatives, the agreements are usually governed by an International Swaps and Derivatives Association (ISDA) agreement.

2.2.2 Dark Pools and Multilateral Trading Facilities (MTFs)

Dark pool is the term that generally refers to an off-exchange trading venue where stocks are traded in large quantities without the prices being displayed until after the trade is done. The term 'dark' is used to describe the fact that pricing information cannot be seen. The opposite of dark pools are known as 'lit pools'. Trading undertaken in this way is also commonly described as **dark liquidity**. The venues include both specialist crossing networks, such as Liquidnet and ITG Posit, as well as systems run by banks, such as Credit Suisse's Crossfinder and Goldman Sachs' Sigma X.

One investment manager has described the appeals of dark liquidity pools as follows:

A dark pool is a very simple way you can hopefully capture lots of liquidity and achieve a large proportion of your order being executed without displaying anything to the market.

In the US, the influx of crossing networks and alternative venues, and the rapid adoption of electronic trading technologies, has been driving the growth of dark pools for several years. Recent estimates state that there are currently more than 50 dark pools of liquidity in the US, and more than 30 in Europe. In the US, the dark pools are a form of what are referred to as **alternative trading systems (ATSs)** and, in Europe, they are a form of **multilateral trading facility (MTF)**.

In Europe, by making use of certain waivers for pre-trade transparency under MiFID, MTFs allow institutions to execute large volume trades away from the visible order book. As there is no pre-trade transparency, there is no visible price formation. This is essentially what leads to the description 'dark'.

There are a number of different models on which these dark pools are based. While certain models offer a basic dark matching facility, other systems provide a pass-through function that allows a user to send an order through to a 'light' venue. For instance, the order can be passed through to a standard MTF or exchange if it cannot be filled in the dark pool.

2.2.3   Off-Exchange Trading

In 1998 the SEC in the US authorised the introduction of **electronic communication networks (ECNs)**. In essence, an ECN is a computerised trading platform which allows trading of various financial assets, primarily equities and currencies, to take place away from a specific venue such as a stock exchange. The primary motivation for the SEC to authorise the introduction of ECNs was to increase competition among trading firms by lowering transaction costs, giving clients full access to their order books and offering order matching outside of traditional exchange hours.

Since an ECN exists as a large number of networked computers/work stations, it effectively has no **centre** or physical location but rather is decentralised and virtual. ECNs are sometimes also referred to as **alternative trading systems** or **venues**.

Alternative trading systems (ATSs) have come to play a dominant role in public markets for accessing liquidity. The most popular among varieties of ATSs are ECNs and crossing networks.

An example of an ECN is Bloomberg's TradeBook which, according to its website, describes its mission as follows:

(We) believe that traders equipped with advanced algorithms to manage complexity and supported by analytics to provide the right market insights can achieve superior executions. We partner with our clients to develop technology and services that give them better control of their transactions and keep them more informed of market opportunities.

Examples of crossing networks are run by Liquidnet, Aritas Securities (formerly Pipeline) and Posit. Liquidnet, which has a presence in Europe and in Asian markets, provides not only a crossing network, but is also a major provider, among others, of pools of dark liquidity as discussed in Section 2.2.2.

2.2.4   Private Transactions

Private transactions are those offerings of securities which are made, not to the general public, but to a subset of so-called **sophisticated investors**, when the same rigorous kinds of disclosures that have to be made in an IPO prospectus (sometimes known in the US as a **red herring**) can be avoided.

In the US, the SEC has special provisions for what are termed **private placements**. A private placement (or non-public offering) is a funding round of securities which are sold without an IPO, and without the formality of an approved prospectus, usually to a small number of chosen private investors.

Although these placements are subject to the Securities Act of 1933, the securities offered do not have to be registered with the SEC if the issuance of the securities conforms to an exemption from registrations as set forth in the Rules known as Regulation D. Private placements may typically consist of stocks, shares of common stock or preferred stock or other forms of membership interests, warrants or promissory notes (including convertible promissory notes), and purchasers are often institutional investors such as banks, insurance companies and pension funds.

2.2.5 Major Exchanges Worldwide

The major exchanges around the world are detailed in the following table alongside the country (or countries) they operate within and the trading systems they use.

Exchange	Country/Countries	Trading System
Deutsche Börse	Germany	Electronic
LSE	UK	Electronic
NASDAQ	US	Electronic
NYSE Euronext	US and Europe	Electronic plus some open outcry in Wall Street
TSE	Japan	Electronic

3. The London Stock Exchange (LSE)

Learning Objective

2.3.1   Know the regulatory framework for the LSE: Companies Act; FCA; Exchange Rule Book

The regulatory framework that lies behind the way that the LSE operates includes three major constituents: the law (in particular the Companies Act), the requirements of the FCA and the rules laid down by the exchange itself (in its Rule Book).

The **Companies Act** details the requirements for companies generally, such as the requirement to prepare annual accounts, to have accounts audited and for AGMs. Of particular significance to the LSE are the Companies Act requirements to enable a company to be a plc, since one of the requirements for a company to be listed and traded on the exchange is that the company is a plc.

The FCA has to give its recognition before an exchange is allowed to operate in the UK. It has granted recognition to the LSE and, by virtue of this recognition, the exchange is described as a **recognised investment exchange (RIE)**. In granting recognition, the FCA assesses whether the exchange has sufficient systems and controls to run a market. Furthermore, the FCA (through the UKLA) lays down the detailed rules that have to be met before companies are admitted to the official **list** that enables their shares to be traded on the exchange.

The LSE also has its own rules in relation to who can access its systems and become members of the exchange, as well as how those members must behave when trading on the exchange.

3.1 Criteria for Listing: the Official List and the Alternative Investment Market (AIM)

Learning Objective

2.3.2 Know the admissions criteria for listing: trading record; amount raised; percentage in public hands; market capitalisation

2.4.1 Know the admissions criteria: appointment and role of a nominated adviser; appointment and role of a broker; transferability of shares; no minimum shares in public hands; no trading record required; no shareholder approval needed; no minimum market capitalisation

2.4.2 Know the regulatory framework for AIM: London Stock Exchange; AIM Rules; Companies Act; FCA

The LSE has established two markets for company securities: the Official List and the Alternative Investment Market (AIM). The Official (or full) List is the senior market; indeed it is often referred to as the **main market**. Entry rules are stringent, ensuring that only companies of a high quality can be involved. AIM was created to provide a market for smaller, less well-established companies. As we will see in Section 3.1.2, the admission requirements of AIM are less stringent.

3.1.1 The Official List

The criteria for admission to the **Official List** are set out in the Listing Rules and, as was stated in Section 1, this rule book is maintained by the UKLA, itself a division of the FCA.

The main rules contained in the Listing Rules for admission to the full list are:

- Every company applying for a listing must be a plc and must be represented by a sponsor (alternatively referred to as a **listing agent**), which will usually be an investment bank, stockbroker, law firm or accountancy practice. The sponsor provides a link between the company and the UKLA, guiding the company through the listing process.
- The expected market capitalisation of the company should be at least £700,000 for the company's shares to be listed.
- For issuers listing debt securities, the aggregate market value of the debt securities should be at least £200,000.
- The company should have a trading record of at least three years.
- At least 25% of the company's shares should be in public hands, or be available for public purchase. The term **public** excludes directors and their associates and anyone who holds 5% or more of the shares.
- The company and its advisers must publish a prospectus, a detailed document providing potential investors with the information required to make an informed decision on the company and its shares.
- The company must restrict its ability to issue warrants to no more than 20% of the issued share capital.

- Listing is not free, and a further requirement before a company's shares can be admitted to the Official List is that the appropriate fee has been paid.

Once listed, companies are expected to fulfil certain **continuing obligations**: they are obliged to issue a half-yearly report in addition to annual accounts, and they have to notify the market of any new, price-sensitive information.

3.1.2   The Alternative Investment Market (AIM)

In contrast to the Official List, to which access is via application to the UKLA and the UKLA's listing rules must be complied with, AIM companies' application and regulations are set by the LSE. AIM companies are usually smaller than their fully listed counterparts, and the rules governing their listing are much less stringent. There is no restriction on market value, percentage of shares in public hands or trading history and no shareholder approval is required.

The main requirements for a company's shares to be admitted to the AIM are twofold:

1.   That there is no restriction on the transferability of the shares.
2.   That the AIM company appoints two experts to assist it:
     a.   the **nominated adviser** – can be thought of as an exchange expert, advising the company on all aspects of AIM listing rules and compliance;
     b.   the **broker** – AIM companies' shares are usually less liquid than those of fully listed companies; it is the broker's job to ensure that there is a market in the company's shares, to facilitate trading in those shares and to provide ongoing information about the company to interested parties.

As with the full market, the LSE imposes similar continuing obligations on AIM companies.

There are also certain other aspects in relation to AIM companies and the broker and nominated adviser:

- The broker and adviser can be the same firm; they are often firms of stockbrokers or accountants.
- If a company ceases, at any time, to have a broker or adviser, then the firm's shares are suspended from trading.
- If the company is without a broker or adviser for a period of one month it is removed from AIM.

As with the overall exchange, there are three major constituents to the regulatory framework for AIM: the law (in particular, the Companies Act); the requirements of the FCA; and the rules established by the exchange itself (in its own rule book).

The **Companies Act** details the requirements for companies generally, such as the requirement to prepare annual accounts, the need to have accounts audited and for AGMs. As with the LSE generally, the Companies Act requirements to enable a company to be a plc are particularly important because one of the requirements for a company to be listed and traded on AIM is that the company is a plc.

The FCA's recognition of the LSE as an RIE enables the LSE to set up the submarket that is AIM. However, the nominated adviser role removes the need for any UKLA involvement.

The **LSE** also has its own rules in relation to AIM. There is a rule book for the companies admitted to the market (the AIM rules for companies), and a rule book for the nominated advisers (the AIM rules for nominated advisers).

4. Methods of Trading and Participants

4.1 Quote-Driven Versus Order-Driven Systems

Learning Objective

2.5.1 Understand the differences between quote-driven and order-driven markets and how they operate

Stock exchanges exist throughout the world as centralised forums for dealing in investments.

For companies offering shares and bonds, these exchanges provide a means of raising money, in order to develop and expand. For investors, they provide a safe marketplace for buying and selling their investments.

The major example of a stock exchange in the UK is the LSE. The LSE is like a club whose members are able to take advantage of its facilities. In the case of the LSE, the members are investment banks and stockbroking firms. The facilities that the exchange offers are its trading systems.

Trading systems provided by exchanges around the world can be classified on the basis of the type of trading they offer. Broadly, systems are either quote-driven or order-driven:

- **Quote-driven systems** – market makers agree to buy and sell at least a set minimum number of shares at quoted prices. The buying price is the bid and the selling price is the offer. The prime example of a quote-driven equity trading system is NASDAQ in the US.
- **Order-driven systems** – the investors (or agents acting on their behalf) indicate how many securities they want to buy or sell, and at what price. The system then simply brings together the buyers and sellers. Order-driven systems are very common in the equity markets, where the NYSE, the TSE and the LSE's SETS are all examples of order-driven equity markets.

The presence of market makers on quote-driven systems provides liquidity that might be lacking on an order-driven system. Market makers are required to quote two-way prices, resulting in an ability for trades to be executed. In contrast, an order-driven system can lack liquidity, since transactions can only be matched against other orders – if there are insufficient orders, trades cannot be matched.

The orders that await matching are included in the so-called '**order book**'. The buy side of the order book lists orders to buy, and the sell side of the order book lists orders to sell. New sell orders entered into the system potentially match existing orders on the buy side. New buy orders potentially match existing sell side orders in the order book.

Increasingly trading systems are run electronically, allowing participants to trade via computer screens. However, there are notable exceptions: the NYSE still retains a physical trading floor where buyers and sellers gather to trade in an open outcry manner in addition to the electronic system.

Some trading systems combine features of both order-driven and quote-driven systems – these are referred to as **hybrid** systems and include the LSE's SETSqx.

4.2 Participants

Learning Objective

2.5.2 Know the functions and obligations of: market makers; broker-dealers; inter-dealer brokers

Member firms of an exchange like the LSE can act in two different capacities or roles – as a **principal** and as an **agent**. This does not preclude an individual firm from acting in both capacities; at some times it may be acting as an agent and at others it may be acting as a principal.

When a firm is acting as a **principal** it is essentially buying shares for its own account, in the hope of the shares increasing in value before it sells them, or, in the case of a **short** transaction, selling borrowed shares at a higher price at the time of borrowing than the price it has to pay when it wishes to replace or **cover**. Firms acting in this way can also be described as performing their function as **dealers** and, in more specialised cases, as outlined below, as **market makers**.

When a firm is acting as an **agent** it is essentially arranging and making deals on behalf of other third parties, and it makes money, when acting in this capacity, by charging a commission on the deal. This agency role is commonly described as acting as a **broker**. For instance, when acting as an agent or broker a firm will receive orders to buy and sell equities on behalf of its clients, and find matches for the trades that its clients want to make. In return for these services, brokers charge commission.

If a firm decides to focus only on acting as a principal it is known simply as a dealer, and some LSE member firms have chosen simply to buy and sell equities for their own account.

Most exchanges' members, however, are **broker-dealers**. This means they have the dual capacity to either arrange deals (acting as a broker), or to buy and sell shares for themselves (acting as a dealer).

Some of an exchange's member firms have chosen to take on the special responsibilities of a **market maker**. When a firm acts as a market maker, it stands ready to provide a source of liquidity to certain sections of the market. By being prepared to provide a bid for shares that third parties want to sell and an ask for parties that want to buy shares at any time, the market maker smooths out the more erratic price movements that can occur without this additional source of market liquidity.

To become a market maker a member firm must apply to the stock exchange, giving details of the securities in which it has chosen to deal. It must provide prices at which it is willing to buy and sell a minimum number of its chosen shares throughout the course of the trading day. Because some of the exchange systems rely on market makers to honour their commitments, the exchange closely vets firms before allowing them to quote prices to investors. In return for agreeing to take on these extra responsibilities, market makers hope to enjoy the benefits of a steady stream of business, from broker-dealers and from other investors.

An **inter-dealer broker (IDB)** is an exchange member firm that has registered with the exchange to act as an agent between dealers (such as market makers). When one dealer trades with another dealer, it prefers its identity to remain a secret. This is the key benefit of using an IDB. The IDB is acting as agent for the dealer, but settles any transactions as if it were principal, in order to preserve the anonymity of the dealer. An IDB is not allowed to take principal positions, and it has to be a separate firm, not a division of another broker-dealer.

4.3   High Frequency Trading

Learning Objective

2.5.3   Understand high frequency trading: reasons; consequences for the market (eg, flash crashes); types of company that pursue this strategy

High frequency trading has evolved recently, particularly over the past 15 years or so, since the advent of electronic trading systems. Indeed, estimates for exchanges such as the NYSE put the proportion of trading done by high frequency traders at 50% or more.

High frequency trading involves the use of powerful computers that are programmed to transmit orders based on algorithms. These algorithms will respond extremely rapidly to market movements and, because the computers are usually located physically closely to those of the exchange, the orders will arrive ahead of other conventional orders. The high frequency traders will enter into hundreds, or even thousands, of small orders in this way and will then reverse the deals (so if the initial deals were to buy, they will sell or vice versa) to make a 'turn' on each. The amount of money made on each deal might be very small, but because of the quantity of deals being done, the high frequency trader can make a lot of money very quickly.

Potential criticisms of high frequency trading include seeing the traders as 'vultures' exploiting the genuine, longer-term investors and, given their dominance of market turnover, the impact they can have on pricing. The impact on pricing can be substantial, as was exhibited in the so-called 'flash crash' that hit the US markets on 6 May 2010. On that day, stock prices fell rapidly, with around 600 points being wiped off the Dow Jones Industrial Average in five minutes, only to recover again around 20 minutes later. An official report from the SEC and the Commodity Futures Trading Commission (CFTC) put most of the blame for the volatility on high frequency traders' algorithms. The initial impact came from movements in the S&P futures market and spilled over into the wider stock market with the high frequency traders aggressively selling. After the Chicago Mercantile Exchange (CME) paused trading in the S&P futures by triggering a circuit breaker, prices stabilised and then recovered almost as quickly as the losses had crystallised minutes earlier.

Another 'mini' flash crash occurred in the US market on 23 April 2013 in response to a hoax Twitter posting about an attack on the White House and an injury to President Obama. The DJIA fell about 130 points and then rapidly recovered. Again some commentators placed the blame for the excessive volatility on the algorithms of the high frequency traders.

High frequency trading has also been criticised for the systemic risks that it can create. In the event of extreme price movements on one exchange, the arbitrage trades automatically placed by the high frequency traders can rapidly spread the price movements to other exchanges where the same, or related, instruments are traded.

The original operators of the high frequency trading algorithms were small, specialist firms; their success has attracted others, including hedge funds and the large investment banks.

5. Government Bonds

Learning Objective

2.6.1 Understand the basic characteristics and purpose of government bond markets in the UK, US, Japan, France and Germany: ratings and the concept of 'risk free'; currency, credit and inflation risks; inflation indexed bonds

The government bond markets are the facilities that enable investors to buy and sell bonds issued by the relevant government – such as UK gilts, issued on behalf of the UK government, and US T-notes and bonds issued on behalf of the US government. They are important since they are the benchmark bonds on which the return provided by other bonds is judged.

For example, the yield available on UK gilts is considered the risk-free rate for sterling-denominated bonds – after all, it is the UK government that ultimately controls the printing of sterling, so the UK gilts are effectively credit-risk-free. If a 15-year gilt was trading at a price to produce a 5% yield, a 15-year sterling denominated corporate bond would be expected to yield 5%, plus a margin to cover the increased credit risk that the corporate borrower presents.

A conventional government bond still displays two particular risks to investors: inflation risk to all investors, and currency risk if it is an overseas investor. To counter currency risks, governments can, and occasionally do, issue bonds denominated in currencies other than their home currency, for example the US government issuing a euro-denominated bond. This type of bond removes the currency risk for a eurozone investor, but loses an element of the risk-free status, since the US government cannot print euros.

To counter inflation risks, government bonds can be issued that pay a coupon that is linked to an inflation index. If the inflation rate increases, the investors will get a larger coupon to compensate. These bonds also link the redemption amount to an inflation index – like the coupon, the investor will get a greater amount on redemption, if inflation has been significant over the life of the bond.

6.   Corporate Bond Markets

6.1   Characteristics

Learning Objective

2.7.1   Understand the characteristics of corporate bond markets: decentralised dealer markets and dealer provision of liquidity; the impact of default risk on prices; the differences between bond and equity markets; dealers rather than market makers; bond pools of liquidity versus centralised equity exchange; relevance of the retail bond market

The price of a corporate bond is based on the equivalent government bond, less a discount to represent the risk that the corporate may default, compared with the default-risk-free nature of the government bond. Unlike the market for equities, the method of dealing in corporate bonds tends to be away from the major exchanges in what is commonly described as a **decentralised dealer market**. The dealers provide liquidity by being willing to buy or sell the bonds. The systems that the dealers use to display their willingness to deal are numerous, with each being described as a separate pool of liquidity.

6.1.1   Default

In the corporate bond market, unlike the government bond markets where it has, until recently, been assumed that no sovereign borrower will default, the determination of the likelihood that a corporate borrower may default is a vital part in the pricing mechanism for corporate bonds.

6.1.2   Differences between Equity and Bond Markets

The primary difference between the corporate bond market and the equity market relates to the nature of the security being traded. A corporate bond usually has a specified income stream in the form of coupon payments which will be paid to the holder of the bond, and a bondholder has a more senior claim against the assets of the issuer in the case of a bankruptcy or restructuring.

Investors in equities may receive a dividend payment from the corporation, but this is less certain and can fluctuate. Indeed, less mature companies may not even pay a dividend. The equity-holder also has a greater risk that, if the corporation, which has issued the shares, becomes insolvent or undergoes a restructuring, there may be insufficient assets to be liquidated or reorganised and then distributed to shareholders. In such instances shareholders may find that their equity stakes in a corporation have little or no residual value.

6.1.3   Markets and Dealers of Corporate Bonds

The primary function and role of **market makers** in corporate bonds is to provide liquidity to the marketplace and to act as a facilitator or agent in trades between the principals. **Dealers** are those that have been appointed by the corporate issuer to act as distributors on their behalf in the issuance and underwriting of bond issues. There is often a combination of such roles by large financial institutions.

A **decentralised dealer market structure** is one that enables investors to buy and sell without a centralised location. In a decentralised market, the technical infrastructure provides traders and investors with access to various bids/ask prices and allows them to deal directly with other traders/ dealers rather than through a central exchange.

The FX market is an example of a decentralised market, because there is no single exchange or physical location where traders/investors have to conduct their buying and selling activities; trades can be conducted via an interbank/dealer network that is geographically distributed. Much of this trading in corporate bonds is also conducted through a decentralised dealer network that can provide pools of liquidity for the conduct of trade between buyers and sellers, without the requirement of all trades to be cleared through an exchange.

6.1.4   Retail Bond Market

Although most trading of bonds is done by institutional investors through a decentralised network of dealers, there is also an active retail market provided by stock exchanges. An example of this is the LSE's Order Book for Retail Bonds (ORB). The ORB is an order-driven trading service offering access to a selected number of gilts, supranational and UK corporate bonds. Trading is available in more than 60 gilts and over 100 corporate bonds on an electronic order-driven system with continuous two-way pricing provided by market makers.

An example of a retail corporate bond and its trading statistics at the time of writing is the following:

Bond issuer: Tesco Personal Finance
Maturity date: 21 November 2020
Coupon: 5% fixed
Average value traded per month: £7.9 million
Average number of trades per month: 279

Issuers are able to issue bonds via the ORB, which can provide an attractive alternative source of finance for the issuers wanting to raise relatively modest amounts of capital. Issue sizes tend to vary from as little as £20 million up to £300 million, and the minimum denominations that investors can trade are all less than £1,000, typically £100, although the minimum up-front investment is £2,000. The Tesco Personal Finance bond outlined above was a £200 million issue and can be traded in minimum denominations of £100.

Chapter Three
Dealing

This syllabus area will provide approximately 10 of the 100 examination questions

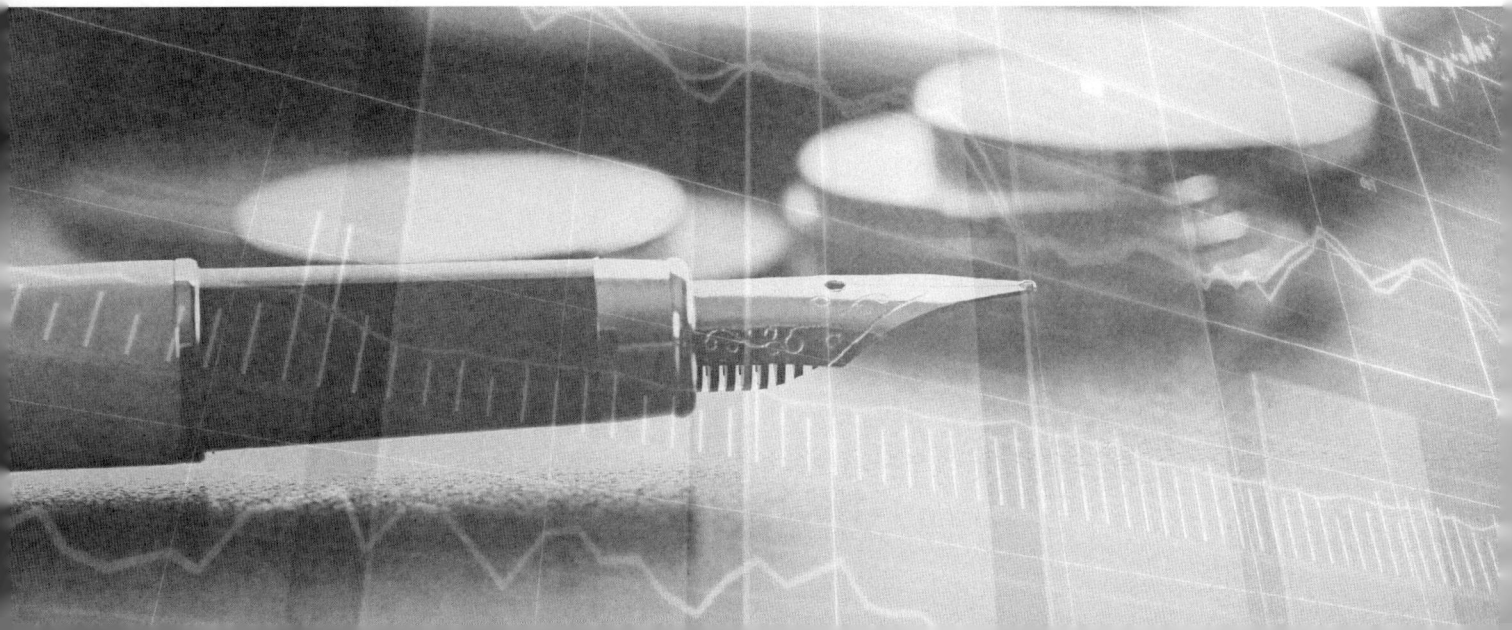

1. The London Stock Exchange (LSE) – UK Equities

1.1 Stock Exchange Electronic Trading System (SETS)

Learning Objective

3.1.1 Understand the rules, procedures and requirements applying to dealing through the Stock Exchange Electronic Trading System (SETS) in the following areas: order book features; order management; limitations and benefits of trading through SETS

The Stock Exchange Electronic Trading System (SETS) is a computer system that automatically matches orders to buy and orders to sell equities. It is formally described as an electronic order-driven system.

It operates an electronic order book into which LSE member firms submit their orders to buy and sell equities, and, when there are orders that can be matched, SETS automatically brings them together. The SETS system is available to all LSE member firms, and automatic trading takes place on it between 8.00am and 4.30pm each business day.

The shares traded on SETS include:

- Shares in companies within the FTSE All Share.
- ETFs and exchange-traded commodities (ETCs).
- The most traded AIM and Irish securities.

Example companies include BP, GlaxoSmithKline, HSBC and Marks & Spencer.

1.1.1 The SETS Order Book

In the order book, orders are given priority first by price and then by time.

The electronic screen reflecting the order book for the shares of the fictional company ABC plc will look something like this:

Company: ABC plc			
Orders to buy		Orders to sell	
Volume	Price	Volume	Price
10,000	315	4,000	316
2,000	315	12,000	317
4,000	314	14,000	318
8,000	313	3,000	318

The order priority adopted by SETS is by price, and then time. The best buy and sell prices are always at the top of the two columns of orders and will be executed first. In the case of the **buy orders** this is the **highest-priced order** (315p in the above example, where the order to buy 10,000 shares must have been entered into the system before the order to buy 2,000 shares).

In the case of the sell orders this is the **lowest-priced order** (316p in the above example). Below the best-priced orders, all the other orders are displayed, giving an immediate picture of the depth of liquidity on the order book.

Essentially, the way that the SETS system works is that LSE members have access to the order book and can enter orders electronically. If a firm of brokers enters a sell order on behalf of a client for up to 12,000 shares in ABC at the best available price, the order will be executed by the system by matching with the best buy orders (10,000 and 2,000 shares). The matched order will proceed to settlement at 315p per share, and be immediately revealed to the market in terms of size (12,000 shares) and price (315p).

The minimum order size is a single share and there is no maximum order size.

1.1.2 SETS Auctions and Automatic Execution

At the start of automatic execution on SETS each day there is an opening auction. Leading up to the auction, the period between 7.50am and 8.00am is known as the **opening auction call period**. In this period no trading takes place; however, three types of order (limit, iceberg and market orders) can be placed on the order book to take part in the opening auction.

The auction itself does not necessarily happen at 8.00am. Instead, it is subject to a **random start** and will occur at 8.00am plus a random number of seconds between 0 and 30. The **auction** uses an **uncrossing algorithm**, through which those orders that overlap on the order book are executed at the single price that maximises the number of shares traded. Simultaneously, the opening price for the security is calculated. During the course of the uncrossing, no further orders can be added and existing orders cannot be deleted or amended.

There is a possibility of the opening auction being delayed beyond its scheduled time. The delay can be caused by either market orders not being fully satisfied, or the price arrived at by the uncrossing algorithm being extreme, or a combination of both of these. The resultant delay is termed an **extension**.

- A **market order extension** occurs if there are unexecuted market orders on the order book following the auction. This extension is two minutes plus an additional 0–30-second random end period.
- A **price monitoring extension** occurs if the opening price is more than the price tolerance level of 5% away from the price of the last automated trade which took place on the previous business day. The price tolerance level is a predefined percentage threshold either side of a base price set by the LSE and currently standing at 5% for the opening auction. The price monitoring extension is five minutes long, again plus an additional 0–30-second random end period.

So, there is the potential for a seven-to-eight minute delay to the opening auction if both the market order and price monitoring extensions are applied.

Once the opening auction is complete, **automatic execution** commences. As orders are entered on to the system, SETS tries to match them. If SETS finds a buyer and seller with agreeable prices and volumes, the trade is automatically executed.

There is a possibility of an interruption to this automatic execution of orders. If the price of a trade is more than the price tolerance level away from the previous trade price, an **automatic execution suspension period (AESP)** occurs to allow investors time to react to large price changes. The price tolerance level during the continuous trading period varies from 5% to 25%, depending upon the share.

The AESP lasts for five minutes (plus a period of 0–30 seconds) and during this time no trades are executed (although orders can be entered, deleted and amended). Automatic execution then recommences after the uncrossing auction programme is run.

If a SETS security is suspended from trading by the exchange, as with an AESP, no execution takes place, although orders can be entered, deleted or amended.

After 4.30pm, when automatic execution is completed, the trading day ends with another auction. The auction call period runs from 4.30pm to 4.35pm, and at 4.35pm (plus a period of 0–30 seconds) the auction uncrossing algorithm is run.

If auction matching occurs in the closing auction, then the day's closing price will be based on the closing auction price. If no execution occurs, the volume weighted average price (VWAP) of the last ten minutes of continuous trading will be used. In the event of no automatic trades in the VWAP period, the last automatically executed trade price will be used.

For the last 25 minutes until 5.00pm, SETS allows participants to delete orders. No execution takes place during this period.

1.1.3   Viewing the SETS Order Book

Any market participant can view the SETS order book for a particular security (by looking at a Bloomberg screen, for example). However, membership of the LSE is required to interact with the order book. It is for brokers and dealers only.

1.2   SETS Order Types

Learning Objective

3.1.2   Understand the following order types and their differences: market; limit; fill or kill; execute and eliminate; iceberg; multiple fills

There are a number of types of order that can be entered into SETS, and each will be treated slightly differently by the system.

1. **Limit orders** have a price limit and a time limit, eg, a limit order may state: *'sell 1,000 shares at 360p by next Tuesday'*. SETS will attempt to sell these shares at a price no worse than 360p by next Tuesday. Any time limit up to a maximum of 90 days can be put on these orders. If no time limit is placed on the order, it will expire at the end of the day that it is entered. Limit orders can be partially filled, and it is only limit orders that are displayed on the SETS order book.

2. **Iceberg orders** are a particular type of limit order. They enable a market participant with a particularly large order to partially hide the size of their order from the market and reduce the market impact that the large order might otherwise have. The term comes from the fact that just the top part of the order is on view (the peak of the iceberg); the rest is hidden (the bulk of the iceberg is below the water). Once the top part of the order is executed, the system automatically brings the next tranche of the iceberg order on to the order book. This process continues until the whole of the iceberg order has been executed, or the time limit for the order expires.

3. **Market orders** do not specify a price. They are submitted to the order book to deal in a specified number of shares.

4. **Execute and eliminate orders** can only be entered during automatic execution. As with the at best order, this type will execute as much of the trade as possible and cancel the rest. However, unlike an at best order, this order type has a specified price and will not execute at a price worse than that specified.

5. **Fill or kill orders** can only be entered during automatic execution. They normally have a specified price (although they can be entered without one) and either the entire order will be immediately filled at a price at least as good as that specified, or the entire order will be cancelled (ie, if there are not enough orders at the price specified or better).

1.3   The Central Counterparty (CCP)

Learning Objective

3.1.3   Understand the operation and purpose of the LSE's central counterparty: LCH.Clearnet Limited; x-clear; benefits and limitations

SETS transactions utilise a central counterparty (CCP). The CCP is either the **London Clearing House (LCH.Clearnet)** or **SIX Swiss Exchange's SIX x-clear**. The impact of the CCP is best illustrated by way of a simple example:

Example

A trade is executed on SETS that involves A agreeing to sell some shares to B. One of the CCPs, say LCH. Clearnet, steps in between the two parties and two new obligations replace the initial obligation of A to sell to B. The two obligations are for A to sell to LCH.Clearnet and then for LCH.Clearnet to sell to B. This transfer of obligation is known as **novation.**

If either of the two parties to this transaction (A or B) were to default, it would no longer affect the other party, as they no longer have a contract with each other. It would only impact LCH.Clearnet.

The use of a central counterparty provides certain benefits to market participants, particularly:

- **Reduced counterparty risk** – the risk that the other side of the transaction will default is reduced because it is replaced by one of the CCPs, both of which are well capitalised and have insurance policies in place lessening the risk of default. This reduces the risk of systemic collapse of the financial system.
- **Providing total anonymity** – both sides of the trade do not discover who the original counterparty was.
- **Reduced administration** – all trades are settled with one of the two CCPs, rather than a variety of counterparties, improving operational efficiency.
- **Facilitating netting of transactions** – because all the trades are with a CCP, receipts and payments for transactions in the same share that settle on the same day can be netted against each other.
- **Improved prices** – because more participants are willing to transact anonymously, it is argued that a CCP results in improvements in price.

The CCP charges a flat fee to both parties for fulfilling its role and also requires margin payments (similar to derivatives margin) to reduce its potential loss, should one party default.

CREST is the settlement system that is used to settle the transactions between the CCP and the member firms.

1.4 Trading Halts

Learning Objective

3.1.4 Know the LSE's right to call for a halt in trading in any listed security: for any reason; length of trading halt

The LSE reserves the right to prohibit any transaction from being dealt on exchange for any reason. This is referred to as a trading halt, and typically arises from the suspension of a security's listing.

If a security is suspended, permission is required from the exchange before a member firm can effect a transaction in that security. The length of the trading halt is at the discretion of the exchange. Trades that have occurred, but have not yet settled at the time of suspension are settled as normal.

1.5 Stock Exchange Electronic Trading Service – Quotes and Crosses (SETSqx)

Learning Objective

3.1.5 Know the features and requirements of SETSqx dealing: SETSqx as a hybrid trading system; relative illiquidity; securities covered; normal market size; minimum number of market makers

The Stock Exchange Electronic Trading Service – quotes and crosses (SETSqx) is the LSE's trading service for less liquid securities.

SETSqx is a hybrid system, combining some of the order-driven features of SETS with the potential for two-way quotes from market makers. Functionally it is similar to the SETS order book, with buy and sell orders displayed in a central order book. However, it is supplemented by one or more market makers also displaying two-way prices. Furthermore, unlike SETS, execution on the central order book is only at periodic auctions (uncrossings) that occur four times per day – at 8.00am, 11.00am, 3.00pm and 4.35pm. Like SETS, these auctions can be subject to **price monitoring extensions**.

The order types that are accepted into the SETSqx central order book are anonymous limit orders and named orders, which detail the firm, as well as the order. Any member firm has the option to phone the counterparty behind a named order and fill the order before the next uncrossing if the two parties agree.

The minimum number of market makers for securities traded on SETSqx is zero, but if there are one or more market makers they must provide continuous liquidity throughout the trading day. They must quote prices to buy or sell at least one times the normal market size (NMS).

1.5.1   Normal Market Size (NMS)

Normal market size (NMS) is the minimum number of shares, determined by the LSE, for which a market maker is obliged to quote firm bid and offer prices. NMS for each security is calculated quarterly and is based on 2.5% of the security's average daily turnover in the preceding year. Most market makers will also be prepared to quote firm prices for sizes greater than the NMS, usually up to a maximum of 200,000 shares.

Example ───

A large company may currently have an NMS of 10,000, yet a market maker may be prepared to quote firm prices for volumes of, say, 30,000 offer and 30,000 bid. Therefore, one would be able to buy or sell up to 30,000 shares through that market maker at the prices quoted on the SETSqx screen by that market maker.

───

2.   The London Stock Exchange (LSE) – International Equity Market

As well as providing trading mechanisms for domestic shares, the LSE is also an important centre for trading international equities. One particular trading service for international equities, the international order book (IOB), is included in the examination syllabus.

2.1 The International Order Book (IOB)

Learning Objective

3.2.1 Understand the rules, procedures and requirements applying to dealing through the International Order Book (IOB) in the following areas: securities covered; minimum and maximum trading sizes; who can access the IOB

The international order book (IOB) is an order-driven trading service primarily for depositary receipts of international securities. It operates in the same way as the SETS order book with one additional feature – the facility for inputting orders that are not anonymous. Such orders are commonly referred to as **named orders** and are placed by LSE member firms dealing in a principal capacity and wanting to display their willingness to deal on the order book. The acronym that identifies the firm appears next to their order on the IOB.

Both GDRs and ADRs are traded on the IOB, mostly from companies in developing countries in Central and Eastern Europe and Asia. Orders are required to be for at least one share, with no restriction on the maximum order size. The IOB is accessible to all LSE member firms.

3. Other Equity Markets

3.1 Trading on the New York Stock Exchange (NYSE)

Learning Objective

3.3.1 Know how trading on the NYSE compares with trading on the LSE

The two main differences between trading on the NYSE and the LSE are:

- the NYSE continues to retain some open outcry trading on the trading floor; and
- the NYSE still employs designated market makers, sometimes known as 'specialists', who act as an official market maker for a given security, whereas the LSE has a more heterogeneous structure, which includes specific market makers in certain securities but no 'specialists' as the term is traditionally understood.

3.1.1 Designated Market Makers or Specialists

A market maker is a financial intermediary, often an investment bank or specialist dealer, that quotes both a buy and a sell price in a financial instrument or commodity, hoping to make a profit on the bid-offer spread, or turn. The market maker often maintains an inventory of positions and stands ready to buy or sell the securities for which it makes a market, on demand from other market participants. The market makers provide a required amount of liquidity to the security's market, and take the other side of trades when there are short-term buy- and sell-side imbalances in customer orders. This helps prevent excess volatility, and in return the specialist is granted various informational and trade execution advantages.

These specialists working on the NYSE floor have been described as fulfilling three main roles to ensure a fair and orderly market:

• The NYSE is an auction market where bids and asks are continuously published to all investors. It is the job of the specialist to ensure that all bids and asks are reported in an accurate and timely manner, that all marketable trades are executed and that order is maintained on the floor.

• Along with posting the daily bid and ask prices, the specialist must also set the opening price for the stock every morning. This price can greatly differ from the previous day's closing price, based on after-hours news and events. The role of the specialist is to find the correct market price based on supply and demand.

• In addition to the notion that a market maker acts as a facilitator, the role of the specialist has been seen as one of encouraging enough market interest in the particular stocks for which they are designated market makers. This is carried out by specialists seeking out recently active investors in cases where the bids and asks cannot be matched. This aspect of the specialist's job helps to induce trades that may not have arisen within the context of a more passive and automated notion of the role of the market maker.

As with a lot of financial terminology, some imprecision has entered the discussion of the role of market makers but, in fairness, with the advent of sophisticated high-frequency trading platforms, where taking a position into inventory could mean holding it for a nanosecond, it becomes harder to separate out the different kinds of liquidity providers in contemporary capital markets. One of the key differentiators which distinguishes the designated market maker role is that the specialist is expected to hold inventory in the stocks which they **represent**. In other words, they act not only as agent and facilitator of liquidity but also as a principal, and hold stocks in their own accounts. In cases where there is a demand-supply imbalance of a particular security, the specialist must make adjustments by purchasing and selling out of their own inventory to equalise the market. For example, a specialist is required to buy shares for their own inventory in the event of a large sell-off.

3.1.2 Comparison with LSE Market Makers

On the LSE there are no equivalents of designated market makers as just described. There are market makers but their role is less formally defined, and even that more loosely defined role is becoming more indistinct, as the changes in the underlying technology more closely resemble an electronic order matching system.

At present on the LSE, there are official market makers for many securities (but not for shares in the largest and most heavily traded companies, which are traded on SETS). These market makers are LSE member firms that take on the obligation of always making a two-way price in each of the stocks in which they make markets. Their prices are displayed on the system and it is they who generally deal with brokers buying or selling stock on behalf of clients.

3.1.3 Liquidity Rebates

Exchanges are having to fight much harder to retain their role within a decentralised market system where investors have many **off-exchange** choices as to where to conduct business. There is also a lot of competition among exchanges as transnational trading and settlement has meant that the actual place or geographical location of an exchange becomes fairly meaningless in a virtual world of electronic trading.

One area of competition among exchanges is to encourage market makers to use their platforms over others by providing liquidity rebates for each share that is sold to or purchased from each posted bid or offer. In this respect, the Archipelago Exchange (ARCA) facility, which is becoming a very significant division of the NYSE/Euronext platform, and hosts the trading of most ETFs, has been one of the most aggressive in providing liquidity rebates as a way of promoting business.

4. Government Bonds

Learning Objective

3.4.1 Know the functions, obligations and benefits of the following in relation to government bonds with respect to the UK, US, Japan, France and Germany: primary dealers; broker-dealers; inter-dealer brokers; government issuing authority such as the UK Debt Management Office

4.1 Participants in Government Bond Markets

In addition to the government itself, there are three major groups of participants that facilitate deals in the government bond markets:

- Primary dealers – such as GEMMs in the UK.
- Broker-dealers.
- Inter-dealer brokers.

These three participants will be illustrated using the UK government bond market as an example.

4.1.1 Government Issues in the UK

Issuing Agency

The DMO is the issuing agency for the UK government. It is an executive agency of the Treasury, making new issues of UK government securities (gilt-edged securities or gilts). Once issued, the secondary market for dealing in gilts is overseen by two bodies, the DMO and the LSE.

The DMO is the body that enables certain LSE member firms to act as primary dealers, known as GEMMs. It then leaves it to the LSE to prescribe rules that apply when dealing takes place.

Gilt-Edged Market Makers (GEMMs)

The GEMM, once vetted by the DMO and registered as a GEMM with the LSE, becomes a primary dealer and is required to provide two-way quotes to customers (clients known directly to them) and other member firms of the LSE throughout the normal trading day. There is no requirement to use a particular system for making those quotes available to clients, and GEMMs are free to choose how to disseminate their prices.

The obligations of a GEMM can be summarised as follows:

- To make effective two-way prices to customers on demand, up to a size agreed with the DMO, thereby providing liquidity for customers wishing to trade.
- To participate actively in the DMO's gilt issuance programme, broadly by bidding competitively in all auctions and achieving allocations commensurate with their secondary market share – effectively informally agreeing to underwrite gilt auctions.
- To provide information to the DMO on closing prices, market conditions and the GEMM's positions and turnover.

The privileges of GEMM status include:

- executive rights to competitive telephone bidding at gilt auctions and other DMO operations, either for the GEMM's own account or on behalf of clients;
- an exclusive facility to trade as a counterparty of the DMO in any of its secondary market operations;
- exclusive access to gilt IDB screens.

A firm can register as a GEMM to provide quotes in either:

- all gilt-edged securities; or
- gilt-edged securities excluding index-linked gilts; or
- index-linked gilts only.

There are exceptions to the requirement to customers, including the members of the LSE. The obligation does not include quoting to other GEMMs, fixed-interest market makers or gilt IDBs.

Broker-Dealers

These are non-GEMM LSE member firms that are able to buy or sell gilts as principal (dealer) or as agent (broker). When acting as a broker, the broker-dealer will be bound by the LSE's best execution rule, ie, to get the best available price at the time.

When seeking a quote from a GEMM, the broker-dealer must identify at the outset if the deal is a small one, defined as less than £1 million nominal.

Gilt Inter-Dealer Brokers (IDBs)

Gilt IDBs arrange deals between gilt-edged market makers anonymously. They are not allowed to take principal positions, and the identity of the market makers using the service remains anonymous at all times. The IDB will act as agent, but settle the transaction as if it were the principal. The IDB is only allowed to act as a broker between GEMMs, and has to be a separate company and not a division of a broker-dealer.

4.1.2   Government Issues in the US

The Federal Reserve is the co-ordinator of the issuance of US government securities. As with the UK, it conducts auctions on a regular basis and appoints primary dealers, which include the major investment banks as conduits in the auction process to place bids and to buy the issue on behalf of their clients or for their own account.

The US government securities are typically issued in one of three forms – bills, notes and bonds – that differ in the length of time between issue and maturity:

- T-bills are issued for terms less than a year.
- T-notes are issued for terms of two, three, five, seven and 10 years.
- T-bonds are issued for terms of 30 years.

T-bills are issued in regular auctions with maturity dates of 28 days (or four weeks, about a month), 91 days (or 13 weeks, about three months), 182 days (or 26 weeks, about six months), and 364 days (or 52 weeks, about one year). T-bills are sold by single price auctions held weekly.

During periods when Treasury cash balances are particularly low, the Treasury may sell cash management bills (or CMBs). These are sold at a discount and by auction just like weekly Treasury bills. They differ in that they are irregular in amount, term (often less than 21 days), and day of the week for auction, issuance, and maturity. When CMBs mature on the same day as a regular weekly bill, usually Thursday, they are said to be on-cycle.

T-notes, and T-bonds pay interest every six months until they mature. T-bonds have the longest maturity of 30 years. Both T-notes and T-bonds are issued by auction.

For T-notes, two-year notes, three-year notes, five-year notes, and seven-year notes are auctioned every month. Ten-year notes are auctioned at original issue in February, May, August, and November, and in reopenings in January, March, April, June, July, September, October, and December. In a reopening, additional amounts of a previously issued security are auctioned. Reopened securities have the same maturity date and interest rate as the original securities.

For T-bonds, original issue auctions take place in February, May, August, and November, and reopening auctions in the other eight months.

4.1.3   Government Issues in Japan

Japanese Government Bonds (JGBs) are issued by the Bank of Japan (BoJ) and, as the name implies, they are the bonds issued by the government, which is responsible for interest and principal payments. Interest is paid every six months, and principal payments are secured at maturity.

JGBs are available with various maturity periods. Coupon-bearing bonds, which feature semi-annual interest payment and principal payment at maturity, have maturities of two, five, five (for retail investors), ten, ten (inflation-indexed), ten (for retail investors), 15 (floating rate), 20, 30 and 40 years.

The Japanese government also offers a separate strips programme.

4.1.4   Government Issues in the Eurozone

The eurozone consists of the 18 states which have adopted the euro as their currency and for whom their monetary policy is determined by monthly meetings of the European Central Bank (ECB). Each of the member states issues government bonds which have the credit rating associated with the country of issue rather than the eurozone as a whole. In the syllabus, the focus is on Germany and France.

German government securities offer original maturities ranging from three months to 30 years. In the money market segment, the Federal Government issues Treasury discount paper (**Bubills**) with maturities of six and 12 months. The offering of capital market products begins with Federal Treasury notes (**Schaetze**) with a maturity of two years, followed by five-year Federal notes (**Bobls**) (Bundesobligationen) and Federal bonds (**Bunds**) with maturities of ten and 30 years.

The German Federal Government usually places single issues by auction. Only credit institutions domiciled in an EU member state can be members of the auction group and participate directly in these auctions. The Bund uses a multiple price auction procedure. In other words, bids for Bunds, Bobls and Schaetze accepted by the government are allocated at the price quoted in the respective bid and are not settled at a uniform price. Bids priced above the lowest accepted price are allotted in full, while bids priced below the lowest accepted price receive no allotment. Non-competitive bids are allotted at the weighted average price of the accepted price bids. The government reserves the right to re-allot the bids at the lowest accepted price as well as the non-competitive bids, eg, to allot them only at a certain percentage rate. The same procedure is applied on a yield basis for Bubills.

To remain a member of the auction group, a credit institution must subscribe to at least 0.05% of the total issuance allotted at the auctions in a calendar year, weighted according to maturity. Members who do not reach the required minimum allotment drop out of the auction group bund issues. There are no other requirements placed on the members of the auction group.

French government securities consist of Obligations Assimilable du Trésor (OATs), Bons du Trésor à Taux Fixe et à Intérêts Annuels (BTANs) and Bons du Trésor à Taux Fixe et à Intérêts Précomptés (BTFs).

OATs, or fungible T-bonds, are the government's long-term debt instruments with maturities from seven to 50 years. Most OATs are fixed-rate bonds redeemable on maturity. OATs are auctioned on the first Thursday of each month.

BTANs, or negotiable fixed-rate medium-term T-notes with annual interest, represent medium-term government debt. On issue, their maturity is either two or five years. They are auctioned on the third Thursday of each month.

BTFs, or negotiable fixed-rate discount T-bills, are the government's cash management instrument. They are used to cover short-term fluctuations in the government's cash position (less than one year), mainly due to differences in the pace with which revenues are collected and expenses are paid and in the debt amortisation schedule. On issue, BTFs have a maturity of less than one year. They are auctioned every Monday.

The principal method of issuing French government securities is the **bid price system** where participants compete in the auction, on an equal footing, through a transparent system of open bidding according to a planned issuance programme.

In the bid price system the highest bids are first served, followed by lower bids and so on, up to Agency France Trésor's target amount. Participants pay different prices, precisely reflecting their bids. Only institutions affiliated to Euroclear France and holding accounts with the Banque de France are eligible to bid.

5. Dealing Methods

Learning Objective

3.5.1   Know the different trading methods for bonds: OTC inter-dealer voice trading; inter-dealer electronic market; OTC customer to dealer voice trading; customer to dealer electronic market; on-exchange trading

5.1   Trading Methods for Bonds

Bond trading, including both corporate and government bonds, is either conducted between dealers, some of which is arranged by IDBs, or between dealers and their customers, like asset managers.

Dealer-to-dealer trading can occur in three ways:

*   Direct telephone contact.
*   Indirect via an IDB voice broking the deal.
*   Via an electronic market, known as an electronic trading platform, such as Message Transfer System (MTS) or BrokerTec.

Dealer-to-customer trading is done either by voice trading between the two parties, or via an electronic platform, such as TradeWeb, BondVision or proprietary single dealer systems developed by some of the larger banks.

A relatively small proportion of corporate bond dealing takes place via the exchanges, like the LSE.

5.2 Trends in Trading Methods

Learning Objective

3.5.2 Understand the different trends between trading methods: characteristics of electronic trading; OTC; exchange-traded; price driven via inter-dealer brokers (IDB) – dealer to dealer; request for quote (RFQ) – customer to dealer

Investors can trade marketable bonds among themselves in principal-to-principal deals and this can be done at any time. However, most trading is done through the network of bond dealers, and more specifically, the bond trading desks of major investment dealers. The dealers occupy the pivotal position in the vast network of telephone and electronic platforms that connect the interested players. Bond dealers usually **make a market** for bonds. What this means is that the dealer has traders whose responsibility is to know all about a group of bonds and to be prepared to quote a price to buy or sell them.

Dealers provide liquidity for bond investors, thereby allowing investors to buy and sell bonds more easily (business to client (B2C)) and with a limited concession on the price. Dealers also buy and sell among themselves (business to business (B2B)) either directly or anonymously via bond brokers, an exercise which is known as proprietary trading, as the profit and loss for such trades are taken on to the dealer's books rather than its customers or clients.

The primary incentive for trading bonds among dealers is to take a spread between the price the bonds are bought at and the price they are sold at. This is the main way that bond dealers make (or lose) money. Dealers often have bond traders located in the major financial centres and are able to trade bonds 24 hours a day (although not usually at weekends).

Electronic trading volumes of credit through single-dealer platforms struggled to recover following the 2008 financial crisis, but demands from US and European regulators for best execution are leading to an increase in volumes once more and the creation of new platforms.

The development of electronic trading has advanced furthest in the most liquid US fixed income segments — US Treasury and mortgage-backed securities (MBSs). Currently, electronic trading represents nearly 80% of Treasury segment volume and 32% of MBSs. Many US corporate bonds are infrequently traded in the secondary market, so they are less likely to be traded electronically. Overall, standardisation of the fixed-income product and the resultant liquidity is the key deciding factor whether a bond will be traded electronically or not.

The development of fixed-income electronic platforms has led to a change in market structure and a diversification of product offerings. Major platforms have expanded their product coverage either geographically in Europe and Asia or by entering other markets such as derivatives products.

In order to offer differentiation and create competitive advantage, some electronic trading platforms are including and enhancing value-added services such as straight-through processing (STP) solutions, expansion into OTC derivatives, and multi-asset trading platforms.

5.2.1   OTC Platforms

To illustrate the highly specialised manner in which the trading of most bonds is presently conducted, the following material from a research note entitled *Transparency Proposals for European Sovereign Bond Markets*, by Peter Dunne at Queens University in Belfast, is very helpful. The paper explains the current system and electronic trading facilities in the two segments of the euro-denominated sovereign bond market.

Two kinds of trading interfaces are provided one for dealer-to-dealer trading (B2B) and one for dealer-to-buy-side clients such as asset managers and pension funds (B2C):

1. B2B electronic trading platforms include BrokerTec, Euronext and MTS (the MTS platforms combine country-specific and euro-benchmark markets).
2. B2C segment mainly consists of request-for-quote (RFQ) platforms, including BondVision (a subsidiary of euro-MTS), TradeWeb and Bloomberg Bond Trader (BBT).

Request for quote (RFQ) systems allow investors to request quotes from a number of dealers simultaneously. Dealers can respond to such requests very quickly and trades can be executed electronically.

There are no significant B2C electronic order books, so pre-trade transparency of the B2B market must suffice as the best guide to prices that investors can expect to obtain in potential B2C trades. Investors can request quotes simply to gain pre-trade information but investors can't be sure that they are receiving the same information as other investors. It should also be noted that dealers do not generally know what prices are being quoted by other dealers (although on most RFQ platforms the under-bidder is informed that they quoted closest to the accepted price).

Despite their limited transparency, RFQ systems are a significant improvement over voice communication in terms of ease and speed of trading. RFQ systems also bring dealers into direct competition with each other and this is expected to deliver price improvement for investors.

Since the RFQ system does not provide pre-trade transparency, except on request, the information provided by the B2B segment must substitute. Thus, while the success of an RFQ trading system is at odds with the smooth running of the B2B electronic platform, the RFQ system itself cannot function very well without B2B transparency.

A **catch-22** for transparency regulators is, therefore, that imposing increased transparency on B2C activity increases the risks and reduces the incentives for dealers to provide continuous liquidity in the inter-dealer market. Indeed, any form of transparent trading in the B2C segment (such as the introduction of a parallel electronic order book) could represent a large threat to the efficient working of the B2B electronic trading system and this might in turn alter the entire structure and approach to primary issuance.

5.2.2   Summary of OTC Trading and Current Regulatory Issues

Innovations in the technology used in both OTC markets and in more traditional exchange-based markets are converging and it is becoming harder to distinguish between them. Price transparency, issues related to fees and the risk of counterparty default have become the focus of attention from policy makers and regulators following the collapse in 2008 of firms such as Bear Stearns and Lehman Brothers who were some of the principal players in the development of OTC trading methods for bonds and derivatives.

Recent legislation in the US, which is collectively known as the Dodd-Frank Act, has turned greater focus on the need for more transparency and safety from counterparty risk in the transactions which have hitherto been conducted in the OTC market. OTC-traded instruments are increasingly required to be centrally cleared, like exchange-traded instruments.

IDBs are also facing the prospect of lower revenues, as regulatory pressures both in the US and Europe are having an impact on the scope and volume of proprietary trading activities of the large investment banks and other financial intermediaries, and many are shrinking their balance sheets and trading less.

Futures exchanges have been attracted by the high margins of OTC products and are seeking to benefit from the heightened regulatory scrutiny of IDBs. NYSE Euronext's Liffe, the London-based derivatives market, has launched a clearing house for credit derivatives. The Chicago Mercantile Exchange (CME), Deutsche Börse-owned derivatives market Eurex and Atlanta-based InterContinental Exchange are also now active in this area. Indeed, the InterContinental Exchange has acquired NYSE Euronext to become the world's leading network of global derivatives and equity exchanges, as consolidation accelerates.

IDBs are increasingly implementing trading platforms that are similar to the exchange model. Some have argued that the exchange model is morphing into a similar electronic matching network that has been a characteristic of the OTC market for many years. In essence, the difference between OTC trading and exchange-based trading is blurring.

IDBs play a useful role in locating liquidity in the European options market, which is fairly illiquid. That usefulness may be most pronounced when market conditions are volatile, as banks tap the expansive knowledge of voice brokers to locate products.

Some parts of the swap market are now being cleared by clearing houses. A substantial share of interest rate swap trades are cleared through SwapClear, the oil derivatives market is cleared through Nymex Clearport or ICE Clear and the EU emissions market is cleared through LCH. Clearnet.

5.3 Factors that Influence Bond Pricing

Learning Objective

3.5.3 Know the factors that influence bond pricing: issuer factors: yield to maturity, seniority, structure, technical factors, credit rating; market factors; benchmark bonds; liquidity premiums for highly traded bond issues; indicative pricing versus firm two-way quotes; availability of a liquid repo market and the difficulty in offering illiquid bonds; inability to borrow or cover shorts

Broadly, the factors that influence the prices of bonds can be subdivided into two: issuer factors, and market factors.

The characteristics of a particular issue and the quality of the issuer encompass the following:

- Issuer's current credit rating (which itself will reflect the issuer's specific prospects) and highlight the issuer's default risk.
- The structure and seniority of the particular issue, for example, the bonds may be high- or low-priority in the event of default by the issuer and may be structured in a way that gives the bonds particular priority in relation to particular assets (such as mortgage-backed bonds).
- The above aspects, combined with prevailing yields available on other benchmark bonds (such as government issues in the same currency, with similar redemption dates), will determine the required yield to maturity (YTM) and, therefore, the appropriate price.

Additionally, market factors will include the following:

- **Liquidity** – the more liquid bonds tend to be more expensive, encompassing a liquidity premium and having lower bid/offer spreads.
- **Method of trading** – some bonds attract firm quotes while others are traded with indicative quotes only; the precise price will only be arrived at by negotiation.
- **Ability to borrow** – bonds with active repo markets, and the ability to short positions relatively easily, will inevitably react more quickly to underlying interest rate changes and therefore yield changes.

The difficulties that can arise in the trading and pricing of bonds were especially acute during the 1998 crisis which began with the default by Russia on its bonds and led to the collapse of Long Term Capital Management – a major fund that specialised in the trading of fixed-income instruments and various arbitrage strategies. One of the difficulties that arose during this crisis was the mispricing in the US Treasury market, where the most recently issued long-term bond, which is known as the **on the run** bond, trades at a premium to those bonds which had been issued previously and which are known as **off the run**. If investors have a preference, during a crisis, for the most liquid instruments, they may hoard the on the run bonds and force their price to be out of normal alignment with similar bonds which have slightly different maturity dates. This can result in a breakdown in complex strategies designed to exploit the spreads or price differences across the yield spectrum.

5.4 Quotation Methods

There are two major elements of a quote for a bond – the **price** and, as a result of the price, the **yield**. Most traders will be looking for particular yields and then adjust the price to achieve that yield.

When dealing in corporate bonds, or across different bond markets (such as different countries' government bonds), traders and researchers will also be looking at the yield **spreads** that are available and anticipating changes in those spreads – eg, assessing whether the additional yield that is currently available for a BBB-rated sterling-denominated corporate bond over a gilt with similar maturity is likely to increase or decrease.

5.5 Bond Prices and Bond Futures

The price of a bond is driven by a number of factors, such as credit rating and required yields. Clearly, the required yield will itself be driven by expected future interest rates. A key indicator of the market's collective expectation of **future** interest rates is implicit within derivatives of bonds, such as bond futures. As a result, the prevailing prices of bonds are to an extent driven by the price at which derivatives of those bonds are trading, such as bond futures.

One of the most actively traded global futures contracts is the US Thirty-Year T-Bond contract which trades on the Chicago Board of Trade (CBOT). This contract has excellent liquidity and provides a vehicle for hedging one's exposure to a broad variety of fixed income instruments, as well as an opportunity for speculating on the future direction of interest rates and specifically as one component in a speculation about interest rate spreads, between, for example, corporate investment grade bonds or high-yield bonds versus US Treasuries.

The futures contracts can be settled by a cash payment at the time of the contract's maturity or by the owner of a contract delivering certain bonds, which are subject to a standardised definition or conversion factor. This gives rise to the practice among participants in the futures and cash markets for bonds of making continuous and precise calculations as to which particular bonds are the **cheapest to deliver** at the time of settlement of a futures position.

The relationship between the cash market for bonds and the futures markets in government bonds exemplifies the manner in which all cash and derivatives markets are driven by a relatively simple arbitrage mechanism. The concept of cheapest to deliver is a vital component in this arbitrage strategy, which will tend to eliminate discrepancies arising in price between the trading of actual bonds in the cash market and the trading of, for example, US T-bond futures. If pricing discrepancies should arise on a temporary basis, these will tend to be eliminated, as in any arbitrage, by selling the relatively more expensive item (ie, the cash bond or the derivative depending on the particular circumstances) and buying an offsetting position in the corresponding alternative position of either the underlying asset or the futures contract.

The interaction between the cash price of bonds and the futures prices is a dynamic two-way process in which prices are constantly being adjusted through arbitrage and through the activities of **hedgers** as well as speculators.

Chapter Four
Offers and Capital Adjustments

This syllabus area will provide approximately 19 of the 100 examination questions

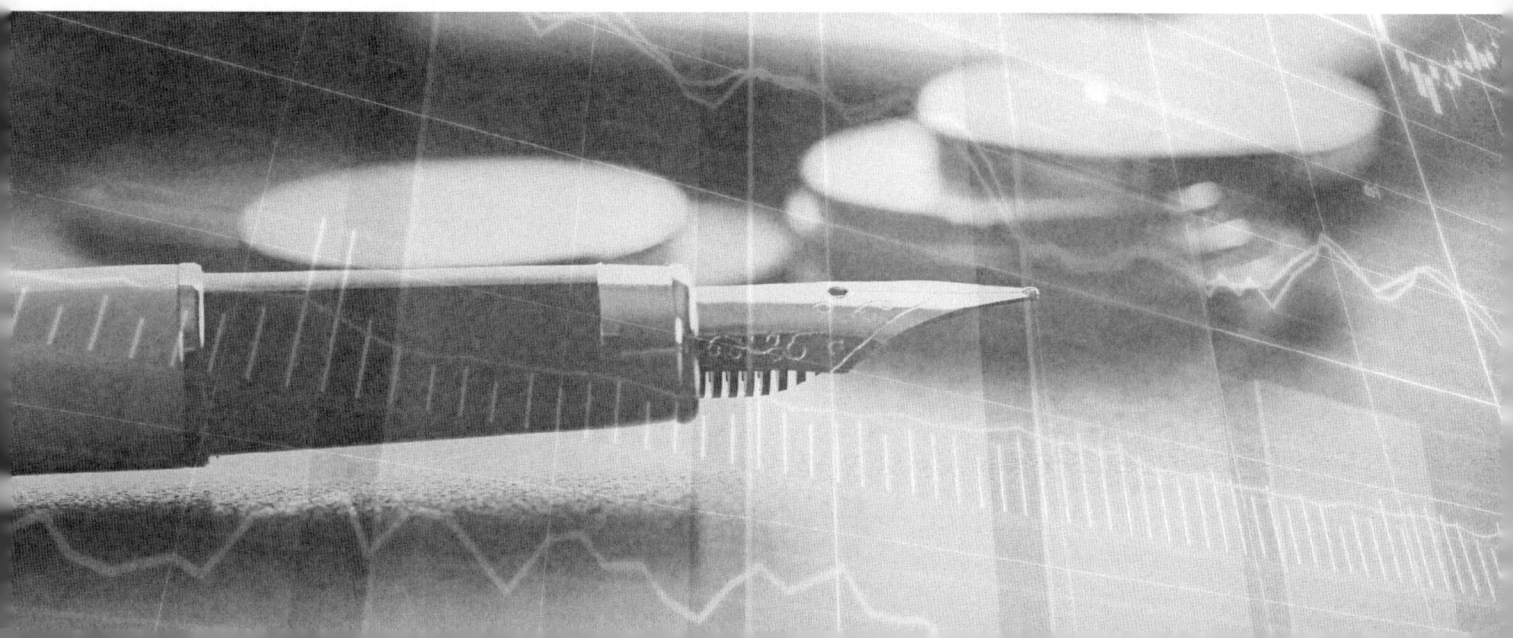

1. Listing Securities

Deciding to list (or **float**) securities on a stock exchange such as the LSE is a significant decision for a company to take. Flotations have both pros and cons – the fact that the company can gain access to capital and enable its shares to be readily marketable are often-quoted positives. The most often-quoted negatives are the fact that the original owners may well lose control of the company and that the ongoing disclosure and attention paid to the company after listing is much greater than previously.

1.1 Listing Advisers and Continuing Obligations

Learning Objective

4.1.2 Know the role of advisers: listing agent; corporate broker

4.1.3 Know the issuer's obligations: corporate governance; reporting

In order to have its securities listed, the company concerned will have to find and appoint certain advisers. The precise requirements and roles are laid down in the local regulations that apply to the particular exchange. Generally, the advisers will include both a listing agent (at the IPO stage) and a corporate broker (both at IPO and afterwards).

Once the decision has been made to list, the company will have to find and appoint a listing agent, alternatively referred to as a **sponsor**. The sponsor is likely to be an investment bank, a stockbroking firm or a professional services firm such as an accountancy practice. The role of the sponsor includes assessing the company's suitability for listing, the best method of bringing the company to the market, and co-ordinating the production of the **prospectus**. The prospectus is a detailed document about the company, including financial information that should enable prospective investors to decide on the merits of the company's shares.

The sponsor is only part of the **origination team** helping the company in the flotation. In addition to the sponsor, the issuing company will appoint a variety of other advisers, such as reporting accountants, legal advisers, public relations (PR) consultants and a corporate broker.

The **reporting accountants** will attest to the validity of the financial information provided in the prospectus. The **legal advisers** will make sure that all relevant matters are covered in the prospectus and the statements made are justified. The combination of the reporting accountants and the legal advisers is said to be providing **due diligence** for the prospectus – making sure the document is accurate and complies with the regulations.

A **PR consultant** is generally appointed to optimise the positive public perception of the company and its products and services in the run-up to listing.

Finally, the origination team may require a **corporate broker**, who may be the same firm as the listing agent. The responsibilities of the corporate broker are to act as an interface between the company on the one hand, and the stock market and investors in the company's securities on the other. In particular, the corporate broker advises the company on **market conditions** – the way existing and potential investors are viewing the company in relation to its peers, and the general direction of the market.

An issuer that is planning to have its securities listed will have to undertake certain obligations. Like the requirements for advisers, the precise obligations can vary across jurisdictions, but they always include obligations in relation to corporate governance and reporting.

Corporate governance is the way a company (the corporate) manages and controls its activities (governs itself). Corporate governance is often described as the set of laws, rules, customs and both external and internal policies that guide how a company is directed and managed. In particular, it is expected (and, in some jurisdictions, required) that the listed companies have put in place appropriate corporate and management structures. Examples include reducing the influence of a single individual by splitting the roles of chairman and chief executive of the company, appointing a reasonable proportion of non-executive directors (NEDs) to the board, and having a suitably qualified finance director.

Reporting requirements are designed to make sure that existing and potential investors are kept informed of progress and developments at the listed company. It is particularly important that financial information is provided regularly and that the information is reliable, and so listed companies are generally required to provide audited annual accounts and less detailed half-yearly, or perhaps quarterly, reports.

1.2   The Syndicate Group

Learning Objective

4.1.1   Understand the role of the syndicate group: different roles within a syndicate: bookrunner, co-lead, co-manager; marketing and bookbuilding

For large listings, when the issuing company is planning to issue substantial quantities of shares to interested investors, the sponsor will gather together a **syndicate** of investment banks and stockbrokers to market the share issue to their clients. These clients may be a mixture of both institutional clients (such as insurance companies and asset management firms) and retail clients. The sponsor will generally act as the **lead manager** of the syndicate, appointing a host of **co-managers** to assist. Sometimes the issue may be large enough to warrant the appointment of more than one lead manager, perhaps with each **co-lead manager** taking responsibility for particular geographical areas – for example, one lead manager for Europe, another for the US.

The process of finding buyers for the issuing company's shares is known as **bookbuilding**, and the lead managers co-ordinate the overall level of demand across the syndicate. This role is commonly referred to as that of the **book runner**.

During the bookbuilding, the syndicate will gather the willingness of investors to purchase the shares, which will be sensitive to the price at which the shares are sold. Usually, the bookbuilding begins with an indicative range of prices; the finalisation of the price will come just prior to listing. This is illustrated in the following example.

Example

Cauldron Stanley is a large investment bank. It is acting as lead manager and sponsor for a new issue of shares for a client, Wizard Enterprises plc, which is looking to raise several billion pounds. Because of the size of the issue, Cauldron Stanley sets up a syndicate of ten investment banks to assist in the marketing and act as co-managers.

The syndicate initially markets the shares at an indicative price range of £2 to £2.20 each. The strength of demand is strong so that, as listing approaches, the final price is set at the top of the range, at £2.20 per share.

1.3 Underwriting

Learning Objective

4.1.4 Understand the purpose and practice of underwriting, rights and responsibilities of the underwriter: benefits to the issuing company; risks and rewards to the underwriter

In circumstances where a company is attempting to sell shares to the investing public, there is a danger that the demand is not sufficient, perhaps because of a general fall in share prices near to the flotation date. This could lead to the flotation failing, so it is usual to **underwrite** new issues of shares. Underwriting is agreeing with financial institutions, such as banks, insurance companies and asset managers, that, if the demand is insufficient, the financial institutions will buy the shares. Effectively, underwriting creates an insurance policy that the issue will happen because, in the worst case, the underwriters (the financial institutions that have agreed to underwrite the offer) will buy the shares. The underwriters also work closely with the issuing company, prior to an offering period, to determine demand for the shares, to help determine an appropriate share price for the listing and in the distribution of the shares to their network of institutional or retail clients.

In such circumstances the price at which the underwriters guarantee to buy is generally at a discount to the share price at which the shares are offered to the public, eg, shares offered to the public at £5 each might be underwritten at £4.75 each.

The benefits to the issuing company of an underwriting arrangement are obvious – the sale of the shares and minimum proceeds are guaranteed. For the underwriters, the risk is that they may end up buying shares for more than they are worth. However, in return for accepting this risk, the underwriters will be paid fees, regardless of whether or not there is a lack of demand for the shares from the public.

1.4   Stabilisation

Learning Objective

4.1.5   Understand stabilisation and its purpose: governing principles and regulation with regard to stabilisation activity; who is involved in stabilisation; what does stabilisation achieve; benefits to the issuing company and investors

Stabilisation is the process whereby, to prevent a substantial fall in the value of securities when a large number of new securities is issued, the lead manager of the issue agrees to support the price by buying back the newly issued securities in the market if the market price falls below a certain predefined level. This is done in an attempt to give the market a reasonable chance to adjust to the increased number of securities that have become available, by stabilising the price at which they are traded.

By increasing the demand for the securities in the market at the same time as more securities become available, the price should remain more stable. This will mean the issuing company's securities appear less volatile, and existing investors will be less likely to begin panic-selling, creating a downward spiral in the securities' price. The securities that are bought back by the lead manager of the issue will then be sold back into the market over time.

There are strict rules laid down by regulators regarding stabilisation practices. For example, the FCA requires disclosure to the market that stabilisation is happening, and that the market price may not be a representative one because of the stabilisation activities. Prices can also be stabilised by exchanges using circuit breakers to temporarily suspend trading in periods of volatility.

1.5   Initial Public Offerings (IPOs)

Learning Objective

4.2.1   Understand the use of an initial public offering: why would a company choose an IPO; structure of IPO – base deal plus greenshoe; stages of an IPO; underwritten versus best efforts

An IPO is when a company sells equity that is currently privately owned (and controlled) to a wider group of investors (the public). The current owners are likely to be the founders of the company and/or relatives or close acquaintances. By issuing shares via an IPO, which is known as 'going public', they are giving up a substantial amount of control, as the new owners (shareholders) will not only own shares, but will also have voting rights and be included in decision making that affects the company and the board of directors. It is possible that public shareholders may have different interests from the existing owners, as owners of listed shares are usually most interested in an increased share price. Furthermore, they can sell the shares on the market and the existing owners will lose control over who becomes a shareholder (and, therefore, a decision maker) in the future.

The key advantages of initial public offerings (IPOs) over other capital-raising methods are that IPOs can raise substantial sums of capital and create a great deal of publicity for the issuing companies. The money raised in the form of an IPO is known as **risk capital** and the company assets are not encumbered or hypothecated in the same manner as they would be if the capital were raised from a debt offering.

An IPO is usually structured with a **base number** of shares that the company is planning to issue. However, the issuing company may also reserve the right to increase the number of shares it issues, if significant levels of demand would remain unsatisfied if only the base number of shares were issued. The option to increase the number of shares is referred to as a **greenshoe**.

As seen, there are three broad stages to an IPO:

1. **The decision** – the issuing company (in conjunction with its advisers, particularly the investment bank) makes a decision to raise capital via an IPO. This will involve careful consideration of the pros and cons of a public offer.
2. **The preparation of the prospectus** – this is the necessary document that must accompany an IPO, involving the whole team of advisers, including the investment bank, reporting accountants and legal advisers.
3. **The sale of securities** – the investment bank will lead manage the sale and may well establish a syndicate of co-managers to assist in selling the securities to their clients.

Underwriting of the offer is generally the responsibility of the investment bank(s) and they typically arrange **firm underwriting** when there are guarantees in place to buy the securities. Investment banks may not provide a **firm undertaking** to place all of the securities on behalf of their clients. Instead the lead underwriter, along with the co-managers of the offer, may provide a **best efforts underwriting**, in which they will do their best to sell the shares involved in the offering but when there is no formal guarantee that this will be achieved. In practice this means that the managers of the underwriting are not committing to purchase any unplaced securities for their own account in an unconditional manner. By an underwriter and the co-managers inserting the **best efforts** conditionality, should there be a failure to fully complete a sale of the offering, there is less risk to the underwriter of reputational damage and not being invited to participate in future IPOs.

1.6 Follow-On Offerings

Learning Objective

4.2.2 Understand the use of follow-on offerings: why would a company choose a follow-on offering; structure of follow-on – base deal plus greenshoe; stages of follow-on offering; underwritten versus best efforts

An already listed company looking to raise more capital can choose to go through a follow-on offering. A follow-on offering is alternatively referred to as a **secondary** offer. Clearly, issuing more shares in a follow-on offering will only be considered if the equity markets are sufficiently robust. In a bear market there is unlikely to be sufficient demand for the shares at the price the issuing company wants.

Like an initial public offering, a follow-on offering will be structured with a **base number** of shares that the company is planning to issue. Again, the issuing company may also retain a greenshoe option to increase the number of shares that it issues, if significant levels of demand would otherwise remain unsatisfied.

A secondary offering will inevitably be quicker, easier and cheaper than an IPO, simply because the company has been through the stages before in its IPO. The broad stages of a follow-on offer are the same as an IPO:

1. **The decision.**
2. **The preparation of the prospectus.** This should be relatively easy, since the issuing company has prepared a prospectus before, when it first became a listed entity.
3. **The sale of securities.** As in an IPO, the appointed investment bank will lead manage the sale and may well establish a syndicate of co-managers to assist in selling the securities to their clients.

As with an IPO, the follow-on offering may also be underwritten, with a potential combination of firm underwriting by the investment bank(s) and best efforts underwriting by clients such as stockbroking firms.

As with an IPO, a follow-on offering is said to be underwritten when there is a firm undertaking by the investment bank(s) that is conducting the offering that all of the offering will be fully subscribed. In other words, the underwriting bank(s) will guarantee that any shortfall by subscribers will be purchased by the bank(s) for its own account.

A best efforts agreement provides no such guarantee. In this case the underwriting bank(s) agrees to use its best efforts to sell as much of an issue as possible to the public. If the underwriter is unable to sell all of the offering because of adverse market conditions, he does not take responsibility for placing any of the unsold inventory. Arrangements that are made on a best efforts basis are often found with high-risk securities.

1.7   Open Offers and Offers for Subscription

Learning Objective

4.2.3   Understand the use of open offers and offers for subscription: why would a company choose an open offer; structure of offer; stages of offer; tenders, strike price, who is involved in the offer process

---

A company applying for admission to the Official List in the UK needs to have at least 25% of its ordinary shares in the hands of the public. In order to achieve this, and to raise capital through its listing, a company can have an IPO of ordinary shares by making an **offer for subscription**.

An offer for subscription involves the company sending a prospectus (including the share price) and an application form to potential investors. The company's sponsor, along with reporting accountants and legal advisers, will assist in the preparation of the prospectus. Those potential investors who want to invest in the company apply for shares. The company then issues **allotment letters** to successful applicants.

Only new (not previously issued) shares may be issued in this way.

Diagrammatically:

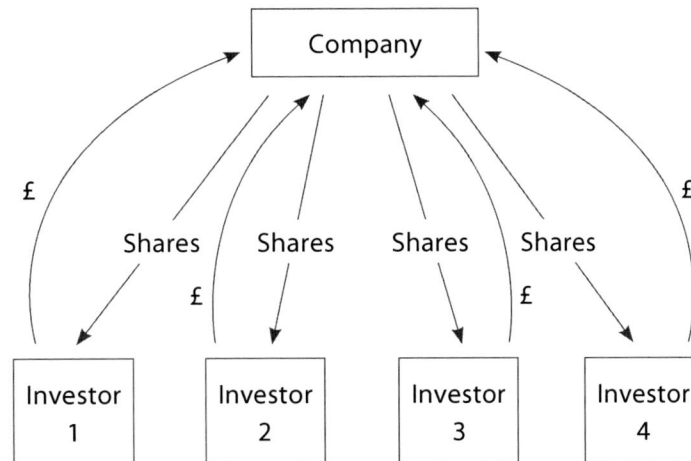

This method is rare in large IPOs, mainly because issuing companies like to use the expertise of the investment banks to facilitate their IPOs, in particular their ability to price and sell shares to their substantial client base. As a result, large IPOs tend to follow the offer for sale route outlined in Section 1.8.

An **open offer** is similar in that it is an invitation to subscribe for new shares. However, open offers are follow-on offers that only offer new shares to the existing shareholders, in proportion to their existing shareholding. This meets the pre-emptive rights of the shareholders, but it differs from a rights issue in that the rights are not able to be sold nil paid. The offer is simply open for the existing shareholders to take up, or not.

1.8   Offers For Sale

Learning Objective

4.2.4   Understand the use of offers for sale: why would a company choose an offer for sale; structure of an offer for sale; stages of an offer for sale; tenders, strike price, who may receive an allotment, who is involved in the offer process

Offers for sale are a much more common way of achieving a listing. The company seeking to sell the shares approaches an **issuing house** (usually an investment bank) that specialises in approaching potential shareholders and preparing the necessary documentation. The issuing company sells its shares to the issuing house (usually an investment bank), which then invites applications from the public at a slightly higher price than the issuing house has paid and on the basis of a detailed prospectus, known as the **offer document**. For a company applying for a full listing, this provides comprehensive information about the company and its directors and how the proceeds from the share issue will be applied. As seen, this document must be prepared by the company's directors and assessed by their sponsor to satisfy the UKLA of the company's suitability to obtain a full listing.

Diagrammatically:

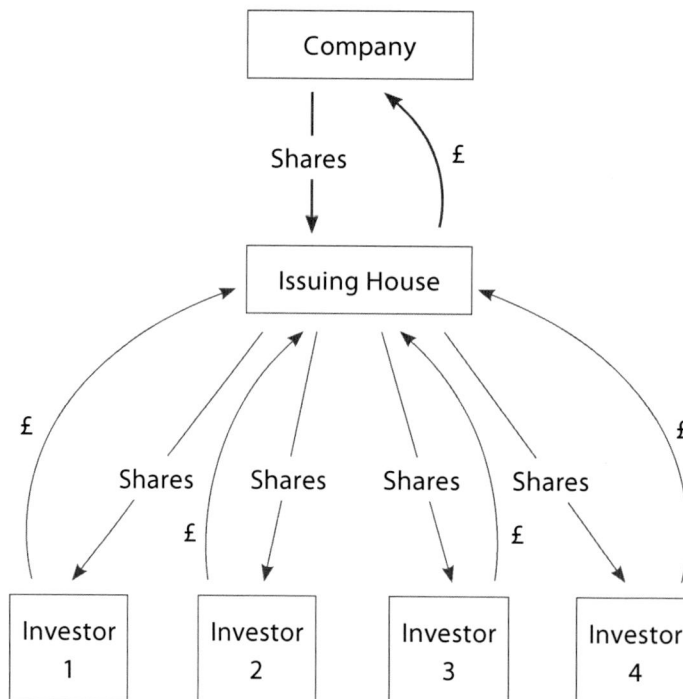

Offers for sale do not necessarily require the company to create new shares specifically for the share issue. Indeed, offers for sale are often used by a company's founders to release part, or all, of their equity stake in their company, and have also been the preferred route for government privatisation programmes, when former nationalised monopolies have been sold to the public. In both cases, existing shareholdings are disposed of, rather than new shares created, in order to obtain a listing.

An offer for sale, or an offer for subscription, can be made on either a fixed or a tender price basis:

Fixed-price offer – when a fixed-price offer is made, the price is usually fixed just below that at which it is believed the issue should be fully subscribed, so as to encourage an active secondary market in the shares. Subscribers to a fixed-price issue apply for the number of shares they wish to purchase at this fixed price. If the offer is oversubscribed, as it nearly always is, given the favourable pricing formula, then shares are allotted either by scaling down each application or by satisfying a randomly chosen proportion of the applications in full. The precise method used will be detailed in the offer document.

Tender offer – given the judgement required in setting the price at a level that does not lead to the issue being excessively oversubscribed but which leads to a successful new issue, and the fact that market sentiment can and often does change between the announcement of the IPO and the end of the offer period, offers for sale and offers for subscription can be made on a tender basis when the issuer does not stipulate a fixed price for the shares but invites tenders for the issue, usually by setting a minimum tender price. Investors state the number of shares they wish to purchase and state the price per share they are prepared to pay.

Once the offer is closed, a single **strike price** can then be determined by the issuing house or by the company, as appropriate, to satisfy all applications tendered at, or above, this price.

Although this auctioning process is the more efficient way of allocating shares and maximising the proceeds from a share issue, tender offers are also more complex to administer and, as such, tend to be outnumbered by fixed-price offers.

1.8.1 Over Allotment Options

An allotment provision used in the case of an IPO that has become almost standard in the case of new offerings undertaken by US investment banks is the greenshoe. It is known as the **greenshoe option** because the term comes from a company founded in 1919 as Green Shoe Manufacturing Company, now called Stride Rite Corporation, which was the first company to be permitted to use this practice in an offering.

More properly known by its legal title as an **over-allotment option**, the greenshoe provision gives the underwriters of an IPO the right to sell additional shares in a registered securities offering, if demand for the securities is in excess of the original amount offered. But it is also used as a tool in providing price stabilisation and a successful execution of the offering on behalf of the issuer. At the time of issuance the timing of the sale of shares can often be quite sensitive, and the underwriters have developed strategies which enable them to smooth out price fluctuations if demand surges on the one hand and to help support the IPO if there are adverse market conditions. By using the over-allotment provision the issuer may ensure a more successful marketing and distribution of the offering. However, some issuers have refrained from providing their underwriters with a greenshoe option.

The LSE has ratified the requests from sponsoring member firms enabling them to exercise an over-allotment option for initial offerings conducted for issuers that wish to be listed on its exchange.

The situation is outlined in the following memorandum from the LSE:

Greenshoe arrangements are commonly agreed by a sponsoring member firm as part of the stabilisation and underwriting arrangements for an introduction to either the UKLA's Official List or AIM, as well as for further new issues of shares. Whether the option is ever exercised, and the extent to which it is utilised, will depend on the take up of the issue, the underlying share price in the market and the stabilisation transactions undertaken.

The Exchange has agreed that such transactions can be brought on Exchange under the following circumstances:

- *the terms of the greenshoe option must be agreed and included in the circular or prospectus prior to sign-off, including confirmation that the option writer holds sufficient shares to meet any obligation under the option;*
- *at the point of exercise the shares to be delivered are admitted to trading; and*
- *a regulatory news announcement has disclosed that exercise has taken place.*

1.9   Selective Marketing and Placing

Learning Objective

4.2.5   Understand the basic process and uses of selective marketing and placing: advantages to the issuing company; what is a placing; what is selective marketing; how is a placing achieved; how is selective marketing achieved

In placing its shares, a company simply markets the issue directly to a broker, an issuing house or other financial institution, which in turn places the shares with selected clients. Although the least democratic of the three IPO methods, given that the general public does not initially have access to the issue, a placing is the least expensive, as the prospectus accompanying the issue is less detailed than that required for the other two methods and no underwriting is required.

A placing is often referred to as a **selective marketing**, because the intermediary is selecting the clients to whom the offer is directed.

Diagrammatically:

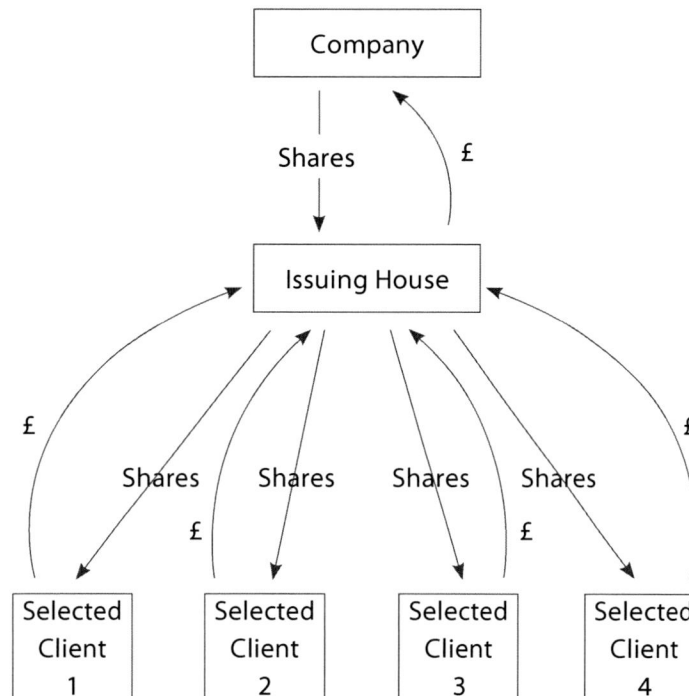

1.9.1 The Prospectus

For most public offerings of securities a vital prerequisite is a prospectus or offering document which the issuer has to make available to all prospective investors and the exchanges upon which it intends to list its securities. Such a prospectus has to fully disclose all the pertinent details regarding the offering, including a detailed business plan, an explanation of how the proceeds from the offering will be used, details of all owners/directors of the entity, and most importantly a comprehensive disclosure of all of the risks associated with the investment.

A special provision exists for offerings marketed to a restricted class of investors in Europe, known as either 'sophisticated' or 'qualified' investors. These investors, and the investment banks who advise them, are able to purchase investments through which a formal prospectus is either not issued, or when the regular disclosure requirements associated with issuing shares are far less onerous than those which would be required for a public offering.

The specific requirements for this type of offering are outlined in the Prospectus Directive (PD), which forms part of the EU initiative known as MiFID. In the US, the SEC also has special provisions for private placements.

1.10 Introductions

Learning Objective

4.2.6 Understand the use of introductions: why would a company undertake an introduction; structure of an introduction; stages of an introduction

An introduction is not actually an issue at all. It is used by a company that wishes to become listed (eg, on the LSE) in order to gain access to the secondary market that the exchange provides.

An introduction is unusual because most companies use listing as an opportunity to raise extra funds, and some companies are forced to issue more shares to comply with the listing rules.

An introduction is used by a company that does not need to raise extra capital through share issues, but wishes to gain the extra liquidity in its shares that a listing provides. This might be a company that is already listed on another, overseas stock exchange, a new company formed from two previously listed companies that have merged, or a demutualised organisation.

Because an introduction raises no funds, it is not a marketing operation in the same way as an offer for sale, offer for subscription or placing.

1.11 Exchangeable/Convertible Bond Offerings

Learning Objective

4.2.7 Understand the use of exchangeable/convertible bond offerings: the difference between exchangeable and convertible bonds; structure of offering – base deal plus greenshoe; stages of offering; underwritten versus best efforts

Exchangeable bonds and convertible bonds are similar instruments – they both can be described as hybrid instruments, with characteristics of both equities and bonds. A **convertible bond** is a bond, paying a coupon and with a nominal value to be repaid on maturity, that offers the holder of the bond the right to convert the bond into a set number of ordinary shares of the company that issued the bond.

Example

XYZ issues convertible bonds paying a 6% annual coupon and redeeming in five years' time. The holder of the convertible can choose to convert £100 nominal value of the bonds into 25 XYZ shares at redemption.

Clearly the holder of the bonds will convert as long as the shares are trading at more than £4 each at the redemption date.

An **exchangeable bond** is also a bond that pays a coupon and has a set redemption date. Like a convertible, it gives the holder the right to exchange the bond for a set number of shares, but these shares are not those of the bond issuer, but of another company's shares that are held by the issuer.

Example

XYZ plc holds ABC plc shares and issues exchangeable bonds paying a 6% annual coupon and redeeming in five years' time. The holder of the exchangeable can choose to convert £100 nominal value of the bonds into 20 ABC shares at redemption.

Clearly the holder of the bonds will exchange as long as the shares are trading at more than £5 each at the redemption date.

The holder of either a convertible or an exchangeable bond has the safety of coupons and repayment, combined with the potential upside of equity growth. Both types of bond will enable the issuer to raise borrowed funds more cheaply, because the bonds have the upside potential of the conversion/exchange into shares.

The structure of an offering of a convertible or exchangeable bond mirrors that of equities – the issuer will set a base amount of bonds it wishes to issue and perhaps retain a greenshoe, reserving the right to issue more if demand is strong.

The stages of the convertible/exchangeable offer are the same as an IPO:

1. The decision.
2. The preparation of the prospectus.
3. The sale of securities.

As with an IPO, the offer may also be underwritten, with a potential combination of firm underwriting by the investment bank(s) and best efforts underwriting by clients of the investment bank(s) such as stockbroking firms.

2. Bond Offerings

2.1 Types of Issuer

Learning Objective

4.3.1 Know the different types of issuer: supranationals; governments; agency; municipal; corporate; financial institutions and special purpose vehicles

Bonds are essentially IOU instruments that specify a face value, coupon rate and redemption date. They are issued by a variety of organisations including:

- **Supranationals** – organisations like the World Bank raise money through issuing bonds.
- **Governments** – most governments have a requirement to borrow money at some stage, and the long-term borrowing is generally financed by bond issues, such as UK gilts and US T-bonds.

- **Agencies** – agencies (often backed by the government) issue bonds for particular purposes. These are common in the US, where examples include the Federal National Mortgage Association ('Fannie Mae'), created to provide mortgage finance for the disadvantaged, and the Student Loan Marketing Association ('Sallie Mae') created to finance student education. Recent developments in the US credit markets have seen government-sponsored entities such as Fannie Mae and Freddie Mac (the Federal Home Loan Mortgage Corporation) come under the conservatorship of the US Treasury and a public underwriting of their entire obligations.
- **Municipalities** – municipalities in the US issue municipal bonds to finance local borrowing. These municipal bonds are often tax efficient, particularly for investors who reside in that municipality. Municipal bonds are usually guaranteed by a third party, known in the US market as a **monoline insurer**, and their credit quality may be enhanced by such a guarantee, which enables the municipality to secure funds on more advantageous terms. Some of the well-known monoline insurers in the US extended their activities to providing a range of far more risky guarantees for asset-backed securities, and have since lost their own investment grade ratings.
- **Corporates** – large companies often use bonds to finance borrowing needs.
- **Financial institutions and special purpose vehicles (SPVs)** – like other corporates, financial institutions issue bonds to finance borrowing. These financial institutions also arrange borrowing for themselves and others by creating SPVs to enable money to be raised that does not appear within the accounts of that entity. This type of finance is often described as **off-balance-sheet finance**, because it does not appear in the balance sheet that forms of part of the company's accounts. Owing to illiquidity and critical developments in the credit markets during 2008, many parent institutions have had to abandon SPVs including structured investment vehicles (SIVs) and have had to move these off-balance-sheet accounts back on to the parent entity's balance sheet. In particular, Citigroup was forced to come to the rescue of certain funds within its own SIV, and this resulted in almost $50 billion being returned to the company's balance sheet.

2.2 Bond Issuance

Learning Objective

4.3.2 Know the methods of issuance: scheduled funding programmes and opportunistic issuance, eg, medium-term notes (MTN); auction/tender; reverse inquiry (under MTN)

Traditionally, borrowing money via a bond issue was only sensible when large sums of money were being raised in a single capital-raising transaction. The sums had to be large enough to make the costs involved in issuance worthwhile. The details of the bond would be established, including its coupon and maturity, and the bonds would be marketed to potential investors. The investors would either be invited to bid for the bonds in an auction-type process, or a tender method was adopted. Both of these are illustrated in the examples that follow in relation to UK government bonds.

The **DMO** is the part of the **Treasury** that oversees gilt issues. It uses a number of different issue methods, depending on the circumstances. Most commonly used is the **auction method**, when the DMO announces the auction, receives bids and allocates the gilts to those that bid highest, at the price they bid. GEMMs are expected to bid for gilts when the DMO makes a new issue, and the DMO reserves the right to take the gilts on to its own books if the auction is not fully taken up. Applicants bid for the gilt and successful bidders pay the price at which they bid.

Example

Imagine the auction is for £1m nominal and the price is £100 for £100 nominal.

- A offers to buy £0.5m nominal, willing to pay £101.50 for every £100 nominal.
- B offers to buy £0.5m nominal, willing to pay £100.75 for every £100 nominal.
- C offers to buy £0.5m nominal, willing to pay £100.50 for every £100 nominal.

A and B are awarded the gilts for **the prices that they bid** and there is nothing left for C.

Up until 1987 the tender method was standard, when all bidders paid a common strike price. A minimum price is set by the DMO and investors make bids. The gilts are awarded at the highest price at which they can all be sold.

Example

Imagine the tender is for £1 million nominal and the minimum price is £100 for £100 nominal. The bids submitted are:

- A offers to buy £0.5 million nominal, paying £101.50 for every £100 nominal.
- B offers to buy £0.5 million nominal, paying £100.75 for every £100 nominal.
- C offers to buy £0.5 million nominal, paying £100.50 for every £100 nominal.

In this instance, A and B are awarded the gilts, but both pay the lower price: £100.75 (the highest price at which all the gilts could be sold).

Because many issuers, particularly companies, needed to borrow money regularly in line with the developments of their business, they tended to prefer to set up **scheduled programmes** with their banks under which they would be able to borrow money, instead of issuing bonds.

However, a US innovation has been introduced that has been subsequently adopted in many other jurisdictions which enables bond financing to be much more flexible. Traditionally, it was awkward and expensive to regularly raise bond finance because each bond issue had to be separately registered with the financial regulator (the SEC in the US). A process known as '**shelf registration**' was introduced that enabled a single registration to be used for a number of bond issues over a period of up to two years. This has been heavily used in the **medium-term note (MTN)** market for bonds with generally two to 10 years between issue and maturity. Shelf registration introduced flexibility to the bond market, allowing companies to issue smaller batches of bonds, with the coupons and maturity varying according to market demand at the time.

The process involves the bond issuer finding two or more dealers that are willing to offer their services to market the bonds to their clients on a best efforts basis. The issuer will then issue bonds as and when the money is required, with coupon rates and maturity in accordance with market demand. Indeed, it is not unusual for some MTNs to be issued in response to an enquiry from clients of the dealers that want a particular maturity and coupon. These are termed **reverse inquiries** in the US, and the issuer can decide whether to accept the terms and issue the bonds or not.

2.3 The Role of the Origination Team

Learning Objective

4.3.3 Understand the role of the origination team including: pitching; indicative bid; mandate announcement; credit rating; roadshow; listing; syndication

Many of the activities in originating bond issues are similar to those in originating equity issues, particularly if the bonds are going to be listed and therefore need a prospectus. In such cases there will be a whole **origination team** involving the issuer, its investment bank, reporting accountants, legal and PR advisers.

A typical new issue of bonds could contain any, or all of the following stages:

1. **Pitching** – the issuer of the bonds will need to decide that a bond issue is appropriate and which investment bank(s) it wants to assist in the issue. The final decision will be dependent upon an assessment of the qualities of the potential banks. A final decision is usually made on the basis of a presentation (pitch) made by the banks, to the issuer.
2. **Indicative bid** – during the pitching stage, the banks will detail their views of how much finance the issuer is likely to raise given the terms of the bond issue.
3. **Mandate announcement** – once the issuer has decided upon the bank(s) to raise the finance on its behalf, it will announce the names of the banks that have been given the mandate to arrange the issue on its behalf.
4. **Credit rating** – given by one of the credit rating agencies, this will be vital to the amount of finance that can be raised. The details of the proposed terms and conditions of the bond will have to be provided to the agency to get a credit rating, and there may be a need for credit enhancements, such as insurance, to enable a higher rating to be achieved.
5. **Roadshow** – once the bank running the issue has been appointed, it will arrange and run a series of visits to the potential buyers of the bonds. This is commonly described as the roadshow, because it involves travelling around a number of major financial centres to see the key investors.
6. **Listing** – if the bond is to be listed it will need a prospectus to submit to the relevant listing authority.
7. **Syndication** – for larger bond issues there will be a number of banks acting for the issuer, described as a lead manager (the primary contact with the issuer) and the other co-managers that will sell into their particular client base, perhaps based on geographical regions. The total of all the banks involved is the syndicate.

3. Corporate Actions

3.1 Rights Issues

Learning Objective

4.4.1 Understand the use of rights issues: reasons for a rights issue; structure of rights issue; stages of rights issue; pre-emptive rights; trading nil paid

---

A rights issue is an issue by a company of new shares (a secondary issue) for cash to the existing shareholders in proportion to their existing holding. It is usually at a discount to the current market price. The holder of the right, as the name suggests, has the right, but not the obligation, to purchase additional shares directly from the company, usually at a discount. The right will have an expiry date, upon which it is no longer valid. Rights are usually short-term privileges and can be traded on the exchange until they expire.

A rights issue is an attractive way for a company to raise new finance for the following reasons:

- There is no dilution of shareholders' interest, ie, someone who held 20% of the shares before the issue will hold 20% after (assuming they take up their rights).
- The issue is at a discount to the current market price to make it attractive.
- Existing ordinary shareholders of a company will receive a provisional allotment of new shares. After being granted such an allotment, each may decide to exercise the rights to add to their holding, but there is no obligation to take up the offer.
- A shareholder who does not want to subscribe more cash and take up their rights can sell them, receiving cash as payment for the dilution of interest that they will suffer.
- Such issues are generally underwritten to cater for those individuals who do not want to exercise their rights, thus the company can be sure of raising all the finance it requires.

In essence, a rights issue is a way of avoiding the negative effects of **dilution** on shareholders. Dilution occurs when new shares in a company are issued, diluting the influence and value of the existing shares.

The reason for a rights issue is usually to fund expansion, perhaps to take over a rival or to diversify into a new business area. Existing shareholders receive a provisional allotment letter, which tells them how many shares they are entitled to and what the price will be.

Existing shareholders do not have to participate in the rights issue but can sell the rights nil paid, either in part or in full. A fuller discussion of the method of calculating the nil paid value is discussed below, but the essential feature is that the issuer provides the current shareholders with a transferable security (known as a provisional allotment letter) which can be sold to other investors.

3.1.1 Pre-Emption Rights

Legally, the current shareholders of a company have prior rights to subscribe for any new issues of shares for cash before they can be offered to anyone else. These are called their pre-emption rights and their purpose is to ensure that the level of influence or control that a shareholder has is not diluted by any issue without his prior knowledge and agreement. The rights issue outlined above complies with pre-emption rights.

The existence of pre-emption rights means that listed companies cannot issue equity shares, convertibles or warrants for cash other than to the current equity shareholders of the company, except with their prior approval in general meeting.

It is quite common to see the waiving of pre-emption rights as a proposed special resolution at the AGM of public companies. Shareholders can vote to forgo their pre-emption rights for a period of up to five years, though the stock exchange's rules for listed companies are stricter, requiring such a resolution to be passed at each AGM.

Example of Dilution

Suppose an investor holds 400 shares out of a total of 10,000 shares in XYZ plc, a 4% stake in the company. XYZ then decides to issue 10,000 further shares. That means that there are now 20,000 shares in issue. The investor's original 400 shares now represents a 2% stake rather than a 4% stake. This is dilution.

UK company law offers some protection against dilution, with most companies requiring a special resolution from shareholders for new shares to be allotted in cash to anyone other than the existing shareholders in proportion to their existing holding. This is known as the shareholders' pre-emptive right.

In the above example, the investor's pre-emptive right would be to be offered 400 of the further issue of 10,000 shares.

3.1.2 Mechanics of a Rights Issue

New shares are offered in proportion to each shareholder's existing shareholding, usually at a price deeply discounted to that prevailing in the market, to ensure that the issue will be fully subscribed and sometimes to reduce, or even avoid, the cost of underwriting the shares. The number of new shares issued and the price of these shares will be determined by the amount of capital to be raised.

The right to participate in such an issue is only conferred upon those shareholders who hold the issuing company's shares cum-rights – that is, those who hold the company's shares before trading in the shares is conducted on an ex-rights, or without rights, basis. The ex-rights period begins on, or shortly after, the day on which the rights issue announcement is made and runs for a further period that must be a minimum of 10 business days through to the acceptance date, the date by which the shareholder should have decided whether or not to take up these new shares.

Those entitled to participate in the rights issues are advised of their entitlement by means of a **provisional allotment letter**. The provisional allotment letter is renounceable and transferable and it sets out the shareholder's existing shareholding, the rights allotted over the new shares and the acceptance date. The ex-rights period begins on the day after the allotment letter is posted.

As these new shares rank equally, or *pari passu*, with the existing shares in issue, once the existing shares are declared ex-rights, the market price should fall to reflect the dilution effect that the new shares will have on the prevailing share price. The price to which the shares should fall is termed the **theoretical ex-rights price**, and its method of calculation is shown below.

$$\frac{\left[\left(\begin{array}{c}\text{No. shares held cum-rights}\\ \text{x}\\ \text{cum-rights share price}\end{array}\right) + \left(\begin{array}{c}\text{No. rights allocated}\\ \text{x}\\ \text{rights issue price}\end{array}\right)\right]}{\text{Total no. shares held assuming rights exercised}}$$

The difference between the theoretical ex-rights price and the rights issue price is known as the **nil paid value**, and the calculation and significance of this will be illustrated in the following sections.

As noted above, shareholders have a minimum of 10 business days to decide how to react to the announcement following receipt of the provisional allotment letter and must choose between one of the four following courses of action:

- **Option One – Take up the rights in full**
  Take up the rights in full by purchasing all of the shares offered. To take up the rights in full, the shareholder simply sends the company the provisional allotment letter, with a cheque, by the due date.

- **Option Two – Sell the rights nil paid in full**
  If a shareholder entitled to take up the rights issue decides not to, then they can sell the rights to these new shares nil paid. The purchaser of the nil paid rights will be able to take up the shares at the discounted price. Essentially they have a short-dated option on these new shares that can only be exercised, or traded, during the three-week ex-rights period. To sell the rights nil paid in full the shareholder must sign the form of renunciation on the reverse of the provisional allotment letter and send it to their broker by the due date.

- **Option Three – Sell part of rights nil paid to preserve current stake without dilution**
  The shareholder can sell sufficient of the rights nil paid to finance the take-up of the remaining rights. This course of action would be taken by a shareholder wishing to retain their shareholding in the company but without any desire to invest any further capital at this stage. When selling the rights nil paid in part, the shareholder does exactly the same as when selling them in full but requests that their broker split the allotment letter in accordance with the number of rights sold and those to be taken up. One of the split allotment letters will go to the purchaser of the rights, and the other to the original shareholder.

- **Option Four – Take no action**
  Any shareholder not taking any action by the acceptance date stipulated in the provisional allotment letter will automatically have their rights sold nil paid. The proceeds, less any expenses incurred by the company, are then distributed to all such shareholders on a pro rata basis. For the smaller shareholder not wishing to increase their shareholding in the company, this is often the most economical way to proceed.

3.1.3 Impact of a Rights Issue on the Share Price

Learning Objective

4.4.2 Be able to calculate the impact of a rights issue on the share price

To illustrate the impact on the share price for a company which undertakes a rights issue, the following are the key variables in the example discussed below.

- Prior to the rights issue the company has issued one million shares with a nominal value of £1.00 each. The par value is the nominal value which has been determined by an issuing company as a minimum price.
- The share premium account shows a balance of £0.5 million. The share premium account of a company is the capital that a company raises upon issuing shares that is in excess of the nominal value of the shares.
- The company wishes to raise new capital for expansion and undertakes a one-for-four rights issue at a price of £1.50 in order to raise £375,000.
- The company's accounts before the rights issue show that net assets are £2 million and retained profits are £0.5 million.
- The market price of the shares prior to the rights offering is £3.00 per share.

What is the impact on the accounts and the theoretical market price per share of this issue?

A one-for-four rights issue means that for every four shares previously in existence, one new share will be issued. In our example, one million shares were previously in issue, so 250,000 new shares will be issued at a price of £1.50 in order to raise the £375,000 cash required.

In terms of the accounts the 250,000 new share issue will increase the share capital to 1.25 million shares, the profit and loss will remain unchanged but the share premium account will need to be adjusted. The reason for this adjustment is that for the £375,000 raised, each of the 250,000 new shares can be issued at the nominal value of £1 but the additional £125,000 raised in excess of the nominal or face value of the shares is allocated to the share premium account as indicated in the simple balance sheet perspective in the table below.

The total capitalisation of the company will have increased to £2.375 million and can be broken down according to the upper part of the table which reflects the rights issue from an accounting perspective.

The impact on the share price can be seen from the calculation of the theoretical market price in the lower part of the table. The price for the shares should have fallen from £3.00 per share before the rights issue to £2.70 after the issue to reflect the new capitalisation divided by the greater number of shares now outstanding.

Rights Issue			
Impact on the accounts (all amounts in £'000)			
	Before	Issue	After
Net assets	2,000	375	2,375
Share capital			
1m £1 ordinary shares	1,000	250	1,250
Share premium	500	125	625
Profit and loss	500		500
Totals	2,000	375	2,375
Impact on the share price			
	Shares ('000)	Price £	Value (£'000)
Before	1,000	3.00	3,000
Rights Issue	250	1.50	375
After	1,250		3,375
Market price for shares	£2.70		

Another perspective on this can be seen simply by looking at the following formula, which only requires knowledge of the share price before the rights issue and the actual terms of the rights issue.

The formula for the theoretical ex-rights price is as follows:

$$\frac{\left[\left(\begin{array}{c}\text{No. shares held cum-rights}\\ \times\\ \text{cum-rights share price}\end{array}\right) + \left(\begin{array}{c}\text{No. rights allocated}\\ \times\\ \text{rights issue price}\end{array}\right)\right]}{\text{Total no. shares held assuming rights exercised}}$$

Description	Number of shares	Price per share (pence)	Total value of holdings (pence)
Shares held cum-rights	4	300	1,200
Rights allocated – new share entitlement	1	150	150
Post rights issue assuming rights taken up	5		1,350
Theoretical ex-rights price =1,350/5		270	

3.1.4 Value of Nil Paid Rights

Learning Objective

4.4.6 Be able to calculate the value of nil paid rights

As seen above, the formula for calculating the theoretical ex-rights price =

$$\frac{\left[\left(\begin{array}{c}\text{No. shares held cum-rights}\\ \text{x}\\ \text{cum-rights share price}\end{array}\right) + \left(\begin{array}{c}\text{No. rights allocated}\\ \text{x}\\ \text{rights issue price}\end{array}\right)\right]}{\text{Total no. shares held assuming rights exercised}}$$

As can be seen, it is straightforward to substitute the following values from the company provided above:

Number shares held cum-rights	=	4
Cum rights share price	=	£3.00
Number of rights allocated	=	1
Rights issue price	=	£1.50
Total shares assuming rights exercised	=	5
Solving	=	{[4 x £3.00] + [1 x £1.50]}/5 = £13.50/5 = £2.70

Given this example, the price of each nil paid right should be calculated from the ex-rights share price – price of the new shares = 270p – 150p = 120p.

Obviously, it would not be rational to pay more than 120p for the right to purchase a new share for 150p when the ex-rights price of the existing shares in issue is 270p.

3.1.5 Maximum Nil Paid Rights

Learning Objective

4.4.5 Be able to calculate the maximum nil paid rights to be sold to take up the balance at nil cost

As discussed in Section 3.1.2, option three is the situation when investors can choose to sell some of their entitlement and use the cash raised to take up the rest of the offer. In effect, they can buy a sufficient number of shares in the offering to preserve their position without dilution, but without having to invest additional funds into the business.

The number of nil paid rights to be sold to take up the balance at nil cost is given by the equation:

$$\frac{\text{Issue price of new shares x number of shares allocated}}{\text{Theoretical ex-rights price}}$$

As nil paid rights cannot be sold in fractions, the number must be rounded up to nearest integer or whole number value.

The actual process of preserving one's position without suffering any dilution but without having to invest new proceeds is sometimes known as **swallowing the tail** and can be demonstrated in the following table which is expanded from the one shown in Section 3.1.3. The table assumes the investor's current holdings, cum-rights, is 2,000 shares, and all of the information is the same as contained in the rights issue case study discussed in Section 3.1.3.

Description	Number of shares	Price per share (pence)	Total value of holdings (pence)
Shares held cum-rights	2,000	300	600,000
Rights allocated – new share entitlement	500	150	75,000
Post rights issue assuming rights taken up	2,500		675,000
Theoretical ex-rights price = 675,000/2,500		270	
Nil paid rights value = 270 – 150		120	
Number of nil paid rights to be sold	278		
Amount raised from selling nil rights = 278 x 120			33,360
Number of nil paid rights required to avoid dilution = 500 – 278	222		
Cost of purchasing rights to avoid dilution = 222 x 150			33,300
Gain/Loss from financing to preserve current stake			60
Total value of shares post-rights = (2,000 + 222) x £2.70	599,940		
Total value of position post-rights	600,000		
Net change in position			0

As can be seen from the bottom row, the net change in the investor's position is zero, ignoring transaction costs. By selling 278 nil paid rights and using the proceeds to purchase 222 new shares, accompanied by the tiny cash gain of 60p on the proceeds, the investor is in exactly the same position as before the rights issue but now holds an additional 222 shares at no additional cost.

3.2 Scrip or Bonus Issues

Learning Objective

4.4.3 Understand the use of scrip (also known as bonus or capitalisation) issues and why a company will undertake a scrip issue

A company may issue new shares to its shareholders for no consideration or *pro bono*, raising no further capital. The reasons for this are varied; sometimes it is as a public relations exercise to accompany news of a recent success or as a means of reducing the current market price to make its shares more marketable.

It can also be used to tidy up shareholders' funds by converting undistributable capital reserves into share capital. A company simply converts its reserves, which may have arisen from issuing new shares in the past at a premium to their nominal value and/or from the accumulation of undistributed past profits, into new ordinary shares. These shares rank *pari passu* with those already in issue and are distributed to the company's ordinary shareholders in proportion to their existing shareholdings free of charge.

Although as a result of the bonus issue the nominal value of the company's share capital will increase proportionately to the number of new shares issued, the net worth or intrinsic value of the business should remain the same. However, given that the company's earnings, or profits, and dividends will now be spread over a wider share capital base, the company's earnings per share (EPS) and dividends per share (DPS) should fall proportionately with the number of new shares in issue. This should result in the market price of the shares reducing by the same proportion, thereby leaving the company's market capitalisation unchanged.

Traditionally, once a UK company's share price starts trading well into double figures in pounds sterling, or, in the US, once its market price exceeds $200, its marketability starts to suffer as investors shy away from the shares. Therefore, a reduction in a company's share price as a result of a bonus issue usually has the effect of increasing the marketability of its shares. It can also raise expectations of higher future dividends. This in turn usually results in the share price settling above its new theoretical level and the company's market capitalisation increasing slightly.

3.2.1   Impact of a Scrip Issue on the Share Price

Learning Objective

4.4.4   Be able to calculate the impact of a scrip issue on the share price

The table below shows the impact of a one for three scrip issue on a company. The company started with 750,000 £1 ordinary shares in issue and net assets valued at £2.25 million, so the market capitalisation of the company is £2.25 million. A transfer of £0.25 million from retained profits to the share capital account is required to cover the scrip issue. When the market capitalisation of £2.25 million is divided by this enlarged number of 1m shares, the resultant share is £2.25 per share. So the impact of the scrip issue has been to reduce the share price from £3.00 to £2.25.

Bonus, Scrip or Capitalisation			
Impact on the accounts (all amounts in £'000)			
	Before	Issue	After
Net assets	2,250		2,250
Issued share capital			
1m £1 ordinary shares partly paid	750		750
1m £1 ordinary shares fully paid		250	250
Share premium	1,000		1,000
Retained profit	500	(250)	250
Totals	2,250	0	2,250
Impact on the share price			
	Shares (000)	Price £	Value (£000)
Before	750	3.00	2,250
Scrip issue	250		
After	1,000		2,250
Market price for shares	£2.25		

Example

XYZ plc makes a bonus issue to its shareholders on a one-for-four basis to coincide with the launch of a new product. Prior to the announcement of the issue, the company's ordinary shares traded at 200p per share. If the company had one million ordinary shares, each with a nominal value of 25p in issue prior to the announcement, calculate:

- The nominal value of the company's share capital immediately before and immediately after the announcement.
- The new theoretical market price for the shares.
- The market capitalisation of the company immediately before and immediately after the announcement based on the pre-existing share price and the new theoretical market price.

Solution

Nominal value of the company's share capital

- Immediately before = £1m x 25p = £250,000
- Immediately after = £1m x (5/4) x 25p = £312,500

Theoretical market price

The theoretical market price will be 200p x (4/5) = 160p

Market capitalisation

- Immediately before = £1m x 200p = £2m
- Immediately after = £1m x (5/4) x 160p = £2m

3.3   Stock Split and Scrip Issue

Learning Objective

4.4.7   Understand the difference between a stock split and a scrip issue

---

The reduction in the share price, as a result of a bonus issue, may have its advantages, but it also has disadvantages. If share prices are falling, it may result in the price dropping below the nominal value which will prevent a company from raising finance by issuing more shares.

An alternative way of lowering the price per share but avoiding this problem is to undertake a split. A share split is achieved by dividing the existing share capital into a larger number of shares with a lower nominal value per share, though the overall nominal value of all the shares remains the same.

Let us consider the company discussed in relation to the rights issue again.

The company has issued one million ordinary shares at £1 nominal or par value but wishes now to reduce the price of its shares, by replacing that issue with a new issue of 2.5 million shares at a nominal value of £0.40p. The results can be seen on the simplified section of the balance sheet as follows. In effect the company is engaging in a 2.5:1 stock split. Before the split issue the shares are trading at £3 each.

Share Split			
Impact on the accounts (all amounts in £000)			
	Before	Issue	After
Net assets	2,000		2,000
Share capital			
1m £1 ordinary shares	1,000	(1,000)	
2.5m £0.40 ordinary shares		1,000	1,000
Share premium	500		500
Profit and loss	500		500
Totals	2,000	0	2,000
Impact on the share price			
	Shares (000)	Price £	Value (£000)
Before	1,000	3.00	3,000
Split issue	1,500		
After	2,500		3,000
Market price for shares	£1.20		

In terms of market capitalisation it can be seen that the price per share will drop to £1.20 per share. The prior market capitalisation was £3 million based on 1 million shares but there are now 2.5 million shares issued and the market price for the shares is therefore £3 million/2.5 million shares. The new market price for the shares is £1.20, and as this is above the new nominal value of £0.40 per share, the company would not encounter any problem in issuing these new shares with this nominal value.

Exercise 1

A company has a one for one bonus issue. What is the ex-bonus price (the price after the issue) if the cum-bonus price (the price before the issue) is £10? Here is a blank table to help:

	Number of shares	Price per share	Total value of holding
Before			
Bonus			
After			

The answer to this exercise can be found at the end of this chapter.

4. Share Capital and Changes to Share Ownership

4.1 Share Buybacks

Learning Objective

4.5.1 Understand why share buybacks are undertaken: governing regulation: resolution at AGM, limits on percentage of shares and price, use of company's own money; key aspects of share buybacks – criteria to comply with: different structures regarding block trades; accelerated bookbuild – best efforts basis; accelerated bookbuild – back stop price; bought deal

Share buybacks are when a company decides to use its own money to buy back shares from existing investors. There are two obvious situations when share buybacks might be considered:

1. When the company has reduced its activities (perhaps having sold a major part of its business) and has surplus cash to return to shareholders.
2. When the company wants to reorganise its capital structure to include more debt and less equity. In these circumstances the company can borrow money (by issuing bonds or from banks), and use it to buy back and therefore reduce the number of shares it has in issue.

There will inevitably be restrictions on a company's ability to buy back its own shares, partly to prevent shareholders from being unfairly preferred to creditors, and partly to make sure that the company has gained approval to buy back from its own shareholders. To prevent unfair prejudice against the creditors, regulation limits the amount that can be used to repurchase shares. In the UK, there are various accounting tests that need to be satisfied to prevent erosion of what is referred to as the **creditors' buffer**. In simple terms, the creditors' buffer is the money originally paid into the company as capital.

Approval from shareholders generally requires a resolution at the AGM to grant permission to buy shares back. Such permissions inevitably place limits on the percentage of shares to be purchased and the price paid to those shareholders that sell.

The actual mechanics of undertaking a share buyback, once regulatory and shareholder approval has been gained, can follow a variety of forms, such as:

- **Block trades** – when an investment bank acting for the company will seek to do a small number of large trades with investors, perhaps through an exchange.
- **Accelerated bookbuild** – the investment bank will contact a number of institutions, investors in the company, seeking their willingness to sell at particular price points. If the buyback is sufficiently large to require a syndicate (a group of dealers to distribute the issue, rather than just one), some of the more junior members may only be willing to be involved on a **best efforts basis**, and the whole syndicate will have a price which it cannot go above (the **back stop price**). A best-efforts basis means that the dealer(s) will attempt to sell the issue, but do not guarantee any financial compensation, and cannot be held liable if it is not sold. This is the opposite of a **bought deal,** in which the underwriter(s) actually purchase the shares themselves and then attempt to re-sell them to clients. If all of the inventory bought in a bought deal is not sold, the underwriter remains the owner of the issuer, unless the issuer guarantees to buy back any unsold shares from the underwriter (known as a 'buy-back provision').

4.2 Stake Building

Learning Objective

4.5.2 Understand how and why stake building is used: strategic versus acquisition; direct versus indirect: direct – outright purchase, ie, dawn raid; indirect – CFDs; disclosure thresholds, including mandatory takeover threshold

A stake is simply a shareholding, and many investors buy stakes in companies simply for the investment potential. Sometimes, however, stakes are built in companies for reasons over and above the simple investment potential.

Strategic stakes may be accumulated in order to prevent a company being taken over by a competitor and to influence the company concerned. This may be in order to protect supplies. The company may be a key supplier of raw materials to the strategic stakeholder, without which the strategic stakeholder may have difficulty obtaining the quantity and quality of raw materials it seeks.

A stake may be accumulated in the hope of bringing about an **acquisition**. An acquisition of another company is achieved by purchasing more than 50% of the shares, and thereby gaining **control** of the votes and the company. It is usual to talk in terms of the acquiring company being the **predator** or **offeror** and the company being acquired as the **target** or **offeree**.

For a potential predator building a stake in order to eventually acquire a target company, there are certain **regulatory restrictions**.

First, as a stake becomes more significant, there are **disclosure requirements**. In the UK these disclosure requirements are contained within the FCA's **Disclosure and Transparency Rules**. An investor is judged to have a **notifiable interest** in a public company if he holds 3% or more of its shares. At this point he is obliged to inform the company of his holding. Once the investor's holding is above 3%, he must also inform the company if it rises or falls through a whole percentage point.

Indirect exposure to shares acquired under **contracts for differences (CFDs)** are not subject to these disclosure requirements.

The second regulatory restriction, and in addition to the rules relating to notification and disclosure of significant shareholdings, is the rules laid down by the **Panel on Takeovers and Mergers** (**POTAM** or **PTM**) in the UK that apply to stake-building during the course of a takeover bid. Under PTM rules, a **mandatory offer** is required if any person either:

1. acquires shares that take their holding to 30% or more of the voting rights of the target company; or
2. increases their holding from a starting point of 30% or more, but less than 50%.

If a mandatory bid is required, the consideration offered must be in the form of cash, or there must be a cash alternative. The cash offer must not be less than the highest price paid by the offeror in the previous 12 months.

There are some exceptions to this rule, the main one being for additions to the offeror's stake during the course of a formal offer. In any other instances the PTM's permission is required to acquire shares that breach the rule.

During the course of an offer, dealings in relevant securities by the offeror or the offeree company, or any associates, for their own account must be publicly disclosed. The requirement is that disclosure must be made to the Panel and a regulatory information service (RIS) (such as the LSE's Regulatory News Service, (RNS) by noon on the business day following the transaction.

Relevant securities are the shares of the offeror and offeree, and any derivatives such as options on these shares.

Additionally, PTM rules require that anyone holding more than 1% (before or after the transaction) of the offeree or offeror company shares must disclose any further transactions (excluding acceptance of the offer itself) to the PTM and an RIS by noon on the next business day.

Exercise Answers

Exercise 1:

	Number of shares	Price per share	Total value of holding
Before	1	£10.00	£10.00
Bonus	1	£0.00	£0.00
After	2		£10.00

Chapter Five
Clearing and Settlement

This syllabus area will provide approximately 6 of the 100 examination questions

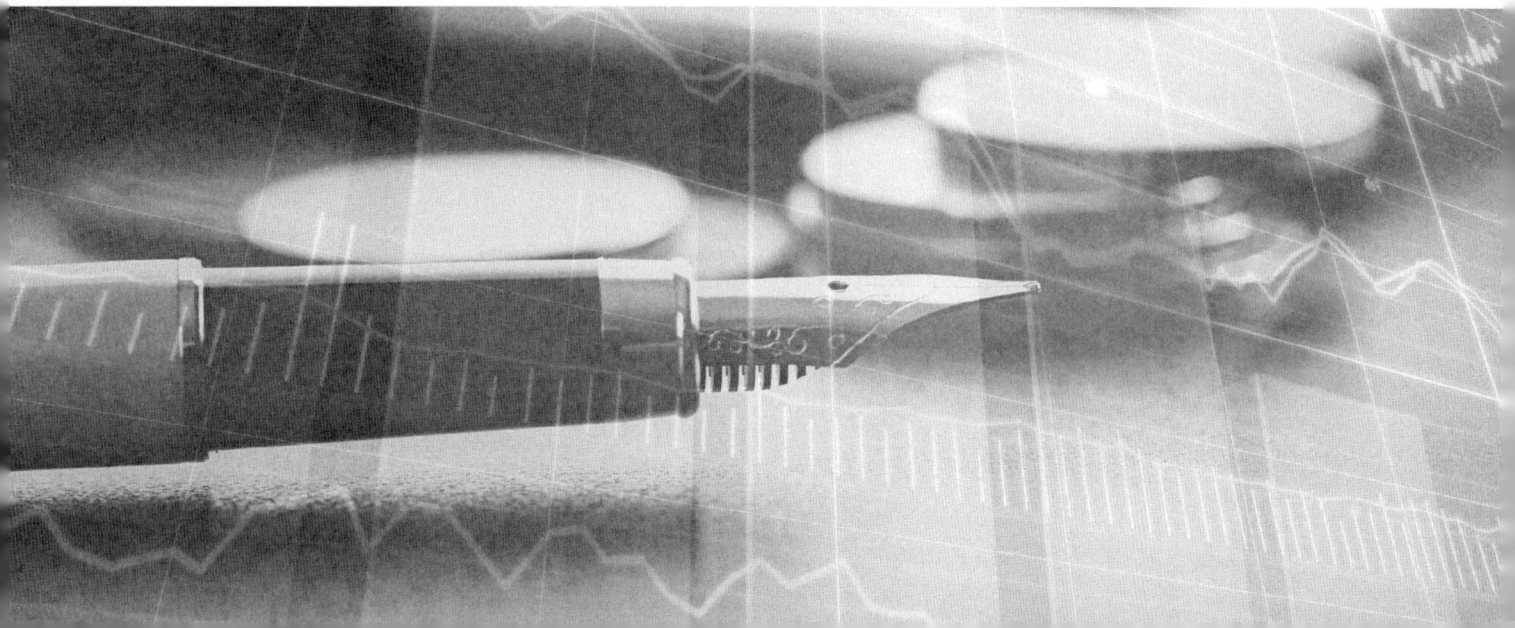

5

1. Introduction to Settlement Systems

Learning Objective

5.1.1 Understand the main stages of clearing and settlement

5.1.2 Know the principal details of settlement in the UK, France, Germany, the US and Japan: DVP; free delivery; potential for financial transaction taxes; trade confirmation; settlement periods; instruments settled; settlement systems: Euroclear UK & Ireland; LCH.Clearnet; Clearstream; DTCC; Jasdec

Settlement occurs after a deal has been executed. It is simply the transfer of ownership from the seller of the investment to the buyer, combined with the transfer of the cash consideration from the buyer to the seller. However, the process actually consists of several key stages, collectively described as **clearing and settlement**:

- **Confirmation** of the terms of the deal by the participants.
- **Clearance (or clearing)** – the calculation of the obligations of the deal participants, the money to be paid and the securities to be transferred.
- **Settlement** – the final transfer delivering the securities in exchange for the payment of funds.

In any situation, the seller is unlikely to be willing to hand over legal title unless he is sure that the cash is flowing in the opposite direction, known as delivery versus payment (DVP). Similarly, the buyer is unlikely to be willing to hand over the cash without being sure that the legal ownership is passing in the other direction, known as cash against delivery (CAD).

There are two basic elements to the settlement of trades that can differ across different instruments and/or markets.

- **Timing of settlement** – this is normally based on a set number of business days after the trade is executed, known as **rolling settlement**.
- **Settlement system** – there are a variety of settlement systems that are used in particular markets. For example, the majority of transactions in UK equities are settled via an electronic settlement facility called CREST.

CREST is a computer system that settles transactions in shares, gilts and corporate bonds, primarily on behalf of the LSE. It is owned and operated by a company that is part of the Euroclear group of companies, called **Euroclear UK & Ireland ltd**. Euroclear UK & Ireland has the status of a recognised clearing house (RCH) and, as such, it is regulated by the BoE.

The financial instruments settled by CREST are **dematerialised**: instead of using paper share certificates, the underlying company uses an electronic entry in its register of shareholders. This allows shares transactions to be settled electronically.

CREST **clears** the trade by matching the settlement details provided by the buyer and the seller. The transaction is then **settled** when CREST updates the register of the relevant company, to transfer the shares to the buyer, and at the same time instructs the buyer's bank to transfer the appropriate amount of money to the seller's bank account.

In summary, to complete the settlement of a trade, CREST simultaneously:

- **updates the register of shareholders** – CREST maintains the so-called **operator register** for UK companies' dematerialised shareholdings;
- **issues a payment obligation** – CREST sends an instruction to the buyer's payment bank to pay for the shares;
- **issues a receipt notification** – CREST notifies the seller's payment bank to expect payment.

If a trading system provides a central counterparty (CCP) to the trades (such as **LCH.Clearnet** for trades on SETS), it is the CCP that assumes responsibility for settling the transaction with each counterparty. The buyer and seller remain anonymous to each other.

For SETS trades, CREST gives the option to LSE member firms to settle with LCH.Clearnet on a gross basis or on a net basis. To illustrate this, if a firm has 20 orders executed in the same security through SETS, they could choose to either settle 20 trades with LCH.Clearnet (settling on a gross basis), or choose to have all 20 trades netted so that the firm just settles a single transaction with LCH.Clearnet (settling on a net basis).

The settlement period (the time between the trade and the transfer of money and registration) for UK equities is on a T+2 basis, where 'T' is the trade date and '2' is the number of business days after the trade date that the cash changes hands and the shares' registered title changes. In other words, if a trade is executed on a Tuesday, the cash and registered title will change two business days later, on the Thursday. So, if the trade is executed on a Thursday, settlement will occur on the following Monday. This is referred to by the LSE as 'standard settlement'. Standard settlement applies to all deals automatically executed on an LSE trading system, such as SETS.

The following table provides an overview of the settlement systems in the UK, Germany, France, the US and Japan:

Country/Region	Instruments settled	Settlement period	System name
UK	Listed equities and corporate bonds	T+2	CREST
	Government bonds (gilts)	T+1 (cash settlement)	CREST
EU	Listed German equities	T+2	Clearstream
	Listed French equities	T+2	Euroclear France
	International bonds	T+2	Clearstream/ Euroclear
US	Listed equities	T+3*	Depository Trust Clearing Corporation (DTCC)
	Government bonds	T+1	DTCC
Japan	Listed equities and convertible bonds	T+3*	Japan Securities Depository Center (JASDEC)

* Although settlement timetables in global markets are generally moving towards T+2, at the time of writing, no announcement had been made regarding any changes to the settlement periods for US and Japanese equities. In view of the uncertainty, these details will not be examined. Candidates should check the Candidate Update section of the CISI's website for further announcements.

The EU is moving towards the introduction of a financial transaction tax. Although the details are yet to be clarified, the EU is planning to phase in the implementation of the tax from 1 January 2016 on transactions involving shares and some derivatives. The UK does not plan to implement the tax and may challenge the tax in the courts if it has implications for the UK financial services industry.

2. Custodianship

Learning Objective

5.1.3 Know the concept of custody and the roles of the different types of custodian: global; regional; local; sub-custodian

2.1 Services Provided by Custodians

When an institutional investor invests in securities, it will commonly employ the services of a custodian to administer these securities by:

- providing safekeeping of the investor's assets in the local market;
- making appropriate arrangements for delivery and receipt of cash and securities to support settlement of the investor's trading activities in that market;
- providing market information to the investor on developments and reforms within that market;
- collecting dividend income, interest paid on debt securities and other income payments in the local market;
- managing the client's cash flows;
- monitoring and managing entitlements through corporate actions and voting rights held by the investor in the local market;
- managing tax reclaims and other tax services in the local market;
- ensuring that securities are registered and that transfer of legal title on securities transactions proceeds effectively;
- ensuring that reporting obligations to the regulatory authorities, and to other relevant bodies, are discharged effectively.

2.2 The Role and Responsibility of a Custodian

The primary responsibility of the custodian is to ensure that the client's assets are fully protected at all times. Hence, it must provide robust safekeeping facilities for all valuables and documentation, ensuring that investments are only released from its care in accordance with authorised instructions from the client.

Importantly, the client's assets must be properly **segregated** from those of the custodian and appropriate legal arrangements must be in place to ensure that financial or external shock to the custodian does not expose the client's assets to claims from creditors or any other party.

2.3 Types of Custodian

An investor faces choices in selecting custody arrangements in regard to a portfolio of global assets. The possible paths can be summarised as follows:

- Appointing a local custodian in each market in which s/he invests (often referred to as direct custody arrangements).
- Appointing a global custodian to manage custody arrangements across the full range of foreign markets in which s/he has invested assets.
- Making arrangements to settle trades and hold securities and cash with a central securities depository (CSD) within each market, or to go via an international central securities depository (ICSD).

2.3.1 Global Custody

A global custodian provides investment administration for investor clients, including processing cross-border securities trades and keeping financial assets secure (ie, providing safe custody) outside the country where the investor is located.

The term **global custody** came into common usage in the financial services world in the mid-1970s, when the Employee Retirement Income Security Act (ERISA) was passed in the US. This legislation was designed to increase the protection given to US pension fund investors. The Act specified that US pension funds could not act as custodians of the assets held in their own funds. Instead, these assets had to be held in the safekeeping of another bank. ERISA went further, to specify that only a US bank could provide custody services for a US pension fund.

Subsequently, use of the term global custody has evolved to refer to a broader set of responsibilities, encompassing settlement, safekeeping, cash management, record-keeping and asset servicing (eg, collecting dividend payments on shares and interest on bonds, reclaiming WHT and advising investor clients on their electing on corporate actions entitlements), and providing market information. Some investors may also use their global custodians to provide a wider suite of services, including investment accounting, treasury and FX, securities lending and borrowing, collateral management, and performance and risk analysis on the investor's portfolio.

Some global custodians maintain an extensive network of branches globally and can meet the local custody needs of their investor clients by employing their own branches as local custody providers. Citi, for example, maintains a proprietary branch network covering 48 markets. Consequently, Citi, acting as global custodian for an investor client, may opt to use its own branch to provide local custody in many locations where the investor holds assets.

2.3.2 Sub-Custody

A sub-custodian is employed by a global custodian as its local agent to provide settlement and custody services for assets that it holds on behalf of investor clients in a foreign market. A sub-custodian effectively serves as the eyes and ears of the global custodian in the local market, providing a range of clearing, settlement and asset servicing duties. It will also typically provide market information relating to developments in the local market, and will lobby the market authorities for reforms that will make the market more appealing and an efficient target for foreign investment.

In selecting a sub-custodian, a global custodian may:

- appoint one of its **own branches**, in cases when this option is available;
- appoint a **local** agent bank that specialises in providing sub-custody in the market concerned;
- appoint a **regional** provider that can offer sub-custody to the global custodian across a range of markets in a region or globally.

Local Custodian

Agent banks that specialise in providing sub-custody in their home market are sometimes known as single-market providers. Stiff competition from larger regional or global competitors has meant that these are becoming a dying breed. However, some continue to win business in their local markets, often combining this service with offering global custody or master custody for institutional investors in their home markets. Examples include Bank Tokyo Mitsubishi, Mizuho Corporate Bank and Sumitomo Bank in Japan, Maybank in Malaysia and United Overseas Bank in Singapore.

A principal selling point is that they are local market specialists. Hence they can remain focused on their local business, without spreading their attentions broadly across a wide range of markets. A local specialist bank may be attractive in a market in which local practices tend to differ markedly from global standards, or where a provider's long standing relationship with the local regulatory authorities and/or political elite leaves it particularly well placed to lobby for reforms on behalf of its cross-border clients.

Reciprocal arrangements may be influential in shaping the appointment of a local provider in some instances. Under such an arrangement, a global custodian (A) may appoint the local provider (B) to deliver sub-custody in its local market (market B). In return, the custodian (A) may offer sub-custody in its own home market (market A) for pension and insurance funds in market B that use provider B as their global custodian.

In summary, the strengths of a local custodian may include:

- They are country specialists.
- They can be the **eyes and ears** of the global custodian or broker-dealer in the local market.
- They will have regular dealings with financial authorities and local politicians – they may be well placed to lobby for reforms that will improve the efficiency of the local market.
- They have expert knowledge of local market practice, language and culture.
- They may offer opportunities for reciprocal business.

A local custody bank may be perceived to have the following disadvantages when compared with a regional custodian:

- Their credit rating may not match up to requirements laid down by some global custodians or global broker-dealers.
- They cannot leverage developments in technology and client service across multiple markets (unlike a regional custodian) – hence product and technology development may lag behind the regional custodians that they compete with.
- They may not be able to offer the price discounts that can be extended by regional custodians offering custody services across multiple markets.

Regional Custodian

A regional custodian is able to provide agent bank services across multiple markets in a region.

For example, Standard Chartered Bank and HSBC have both been offering regional custody and clearing in the Asia-Pacific and South Asian region for many years, competing with Citi and some strong single market providers for business in this region. In Central and Eastern Europe, Bank Austria Creditanstalt/ Unicredit Group, Deutsche Bank, ING Group, Raiffeisen Zentralbank Osterreich AG and Citi each offer a regional clearing and custody service. In Central and South America, Citi and Bank Itau (the Brazilian bank that purchased Bank Boston's established regional custody service) offer regional custody, in competition in selected markets, with HSBC, Bank Santander and Deutsche Bank.

Employing a regional custodian may offer a range of advantages to global custodian or global broker-dealer clients:

- Its credit rating may be higher than that of a single market custodian.
- It can cross-fertilise good practice across multiple markets – lessons learned in one market may be applied, when appropriate, across other markets in its regional offering.
- It can leverage innovation in technology, product development and client service across multiple markets – delivering economies of scale.
- It can offer standardised reporting, management information systems and market information across multiple markets in its regional offering.
- Economies of scale may support delivery of some or all product lines from a regional processing centre – offering potential cost savings and efficiency benefits.
- Its size and regional importance, plus the strength of its global client base, may allow a regional custodian to exert considerable leverage on local regulators, political authorities and infrastructure providers. This may be important in lobbying for reforms that support greater efficiency and security for foreign investors in that market.
- A global client may be able to secure price discounts by using a regional custodian across multiple markets.

In some situations, a regional provider may be perceived to have certain disadvantages when compared with a local custody bank:

- A regional custodian's product offering may be less well attuned to local market practice, service culture and investor needs than that of a well-established local provider.

- A regional custodian may spread its focus across a wider range of clients and a wider range of markets than a single market provider. Hence, a cross-border client may not receive the same level of attention, and the same degree of individualised service, as may be extended by a local custodian.
- Some regional custodians may lack the long track record, customer base and goodwill held by some local custodians in their own market.

3. Registered Title

Learning Objective

5.1.4   Understand the implications of registered title: registered title versus unregistered (bearer); legal title; beneficial interest; voting rights; right to participate in corporate actions

When settling a trade involving UK shares, settlement must involve communicating the change in ownership to the company registrar. This is because the issuing company maintains a register listing all of its shareholders. Whenever shares are bought or sold, a mechanism is required to make the company registrar aware of the change required to the register.

If there were no register, the shares would be described as unregistered or **bearer shares** and physically handing over the shares would be a valid transfer of ownership.

So, **registered title** simply means ownership that is backed by registration. In terms of share ownership, registered title gives shareholders the right to vote on important company matters, to claim dividends on their shares and to participate in other corporate actions such as rights issues.

When shares are bought and sold, it is the **company registrar** who is responsible for updating the **register of members** and giving the new owner registered title.

Busy shareholders often want to avoid the administrative tasks connected with registered title, so they choose to appoint their stockbroker, or another professional, to act as a **nominee**. The nominee takes the registered title to the shares and all the responsibilities that go with it, but the nominee's client retains **beneficial ownership** – it is the client that ultimately receives all of the cash flows generated by the shares. The nominee is referred to as the **legal owner** of the shares, and the client retaining the benefits of ownership, mainly the dividends and capital growth, is known as the **beneficial owner** (see Section 4).

4. Designated and Pooled Nominees

Learning Objective

5.1.5   Understand the basics of designated and pooled nominee accounts and their uses, and the concept of corporate nominees: designated nominee accounts; pooled nominee accounts; details in share register; function of corporate nominees; legal ownership; beneficial ownership; effect on shareholder rights of using a nominee

4.1   The Share Register

Shares in the UK are held in registered form. This means that any share certificate is simply evidence of ownership. The proof that counts is the name and address held on the company's share register.

There is a statutory requirement for UK companies to have a minimum of one shareholder and for the details of shareholders to be put on public record.

4.2   Nominees

Upon the incorporation of a company (be it a new or ready-made shelf company or a tailor-made company), the investor can either act as a shareholder in their own name, or a financial services firm equipped to handle incorporations or a custodian can provide them with a nominee shareholder with a view to securing their corporate privacy. For the purpose of privacy, some clients do not wish to be identified as shareholders of the companies that they have set up and will, therefore, wish to appoint nominee shareholders. These nominee shareholders will hold the shares in trust for the beneficial owners, and only they will be identified on the register of shareholders.

Each nominee shareholder appointed will sign a declaration of trust to the beneficial owner that they are holding the shares on behalf of the beneficial owner and will return the shares into the name of the beneficial owner or will transfer them to another party as requested. A nominee shareholder is normally a company created for the purpose of holding shares and other securities on behalf of investors.

UK company law prevents registrars and companies from recognising anyone other than the **name on register** or, in the case of a corporation, their duly appointed attorney.

Institutional investors employing professional investment management firms to manage their assets are highly unlikely to hold these securities in their own name (**name on register**). The reason for this is simple: the person whose name appears on the share register receives every piece of documentation sent out by the company and is obliged to sign all share transfers and other relevant forms such as instructions for rights issues and other corporate events. To ensure safe custody of assets and remove this administrative burden from the investor thus allowing the speedy processing of transfers, institutional (and, increasingly, private client) shareholdings are held in the names of 'nominee' companies.

Nominee companies have long been established as the mechanism by which asset managers and custodians can process transactions on behalf of their clients. Given that many investment management firms have outsourced some or all of their investment administration activities to the specialist custodians, the vast majority of institutional shareholdings in fact now reside in nominee accounts overseen by those specialist custodians.

As stated in Section 3, as far as the company is concerned, the nominee name appearing on its share register is the **legal owner** of the shares for the purposes of benefits and for voting. However, **beneficial ownership** continues to reside with the underlying client, who is entitled to receive dividends and the capital growth of the shares but does not retain the automatic right to attend company meetings.

It is this separation of ownership which allows the custodians, under proper client authorities, to transfer shares to meet market transactions and to conduct other functions, without the registrar requiring sight of the signature or seal of the underlying client.

Registrars cannot recognise a trust as the beneficial owner of shares, so, in order to look beyond the legal ownership of any holding, the registrar can issue at any time a notice under Section 793 of the Companies Act. This will require the nominee company to disclose the name of the beneficial owner of the shares, so that at least the company may be aware for whom the nominee is acting. A notice issued under **Section 793** of the Companies Act (which came into force on 20 January 2007 and replaced the **Section 212** notice under the Companies Act 1985) allows a public company to issue a notice requiring a person it knows, or has reasonable cause to believe, has an interest in its shares (or to have had an interest in the previous three years) to confirm or deny the fact, and, if the former, to disclose certain information about the interest, including information about any other person with an interest in the shares.

4.3 Types of Nominee Companies

Nominees can be classified into three types:

- **Pooled** (or omnibus), whereby individual clients are grouped together within a single nominee registration.
- **Designated**, where the nominee name includes unique identifiers for each individual client, eg, XYZ Nominees Account 1, Account 2, Account 3, etc.
- **Sole**, where a single nominee name is used for a specific client, eg, ABC Pension Fund Nominees ltd.

How the shareholdings are registered is of vital importance when it comes to voting.

It is now generally accepted that there are no real advantages, from a security point of view, no matter which type of nominee arrangement is used to register the shares. However, clients brought together with others in a pooled nominee have no visibility to the company: it is the single nominee name, covering multiple clients, which the company recognises. Importantly, from a voting perspective it is only the single bulk nominee that is entitled to vote; no separate entitlement accrues from the registrar's standpoint to each individual client making up the total holding.

Some companies offer their shareholders certain perks, such as discounts on their products. By using a nominee (either a designated or a pooled structure), the shareholder perks may not be available to the individual investor. This is simply because the stockbrokers may be unwilling to undertake the necessary administration to facilitate the provision of these perks.

One reason for registering shares in a designated or sole nominee name would be that, if the underlying investor requires dividends to be mandated to a particular bank account rather than being collected by the custodian, registration in an omnibus account is not practicable.

Designation or individual registration can also help some aspects of auditing and it affords a good control mechanism when identical bargains may have been executed for different clients (for example on the same date, for the same number of shares and for the same settlement consideration).

One reason frequently cited by custodians for insisting on pooled nominee arrangements is the vexed question of **costs**. Operating a designated nominee account should give rise to few additional costs from the custodian's point of view, as the existing nominee name can easily be used, with the addition of a unique designation. While there may be a slight increase in the receipt of Section 793 requests and a small amount of extra work involved, eg, in the receipt of separate income payments, the actual procedures are identical and should be capable of being easily absorbed into the existing administration and processing routines.

If the client insists on using a sole nominee name to register the shareholdings, this may involve some costs for the custodian connected with the establishment of a nameplate nominee company and the requisite appointment of directors and the completion of annual returns. The custodian may seek to pass these comparatively meagre costs on to the client, but more usually they will be absorbed within the standard custody tariff.

Neither of these two nominee approaches is likely to give rise to additional transaction charges imposed on the custodian by CREST, the UK's electronic share settlement system, as individual sales and purchases are relayed across the system regardless of how the assets are registered.

One area where additional transactions may occur, giving rise to additional costs, is in respect of securities lending. However, the CREST charges for such transactions are as low as 50p each and a client would need to undertake an inordinate amount of loans and recalls for these transaction charges to become a significant amount. Such small additional amounts need to be seen against the typical custody tariff for UK securities of around 1 basis point (0.01%) of the value of assets under custody and a further charge of approximately £20 for each trade settled. Also, in the case of securities lending, the custodian usually retains a share of the extra income generated. This is often around 30%, again drawing any additional transaction costs in respect of loan movements created by a separately registered or designated nominee account.

4.4   The Corporate Nominee

A corporate nominee (alternatively referred to as a **corporate sponsored nominee**) is when the issuing company itself provides a facility for its smaller shareholders to hold their shares within a single **corporate nominee**.

The corporate nominee is a halfway house between the pooled and the designated nominee structures offered by stockbrokers. It will result in a single entry for all the shareholders together in the company's register (like the pooled nominee) but beneath this the issuing company (or its registrar) will be aware of the individual holdings that make up the nominee. In a similar way to the designated nominee structure, the company will be able to forward separate dividend payments to each of the individual shareholders, as well as voting rights and other potential shareholder perks. Shares held within a corporate nominee in dematerialised form enable quick and easy transfer through CREST.

4.5   Summary

Custodians and their nominees now control the majority of share registrations for institutional investors, even for clients who may not have directly appointed custodians but whose asset management firms have outsourced their investment administration to these providers.

Custodians uniquely identify their clients' holdings by segregating these in their computer systems, as it is largely these systems which drive the calculation and application of dividends and other entitlements. However, this segregation is not the same as having an individually identifiable holding for a particular client on company share registers.

It is largely impractical for an institutional investor to achieve **name on register**, so the recognised practice is to use nominee names whereby the custodian, or other duly authorised agent, is legally entitled to perform the transfer and administration of the assets on behalf of, and under the authority of, the underlying beneficial owner.

Many custodians prefer to pool all their clients into one single nominee registration, but this does remove the visibility of the underlying investor and makes individual client voting much more cumbersome.

Clients can request their custodian to adopt an individual registration solely for their particular shareholdings. Typically this takes the form of a standard nominee name with a unique designation for each client. The costs of such separate registration and its ongoing maintenance are minimal, relative to overall custody and securities lending charges and are often absorbed by the custodians.

5.   Stamp Duty and Stamp Duty Reserve Tax (SDRT)

Learning Objective

5.1.6   Know which securities may be subject to UK stamp duty/SDRT and which transactions are exempt from UK stamp duty

Stamp duty is a tax payable, on documents that transfer certain kinds of property, by the purchaser of that property. If property can be handed over, eg, furniture, there is no charge to stamp duty, because there is no document executed on which to charge the duty. Some property, however, such as houses, land and shares in a company, can only be transferred in a prescribed legal form and the legislation requires that documents liable to stamp duty may not be registered or used unless they have been duly stamped. Since owners want to be able to demonstrate their title to property, they are effectively required to have their document stamped if they want it to be recognised as their own.

There are different rates of stamp duty for shares and for other property. Stamp duty on share transfers is **charged to the purchaser at 0.5%** of the price (excluding any commissions payable to the stockbroker), with no threshold. Normally there is no charge on the issue as distinct from the transfer of shares. The duty is rounded to the next £5, so that a transfer of shares priced at £4,800 will be charged at £25, and a transfer priced at £5,240 will be charged at £30.

However, a charge of **1.5% is made on the creation of a bearer share, or the transfer of shares into a depositary receipt** (eg, an ADR), because subsequent transfers will not attract stamp duty.

In summary:

Rate: 0.5% of the consideration value of the purchase (rounded up to the next £5).

Paid by: The buyer.

Trigger: Transfer to new ownership (not primary issue).

Example: UK equity transfers.

Stamp duty depends upon there being a document to stamp. It cannot therefore be used for paperless transactions. **Stamp Duty Reserve Tax (SDRT)** was, therefore, introduced to cater for the paperless transfer of shares through CREST. The SDRT regulations impose an obligation on the operator of CREST (Euroclear UK & Ireland) to collect SDRT on transfers going through the system.

SDRT applies in place of stamp duty in cases when the agreement is not completed by an instrument of transfer (ie, a document, the stock transfer form). The tax is **charged at 0.5%** on the consideration given for the transfer, **payable by the purchaser**. Unlike stamp duty, there is no rounding to the next £5, and it is calculated to the penny.

The following is a summary of the major instances when SDRT is charged:

Situation	Why can we not charge stamp duty?	Rate of SDRT	Levied when?
Transfer of nominee holdings	No change of name on certificate but beneficial owner has changed	½%	On each transfer
CREST transactions	No paper certificate to stamp	½%	On each transfer

5.1 Exemptions

Gilts and bonds are not liable to stamp duty unless they are **equity-related**, for example, convertible into equity. **Gifts** are not liable to stamp duty, since there is no consideration paid on the transactions.

Securities that are exempt from stamp duty, such as gilts and non-convertible bonds, are also exempt from SDRT. For both stamp duty and SDRT there are also exemptions for purchases by registered charities, on-exchange stock lending transactions, gifts and purchases by LSE member firms (who are granted **intermediary** status) and the clearing house.

According to Schedule 15 of the Finance Act of 1999, which relates to the application of the duty for bearer instruments, the following are relevant exemptions from stamp duty.

Stamp duty is not chargeable under this Schedule on renounceable letters of allotment, letters of rights or other similar instruments where the rights under the letter or other instrument are renounceable not later than six months after its issue.

Stamp duty is also not chargeable under Schedule 15 on the issue of an instrument which relates to stock expressed:

a. *in a currency other than sterling; or*
b. *in units of account defined by reference to more than one currency (whether or not including sterling);*

or on the transfer of the stock constituted by or transferable by means of any such instrument.

Further definitions of instruments which are exempt also include:

A unit under a unit trust scheme or a share in a foreign mutual fund shall be treated as capital stock of a company formed or established in the territory by the law of which the scheme or fund is governed.

*A **foreign mutual fund** means a fund administered under arrangements governed by the law of a territory outside the UK under which subscribers to the fund are entitled to participate in, or receive payments by reference to, profits or income arising to the fund from the acquisition, holding, management or disposal of investments.*

*In relation to a foreign mutual fund **share** means the right of a subscriber, or of another in his right, to participate in or receive payments by reference to profits or income so arising.*

6.   Cum- and Ex-Dividend

Learning Objective

5.1.7   Understand the concepts, requirements, benefits and disadvantages of deals executed cum, ex, special cum and special ex: timetable; effect of deals on the underlying right; effect on the share price before and after a dividend; the meaning of 'books closed', 'ex-div' and 'cum div', cum and ex-rights; effect of late registration; benefits that may be achieved; disadvantages/risks; when dealing is permitted

Cum-dividend means 'with the dividend'. Shares are normally traded cum-dividend, meaning that buyers of the shares have the right to the next dividend paid by the company. However, there are brief periods when the share becomes **ex-dividend**, meaning that they would be sold without the right to receive the next dividend payment. The **ex-dividend** period occurs in the period just prior to a dividend payment, as detailed below.

The sequence of events leading up to the dividend payment is as follows.

1. **Dividend declared** – on this date the company announces its intention to pay a specified dividend on a specified future date. The declaration must occur at least six clear business days before the proposed record date, although it usually occurs well before this date (perhaps a month or two earlier).
2. **Record or books-closed date** – the record, or books-closed date is the date on which a copy of the shareholders' register is taken. The people on the share register at the end of this day will be paid the next dividend. The books-closed date is normally a Friday, except where the Friday is a public holiday, in which case the books-closed date is the next available business day.
3. **Ex-dividend date** – the ex-dividend date is invariably a Thursday: the business day before record date.
4. **Dividend paid** – this date is determined by the company, and is typically within 30 business days of the record date. The dividend is paid to those shareholders who were on the register on the record/books-closed date.
5. **Ex-dividend period** – the period from the ex-dividend date up to the dividend payment date is the ex-dividend period. Throughout this period the shares trade **without** entitlement to the next dividend.

The relationship between the ex-dividend date and the books-closed date is easily explained. Since the equity settlement process takes two business days, for a new shareholder to appear on the register on the Friday they would have to buy the shares by Wednesday at the latest. Wednesday is the last day when the shares trade cum-dividend, because new shareholders will be reflected in the register before the end of the books-closed date. A new shareholder buying their shares on the Thursday will not be entered into the register until the following week – too late for the books-closed date and therefore ex-dividend.

On the Thursday when the shares first trade without the dividend (ex-dividend), the share price will fall to reflect the fact that if an investor buys the share he will not be entitled to the impending dividend.

At all times other than during ex-dividend periods, shares trade cum-dividend, ie, if an investor purchases shares at this time, he will be entitled to all of the future dividends paid by the company for as long as he keeps the share.

During the ex-dividend period, it is possible to arrange a **special cum-trade**. That is when, by special arrangement, the buyer of the share during the ex-dividend period **does** receive the next dividend. These trades can be executed up to and including the day before the dividend payment date, but not on or after the dividend payment date.

In a similar manner to a special cum-trade, an investor can also arrange a **special ex-trade**. This is only possible in the ten business days before the ex-date. If an investor buys a share during the cum-dividend period, but buys it special ex, he will not receive the next dividend.

Using special cum or special ex transactions enables the sellers or buyers to avoid the receipt of a dividend – essentially deciding whether or not they want to collect their right to the dividend. During the period when the LSE allows such trading, it effectively allows the right to the dividend to be traded. The motivation for investors buying or selling with or without the dividend entitlement tends to be related to tax. Dividend income is normally subject to income tax, so selling the right to the dividend may avoid some income tax.

The inherent disadvantage of special cum trades and special ex trades is that they will, potentially, result in dividends from the company being paid to the wrong person. Equally a trade that settles later than usual could mean that the correct owner is not reflected in the shareholders' register on the books-closed date – and the dividend is paid by the company to the wrong person. In such situations, it is the broker acting for the buyers (or seller, as appropriate) that will need to make a claim for the dividend.

In such situations, if the dividend was paid to the wrong person in a special cum-trade, then it is the broker acting for the buyers that should make a claim for the dividend. In contrast, when the dividend has been paid to the wrong person, following a special ex-trade, it is the seller's broker who will have to make the claim for their client to receive their rightful dividend payment.

7.   Continuous Linked Settlement (CLS)

Learning Objective

5.1.8   Understand what continuous linked settlement (CLS) is and its purpose: the settlement of currencies across time zones; receiving and matching instructions; advantages; how it reduces settlement risk

As international trade and investment has increased, so has the foreign exchange market. The average daily volume in the global forex and related markets is continuously growing and was reported to be over US$5 trillion in April 2013 by the BIS.

Continuous linked settlement (CLS) is a process by which most of the world's largest banks manage FX settlement among themselves (and their customers and other third parties). The process is managed by CLS Group Holdings and regulated by the Federal Reserve Board of New York.

CLS settles transactions on a payment versus payment (PVP) basis. The two parties to an FX transaction will buy and sell the respective currencies exchanged and the payments made will occur simultaneously. Unless such simultaneity in payments is ensured, there is a possibility of settlement risk which is also often referred to as **Herstatt risk**. Before the establishment of CLS, FX transactions were settled by each side of a trade making separate payments. The risks implicit in this approach became clear in 1974, when the German banking regulators withdrew the banking licence of Bankhaus Herstatt, putting it into liquidation at the close of business on 26 June. Bankhaus Herstatt had been active in the FX markets and had received currency from counterparties during the day, but had not yet made any payments, when its licence was withdrawn and it was declared bankrupt. Several banks had irrevocably paid over deutschmarks to Herstatt during the day, but had not received the anticipated currency in exchange. In addition, banks had entered into forward trades that were not yet due for settlement, and some lost money replacing the contracts. In short, there were serious repercussions in the FX market after the Bankhaus Herstatt default, thus the intra-day settlement risk highlighted was thereafter termed Herstatt risk.

The result was the impetus to set up a more robust and reliable system that ensured payment from one party was only made if there was a payment coming in the opposite direction to fulfil the other side of the FX deal – PVP. CLS was the result that solved the PVP problem, despite the counterparties potentially being in different parts of the world and time zones.

The CLS process is focused on a five-hour window each business day from 7.00am to 12 midday in Central European Time (CET). This window was created to provide an overlap across the business days in all parts of the world and facilitate global trading.

By 6.30am CET the settlement members must submit their settlement instructions for transactions to settle that day. At 6.30am each settlement member receives a schedule of what monies need to be paid in that day. From 7.00am the settlement members pay in the net funds that are due to settle in each currency to their central banks, and CLS will then begin to attempt to settle deals. In the event that CLS Bank's strict settlement criteria are not met for each side of a trade, then no funds are exchanged. This achieves the PVP system that removes the so-called Herstatt risk. Those trades that can be settled are settled and money is paid out via the central banks.

As outlined above, the payments made to CLS Bank are made via the central banks. In the UK, both sterling and euro payments are made via the Clearing House Automated Payment System (CHAPS). CHAPS is the electronic transfer system for sending payments between banks that operates in partnership with the Bank of England.

In Europe, the system used is the European Central Bank's TARGET2. TARGET stands for the **T**rans-European **A**utomated **R**eal-Time **G**ross Settlement **E**xpress **T**ransfer system; TARGET2 is the second generation of TARGET.

Chapter Six
Special Regulatory Requirements

6

This syllabus area will provide approximately 6 of the 100 examination questions

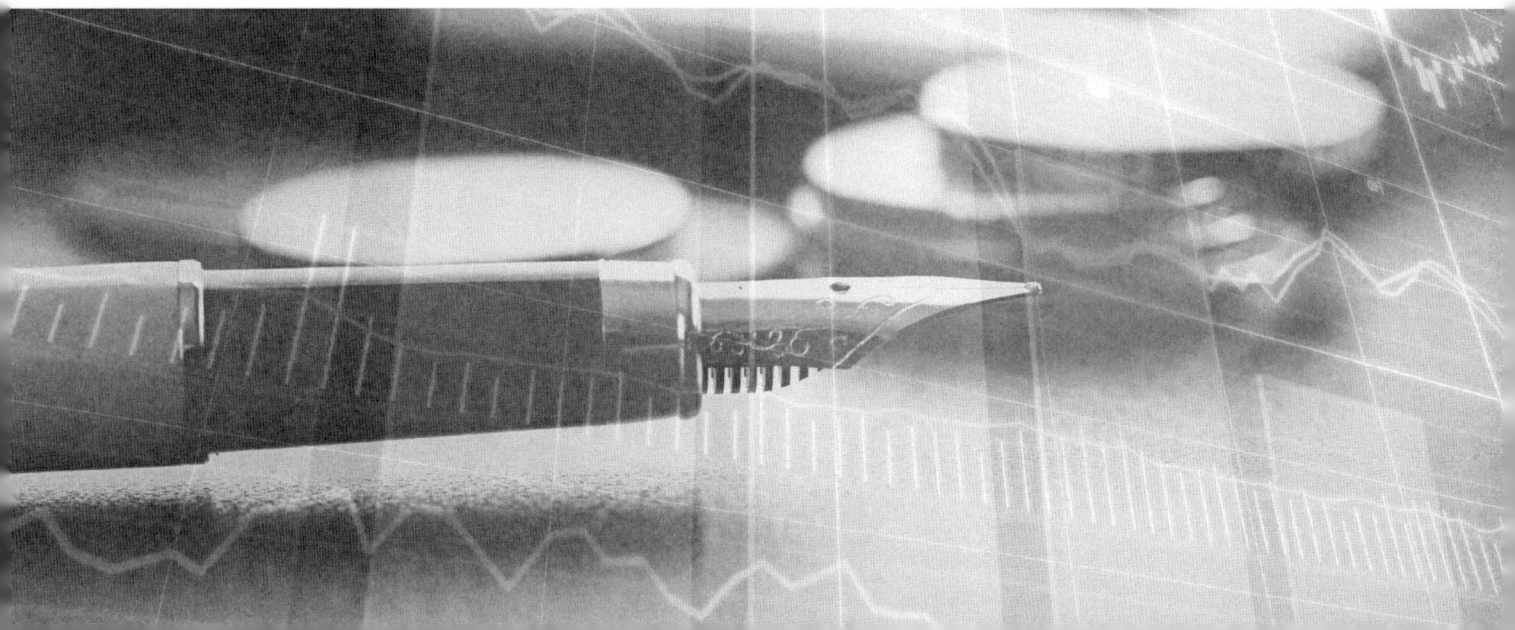

1. The European Union Takeover Directive

Learning Objective

6.1.1   Know the implications of the EU Takeover Directive: that some countries continue with their own rules as minimum standards and that takeover rules vary between states; application to all EU companies trading on an EU regulated market; requirements for a designated supervisory authority and scope for shared supervision; general principles of the Directive (Art. 3); consequences of a mandatory bid and different mandatory bid thresholds; publication of information on the bid (Articles 6 and 10)

A **takeover** occurs if one company buys a majority of the shares of another company; it gains control over the other company and is, therefore, termed the parent company, while the other company is its subsidiary. A **merger** is the term used when the two companies are of a similar size and come together to form a larger, merged entity.

The Takeover Directive is (like MiFID) one of the measures adopted under the EU's financial services action plan (FSAP). It aims to contribute to the creation of a single market in financial services by facilitating cross-border mergers and acquisitions and standardising protections for minority shareholders. The way that the Directive has been constructed is to require member states to implement certain minimum requirements, but to allow the member states to incorporate more stringent requirements if they wish.

The Takeover Directive applies to takeover bids for the securities of an EU company, when all or some of those securities are admitted to trading on a regulated market, such as a stock exchange, in one or more member states.

Under the Directive, member states are required to designate the authority (or authorities) competent for the purpose of supervising any bids, to ensure they meet the appropriate rules. Since the precise rules can vary across member states because of the minimum requirements approach taken by the Directive, there are requirements to determine which member state's rules apply and, therefore, the designated supervisory authority. It is the designated supervisory authority of the member state in which the:

- company subject to the offer (the offeree) has its registered office, where the offeree's securities are traded on a regulated market in that member state;
- offeree's securities are traded, where the offeree's securities are traded on a regulated market in an EU country that is not the country in which it has its registered office.

Due to the possibility of cross-border takeovers involving an offeror in one member state and an offeree in another, the Directive also includes a requirement that supervisory authorities co-operate and supply each other with information when necessary.

The Takeover Directive's minimum requirements include six General Principles that are covered in Section 2 below, and the requirement to launch a **mandatory bid** in certain circumstances. The mandatory bid provision states that a natural or legal person, who as a result of an acquisition by him or in concert with him, reaches a specified percentage shareholding to gain control, is required to make a mandatory bid for the remaining shares at an **equitable price**. The equitable price is the highest price paid by the offeror for the same securities over a period of between six and 12 months prior to the bid.

The Directive also requires information about any takeover bid to be **made public**. The Directive states that the decision to make a bid is made public without delay, and that the supervisory authority is informed of the bid. Furthermore, the offeror is required to draw up and make public, in good time, an offer document containing the information necessary to enable the holders of securities in the offeree to reach a properly informed decision on the bid.

2. The United Kingdom Takeover Code

Learning Objective

6.1.2 Know the legal nature and purpose of the UK Takeover Code (Section 2 of the Introduction): the six General Principles; the definitions of 'acting in concert', 'dealings', 'interest in shares' and 'relevant securities'

The UK supervisory authority that carries out the regulatory functions required under the EU Takeover Directive is the Panel on Takeovers and Mergers, often referred to as the Takeover Panel or just the Panel, or by its initials PTM. The PTM's requirements are set out in a code that consists of six General Principles, and a number of detailed rules.

The Code is designed principally to ensure that shareholders are treated fairly and are not denied an opportunity to decide on the merits of a takeover. Furthermore, the Code ensures that shareholders of the same class are afforded equivalent treatment by an offeror. In short, the Code provides an orderly framework within which takeovers are conducted, and is designed to assist in promoting the integrity of the financial markets.

The Code is not concerned with the financial or commercial advantages or disadvantages of a takeover. These are matters for the company and its shareholders. Nor is the Code concerned with competition policy, which is the responsibility of government and other bodies.

Each of the six General Principles are reproduced in full below. Although the detail of each principle is probably outside the syllabus, it is useful to be able to review the principles to fully appreciate the spirit of the Code. At its broadest, the Code simply requires fair play between all interested parties.

1. All holders of the securities of an offeree company of the same class must be afforded equivalent treatment; moreover, if a person acquires control of a company, the other holders of securities must be protected.

2. The holders of the securities of an offeree company must have sufficient time and information to enable them to reach a properly informed decision on the bid; if it advises the holders of securities, the board of the offeree company must give its views on the effects of implementation of the bid on employment, conditions of employment and the locations of the company's places of business.

3. The board of an offeree company must act in the best interests of the company as a whole and must not deny the holders of securities the opportunity to decide on the merits of the bid.

4. False markets must not be created in the securities of the offeree company, or the offeror company or of any other company concerned by the bid, in such a way that the rise or fall of the prices of the securities becomes artificial and the normal functioning of the markets is distorted.

5. An offeror must announce a bid only after ensuring that s/he can fulfil in full any cash consideration, if such is offered, and after taking all reasonable measures to secure the implementation of any other type of consideration.

6. An offeree company must not be hindered in the conduct of its affairs for longer than is reasonable by a bid for its securities.

It is also important to be aware of the following terms that are used in the Code:

- **Acting in concert** – persons actively co-operating through the acquisition of shares to obtain or consolidate control of a company. The Code presumes that the following will be acting in concert:
    a. a company and other group companies (parent company, subsidiaries and associated companies);
    b. a company and its directors (including the directors' close relatives and related trusts);
    c. a company and its pension fund;
    d. a fund manager and investment vehicles which the manager manages with discretion;
    e. a client and its professional advisers.
- **Dealings** – these include the straightforward acquisition or disposal of securities, as well as involvement in derivative contracts on, or referenced to, the securities and any other action that may result in an increase or decrease in the number of securities a person is interested in.
- **Interests in shares** – a person is treated as having an interest in shares if he owns the shares, has a right to exercise or direct the voting rights on them, or is otherwise interested in those shares through derivatives. A person with only a short position does not have an interest in those shares.
- **Relevant securities** – these include the following:
    a. securities of the offeree company which are being offered for, or which carry, voting rights;
    b. equity share capital of the offeree company and an offeror;
    c. securities of an offeror which carry substantially the same rights as any to be issued as consideration for the offer; and
    d. securities of the offeree company and an offeror carrying conversion or subscription rights into any of the forgoing.

3.   Disclosure of Interests

3.1   Principles Behind the Disclosure Rules

Learning Objective

6.2.1   Understand the principles behind disclosure of interest rules and why they are required

In developed equity markets with a substantial number of listed companies, it is felt appropriate that when investors purchase (or sell) shares to bring about (or remove) a significant stake in a company, such information should be made available to the investing public. This will let others judge the likely impact on the price.

As we will see in Section 3.2, the level at which a shareholding is deemed significant is set at 3% in the UK; for example, if a corporate raider built up a stake of 3% or more in a listed UK company, it would be disclosed to the market. This enables other existing and potential investors to assess the company in full knowledge that there is a new significant shareholding.

3.2   Disclosure Rules

Learning Objective

6.2.2   Know the following disclosure of interest rules: EU under the Transparency Directive: the disclosure thresholds, to whom disclosure has to be made and within what time scale, differing implementation of the Transparency Directive across EEA countries; US Securities and Exchange Commission: the disclosure threshold, to whom disclosure has to be made and within what time scale; UK under the Companies Act 2006, Section 793, in relation to company investigations

The disclosure rules vary in different jurisdictions. In this section we will consider three jurisdictions – the EU generally, more specifically the UK, and the US.

The **EU** has harmonised disclosure rules via the implementation of the **Transparency Directive**. The Transparency Directive establishes disclosure requirements on an ongoing basis for issuers who have securities admitted to trading on a regulated market situated or operated within the EU. Included within the Directive's requirements are notification requirements of both issuers and investors in relation to the acquisition and disposal of significant shareholdings in companies.

The notification requirement is triggered when the size of holdings reach, exceed, or move below certain thresholds. In the Directive these thresholds are set at 5%, 10%, 15%, 20%, 25%, 30%, 50% and 75%. The shareholder reaching or breaching the threshold is required to inform the issuer, and the issuer will then inform the market.

In the **US**, the SEC requires disclosures by any person who directly or indirectly acquires a beneficial interest of 5% or more of any class of shares of a registered (and, therefore, listed) entity. The acquirer is required to issue a statement to both the SEC and the company within 10 days of acquisition.

In the EU, the regulations relating to disclosure of shareholdings can (and do) vary from country to country. This is because, if they wish, EU member states are able to exceed the requirements of the Directive – a process known as **super-equivalence**. On implementation of the Directive, the **UK** chose to retain its thresholds at 3% and each percentage point above that level. So, under UK regulation, an investor is judged to have a **notifiable interest** in a public company if he holds 3% or more of its shares. At this point he is obliged to inform the company of his holding.

Due to changes in the UKLA's Disclosure and Transparency Rules (DTR), an interest is now notifiable if the 3% interest is in the form of voting rights, rather than simply holding the shares. Here for the purposes of clarification are some relevant excerpts from the DTR relating to voting rights.

Voting rights attached to shares are now disclosable, rather than **interests in shares**. Voting rights may arise from holdings of financial instruments as well as shares.

Indirect holdings may result in a requirement for a notification to be made to the issuer, when a person may be able to control the exercise of voting rights.

Appointing a proxy, for example, will (if the holding reaches the relevant threshold) require the shareholder and proxy holder to notify the issuer if, but only if, the appointment includes the power to vote in the discretion of the proxy holder.

Voting rights attached to shares are totally disregarded in six cases, that is:

1. shares acquired for clearing and settlement within a two-trading-day settlement cycle;
2. shares held by a custodian or bare nominee;
3. shares held (if less than 10%) by a declared market maker;
4. shares held (if not more than 5%) by an investment firm or credit institution;
5. shares held as collateral; and
6. shares acquired by a borrower under a stock lending agreement.

Shareholders are deemed to have knowledge of the acquisition or disposal of voting rights (and hence time to notify starts to run from) no later than two trading days following the transaction in question or, if it was conditional upon an event outside the control of the parties to the transaction, when it becomes unconditional.

Furthermore, once the investor's holding is above 3%, they must also inform the company if it rises or falls through a whole percentage point.

- A stake of 3.7% rising to 4.1% must be reported, but a stake of 3.7% rising to 3.9% does not need to be.
- A stake of 5.4% falling to 4.9% must be reported, but a stake of 5.4% falling to 5.1% does not need to be.

An investor must also inform the company if their stake falls back to below 3%.

The reason that this disclosure is deemed necessary, despite the fact that the company maintains a register of its shareholders, is that these notifiable interest rules not only include those shares held directly by the investor, but also those shares held by parties connected to them, known as **connected parties**. These include shares held by the following:

- the investor's spouse;
- the investor's children (less than 18 years old);
- companies controlled by the investor; for these purposes, control is assumed if the investor holds at least one third of the voting rights of the company;
- concert parties: this is simply an agreement between two or more persons to influence the company together, such as voting together; if the combined holding reached 3% or more it becomes notifiable, as if it were a single holding.

As seen above, 3% is the level at which notification starts and this information must be reported in writing to the company within **two business days**. If the company is listed, it must then report the same information to a primary information provider, such as the LSE's RNS, by **the end of the following business day**.

Fund managers and operators of regulated CISs (such as AUTs and OEICs) are deemed to be non-beneficial holders and are exempt from reporting under the notifiable interest (3%) rule. Interests held by investment managers and OEICs, and in general non-beneficial owners, are under the DTR subject to disclosure at 5% and 10% (but not at the percentages in between 5% and 10%) and then at every percentage above 10%. Also, market makers have an exemption for holdings below 10% under DTR and, as long as they are not able to control the voting rights of the shares concerned, custodians are completely exempt from the disclosure rules.

The company is required to maintain a register of notifications of interests in shares and make this available at its registered office.

Companies Act Section 793 Letter

Under Section 793 of the Companies Act 2006, a UK public company is able to send a written notice to any person that the company knows or suspects to be a shareholder and ask them to confirm whether they are holding any shares. The notice requests details of that shareholder's total interest in the company.

The notice can also request details of past shareholdings held at any time in the last three years and, when the interest is a past interest, to give details of the identity of the person to whom the shares were sold if that is known.

However, it is rare for such a notice to be sent by the company registrar to an individual shareholder. These letters are usually sent to the nominee companies that appear on the register. A nominee company is the legal owner of shares on behalf of another beneficial owner.

The letter is sent to the company secretary of the nominee company, requesting details of the true beneficial owner of the securities. This enables the registrar to identify when someone is using the nominee company to hide his identity and accumulate a substantial holding without anyone being aware of the fact.

Notices under Section 793 require a written response from the recipient within a reasonable time as may be specified in the letter. If requests are persistently ignored, the company can apply to court to have the shares held frozen. This means the shareholders would lose their rights to vote on those shares, lose their entitlement to dividends and be unable to sell them.

The company is required to keep a record of the Section 793 letters that have been sent, and the information received, in a separate part of its register of shareholders.

4. Transaction and Trade Reporting

4.1 Reportable Transactions

Learning Objective

6.3.1   Understand the definition of a reportable transaction (FCA and LSE)

In order to keep track of what the various firms are doing, the regulator needs to collect data on the deals that have been done. For example, the FCA requires transactions to be reported if they involve authorised firms and certain designated investments that include shares, bonds and some derivatives. They specifically do not include stock lending or borrowing transactions, repo or reverse repo transactions, asset trading transactions or syndications.

Special requirements were issued by the predecessor to the FCA, the FSA, during turbulent equity market conditions in September 2008, requiring institutions and traders to report transactions, for a limited time period, that fell under the heading of **short selling**. Short selling is the practice of borrowing a security from its owner and selling that security with a view to purchasing and replacing it at a lower price. The FSA, in line with similar directives issued by the SEC in the US and regulators in Australia, took the view that the practice of short selling was disruptive to markets and that requiring institutions to report any such transactions might act as a disincentive to this kind of trading.

4.2 The Role and Purpose of Trade and Transaction Reporting

Learning Objective

6.3.2   Understand the role and purpose of reporting: transaction; trade

Transaction reporting or settlement reporting is done to facilitate settlement of the transaction and provide information to the regulator, enabling review of transactions after the fact – a measure of market completeness. Such details are used by the regulator to monitor for market abuse, including insider dealing and aid the general surveillance of the market.

Trade reporting is a mechanism to feed back to the marketplace on market depth and liquidity – a measure of market transparency. Trade reporting assists in price formation. Trade reports must include a variety of details, including the identity of the reporting member firm, the date and time of the transaction, the security traded and the type of trade. The type of trade is detailed by using a trade type indicator. Trade type indicators include the following:

B	for a broker-to-broker transaction
M	for a market maker-to-market maker transaction
X	for an agency cross trade, arranged by a member firm
K	for a block trade
PN	for a worked principal portfolio trade notification
WN	for a worked principal single security trade notification
NM	for a transaction that is not to mark – used when there is permission not to publish the trade

4.3 Reporting Channels and Systems

Learning Objective

6.3.3 Know which party to a trade is responsible for reporting including trades carried out by overseas branches

6.3.4 Know the reporting channels and systems

In this section, two systems run by the LSE are mentioned. They are the:

- stock exchange electronic trading service (SETS);
- international order book (IOB).

Both were introduced and covered in detail in Chapter 3.

Trade reporting is automatic for all those trades that are executed on the LSE's electronic order books – embracing UK equities traded on SETS and depositary receipts traded on the IOB. Since the trades are executed automatically on the order books, they will generate automatic trade reports and there is no need for participants to report the trades manually.

Off-order book transactions are trades executed by one or more member firms in securities traded on the IOB away from the order book, often over the telephone. Such trades need to be reported by the member firm to the exchange within three minutes of execution.

Trades in **gilt-edged securities** need to be reported to the LSE within the same timetable as trades in equity securities (as close to real time as possible and in any case within three minutes of the trade) by reference to the **trade reporting period**.

- The trade reporting period is the period when the LSE system is able to accept trade reports. It runs from 7:15am to 5:15pm.
- If a trade is executed between 7:15am and 8:00am, the report must be submitted before 8:00am or within three minutes, if later.
- If a trade is executed within the last three minutes of the trade reporting period, it should be submitted before 5:15pm.
- If a trade is executed outside the trade reporting period, it must be submitted before 7:45am in the next trade reporting period.

The responsibility for trade reporting rests with the more senior party to the trade, ie, the market maker member firm, followed by the broker-dealer member firm, followed by the non-member. If the two parties to the trade are of the same seniority, it is the selling member firm that reports the trade.

The main details that need to be included within the trade report are as follows:

- The identity of the reporting member and their counterparty.
- Date and time.
- Whether the trade is a purchase or sale.
- Trade type (for example agency or principal).
- Security and quantity traded.
- Price.
- Settlement due date.
- Any special conditions (such as ex-dividend trades).

The Exchange is then free to publish trade details as it chooses. The trades will be published on a daily basis in the **Stock Exchange Daily Official List (SEDOL)**.

For domestic transactions on systems run by the LSE, transaction reports for settlement purposes are required via CREST by a deadline on each business day of 8.00pm on the day of trade. For international equities, the Thomson Report, an online trade confirmation service provided by an organisation called Omgeo, can be used for settlement reporting, with transactions reported by both participants by 9.00pm on the day of the trade.

In respect of transaction reports, the FCA enables UK branches of European Economic Area (EEA) firms to choose to report all transactions they execute to the FCA, rather than their home regulator. Similarly, EEA branches of UK firms may report all their transactions to the local regulator. If an EEA firm transacts a reportable instrument through a non-EEA branch, no transaction report needs to be submitted to the member state competent authority. If a non-EEA firm executes a transaction from its UK branch, it must report that transaction to the FCA. Any transactions made by a non-EEA firm which are executed from its branches or offices located outside the UK do not have to be reported to the FCA.

4.3.1   TRAX

TRAX is the post-trade, pre-settlement, trade matching and regulatory confirmation system mainly used for bond trades in the OTC market. It was launched by the International Capital Market Association (ICMA) (formerly known as the International Securities Market Association (ISMA)) in 1989, initially to eliminate the costs and risks associated with paper-based trade confirmation, and is currently owned and operated by Xtrakter ltd, a subsidiary of MarketAxess Holdings Inc. TRAX offers an electronic alternative, enabling counterparties to identify potential misunderstandings and problem trades early in the settlement cycle.

It operates as a reporting hub to multiple regulators (competent authorities) within the EU/EEA and is the primary approved reporting mechanism for bonds.

Chapter Seven
Accounting Analysis

This syllabus area will provide approximately 12 of the 100 examination questions

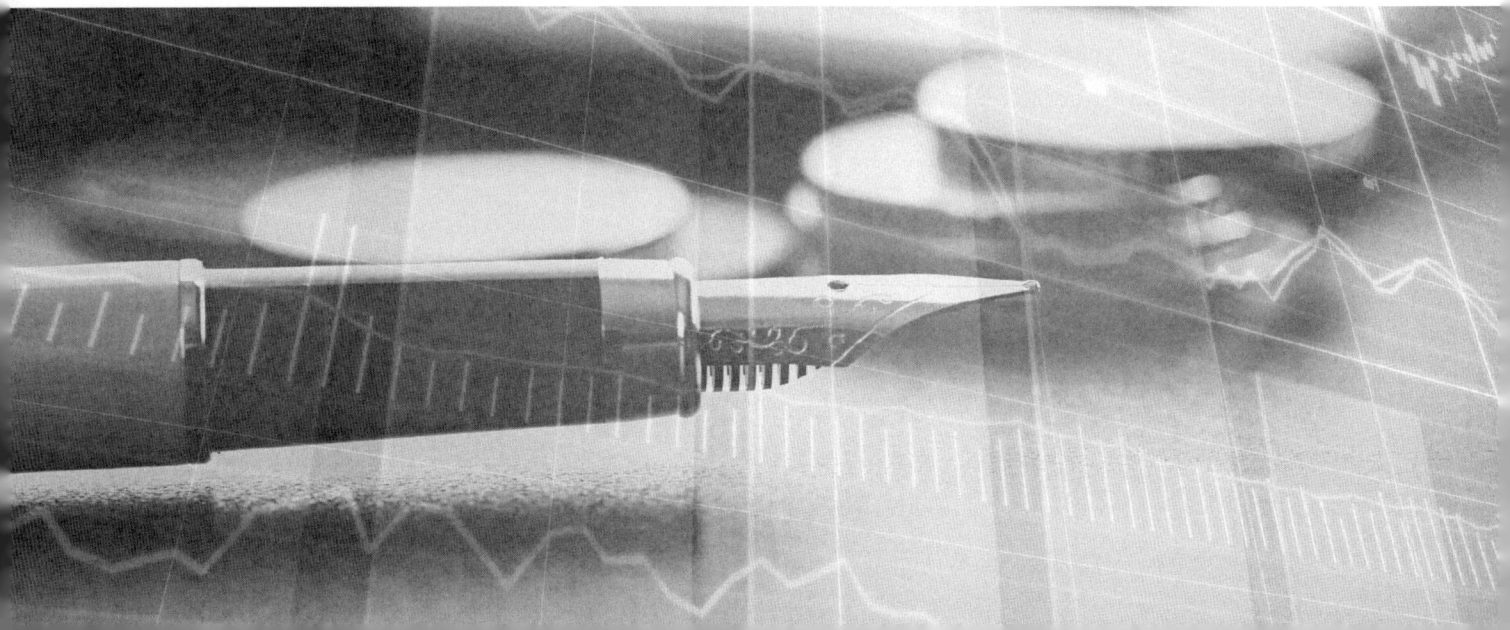

1. Basic Principles

1.1 The Purpose of Financial Statements

Learning Objective

7.1.1   Understand the purpose of financial statements

Accounting can be defined as the recording, measuring and reporting of economic events, or activities, to interested parties in a usable form. It is about providing information relating to the financial and economic activities of a business in the form of a set of accounts. This set of accounts is alternatively referred to as the **financial statements** of the business.

The need for accounting information in the form of financial statements was stimulated by the emergence of the limited liability company in the 19th century and the resulting separation of ownership and control. The financial statements provided information to the owners about the business that may have been managed by someone else.

However, although companies initially provided accounting information to satisfy the informational needs of their shareholders, the form this information now takes, and the way in which it is communicated, must also meet the disparate needs of other parties with a legitimate interest in the company's activities, performance and financial position. These other users include creditors, prospective investors, employees, financial analysts and institutional investors, as well as government, consumers and environmental groups.

The directors of a company are required to prepare financial statements and make other disclosures within an **annual report and accounts**. These set out the results of the company's activities during its most recent accounting period and its financial position as at the end of the period. The accounting period typically spans a 12-month period.

Broadly, these financial statements comprise three major statements:

1. **A balance sheet** – this provides a snapshot of the company's financial position as of a given date, usually at the company's accounting year-end. The assets it owns and how they are financed (liabilities and shareholders' equity) are displayed on opposite sides of the sheet, and must 'balance' each other. The balance sheet is sometimes referred to as the **Statement of Financial Position**.
2. **An income statement** – this statement summarises income (or revenue) that has been earned by the company over the accounting period. Broadly it is a summary of the trading activities of the company over the year. If income exceeds costs, the company has made a profit; if costs exceed income the company has made a loss.

The income statement links the company's previous balance sheet with its current one. This relationship is depicted below.

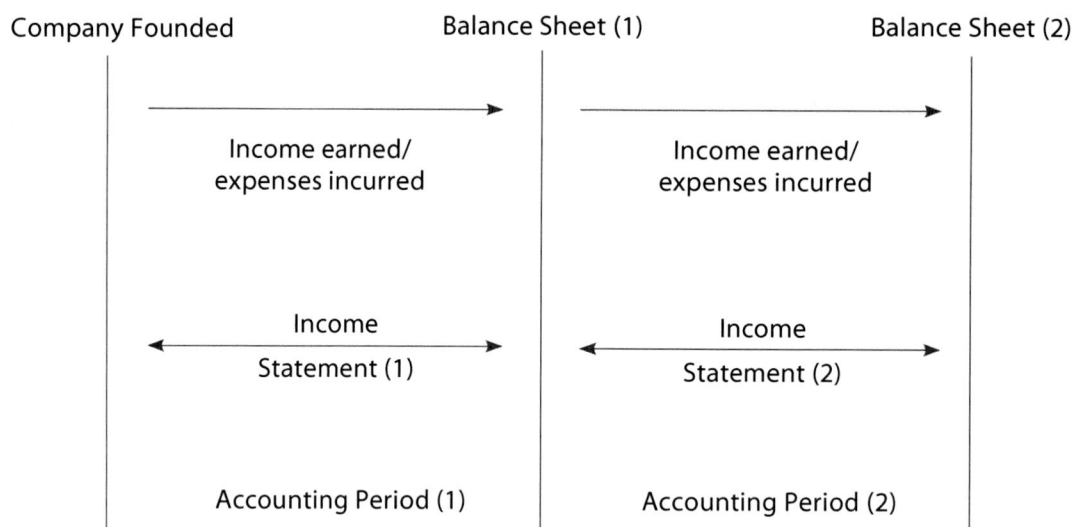

Company Founded	Balance Sheet (1)	Balance Sheet (2)
Income earned/expenses incurred	Income earned/expenses incurred	
Income Statement (1)	Income Statement (2)	
Accounting Period (1)	Accounting Period (2)	

3. **A cash flow statement**. Companies must also publish a cash flow statement within their annual report and accounts. This financial statement identifies how much cash the company generated over the accounting period and how much cash has been spent. The cash flow statement is also referred to as a **Statement of Cash Flows**.

The financial statements also include certain additional disclosures, such as the comparative figures from the previous year's financial statements, explanatory notes to accompany certain individual balance sheet and profit and loss account items, and disclosure of the company's accounting policies. The accounting policies are the basis on which the accounts have been prepared.

The information contained in the company's report and accounts is also required to be independently verified, or **audited**. An audit is an independent assessment of the company's accounts that have been prepared by the directors. This audit is concluded with an auditor's report to the members, or shareholders, of the company confirming whether or not the accounts give a true and fair view of the company's activities and financial position and whether they have been prepared in accordance with the law and other regulations. If they have, an unqualified audit report is issued. If they have not the auditor must issue a qualified report and state the reason for this qualification.

1.2 Accounting Regulations

Learning Objective

7.1.2 Understand the requirements for companies and groups to prepare accounts in accordance with applicable accounting standards and the difficulties encountered when comparing companies using different standards: accounting principles; International Financial Reporting Standards (IFRS); International Accounting Standards (IAS); UK GAAP

The form and content of all company financial statements and their respective disclosures are prescribed by the law and by mandatory accounting standards set by the accountancy profession. Accounting standards are authoritative statements of how particular types of transaction and other events should be reflected in financial statements.

The combination of accounting regulations is often referred to as the **generally accepted accounting principles** or GAAP. Each country's GAAP varies to a lesser or greater extent. For example, UK GAAP is different in a number of respects to US GAAP. This means it is not simply the case of judging whether one company has performed better than another by looking at the amount of profit made by a UK company and a US competitor – adjustments are required to make the accounting principles adopted compatible. However, there are efforts being made to harmonise GAAP throughout the world, spearheaded by the **International Accounting Standards Board (IASB)**. The IASB is an independent, privately funded accounting standard-setter based in London. The board members currently come from 12 countries and have a variety of functional backgrounds. To ensure a broad international diversity, there will normally be:

- four members from the Asia/Oceania region;
- four from Europe;
- four from North America;
- one member each from Africa and South America; and
- two members appointed from any area, subject to maintaining overall geographical balance.

The IASB is committed to developing, in the public interest, a single set of high quality, understandable and enforceable global accounting standards that require transparent and comparable information in general purpose financial statements. In addition, the IASB co-operates with national accounting standard-setters to achieve convergence in accounting standards around the world.

Standards issued by the IASB are designated **International Financial Reporting Standards (IFRSs)**. There were also standards issued by the IASB's predecessor (the International Accounting Standards Committee) that continue to be designated **International Accounting Standards (IASs)**. The IASB has retained the IASs and also issues IFRSs.

One of the key international standards is IAS 1 **Presentation of Financial Statements** that details the objectives and lays down the components of a set of financial statements.

1.3 Group Versus Company Accounts

Learning Objective

7.1.3   Understand the differences between group accounts and company accounts and why companies are required to prepare group accounts (candidates should understand the concept of goodwill and minority interests but will not be required to calculate them)

If a company invests in another company, all that appears in the accounts of the investing company is the original cost of the investment (in the balance sheet), and the dividends received (if there are any) appear in the investing company's income statement.

This treatment is fine when the investment is a small minority shareholding in another company. However, in instances when the investment is so significant that the investing company controls the other company, another accounting treatment is required – the preparation of **group financial statements** (known as group accounts). The investing company is described as the **parent** and the company or companies that the parent company controls are described as **subsidiaries**. As long as a parent/subsidiary relationship exists, the parent company should prepare and present a set of group accounts in addition to their individual company financial statements.

These group accounts present the financial statements as if the parent and the subsidiaries were a single entity, rather than distinct individual companies. This entails the addition of the assets of the parent plus all of the subsidiaries' assets to arrive at the group assets, and similar additions to arrive at the group's liabilities, revenues, expenses and cash flows.

Two particular issues can crop up when amalgamating the figures for the parent company and its subsidiaries:

1. **Goodwill** – when presenting the group accounts as a single entity, the assets and liabilities of the subsidiaries are added to those of the parent company. This replaces the original cost of investment in the group balance sheet. If the cost of investment exceeded the net assets (assets less liabilities) of the subsidiary, the excess is described as **goodwill** and appears as an asset in the group accounts.
2. **Minority interests** – in circumstances when the parent company owns a majority of the shares in a subsidiary, but not all of the shares, there will be minority interests. For example, if a parent owned 75% of the shares of a subsidiary, the minority interest would be 25%; if it owned 51% of the shares the minority would be 49%. Because the presentation of the group accounts adds together all of the assets and liabilities of the subsidiaries, it includes some net assets that belong to the minority interests. These are reflected by including net assets and net income that belong to the minority interests in the group balance sheet and income statement.

2. The Statement of Financial Position

2.1 Purpose, Format and Main Contents

Learning Objective

7.2.1 Know the purpose of the balance sheet, its format and main contents

The balance sheet is a snapshot of a company's financial position at a particular moment. It is split into two halves that must always balance each other exactly, hence the name. The key information it provides to shareholders, customers and other interested parties is what the company owns (its **assets**), what the company owes others (its **liabilities**, or **creditors**) and the extent to which shareholders are providing finance to the company (the **equity**).

The balance sheet should reflect all of the reporting company's assets and liabilities, but over time companies and their advisers developed creative structures to enable items to remain **off balance sheet** rather than **on balance sheet**. The IASB and the adoption of its accounting standards should ensure that everything that should appear on the balance sheet is categorised as **on balance sheet**, and those items that are legitimately not assets or liabilities of the company should remain **off balance sheet**.

The typical format of the balance sheet, with example figures, is provided below, followed by an explanation of each of the headings:

A plc balance sheet as at 31 December 2013	
£000	2013
Assets	
Non-current assets	
Property, plant and equipment	8,900
Intangible assets	2,100
Investments	300
	11,300
Current assets	
Inventories	3,600
Trade and other receivables	2,600
Prepayments	120
Cash	860
	7,180
Total assets	**18,480**
Equity and liabilities	
Capital and reserves	
Share capital – 10m 50p ordinary shares	5,000
Share capital – preference shares	100
Share premium account	120
Revaluation reserve	180
Retained earnings	6,880
Total equity	12,280
Non-current liabilities	
Bank loans	2,000
Provisions	2,000
Current liabilities	
Trade and other payables	2,200
Total liabilities	6,200
Total equity and liabilities	**18,480**

2.2 Assets

An asset is anything that is owned and controlled by the company and confers the right to future economic benefits. Balance sheet assets are categorised as either non-current assets or current assets.

2.2.1 Non-Current Assets

Non-current assets are those in long-term, continuing use by the company. They represent the major investments from which the company hopes to make money. Non-current assets are categorised as:

- tangible;
- intangible;
- investments.

Tangible Non-Current Assets

A company's tangible non-current assets are those that have physical substance, such as land and buildings and plant and machinery, and indeed are often referred to as **plant, property and equipment** (PPE). Tangible non-current assets are initially recorded in the balance sheet at their actual cost, or **book value**. However, in order to reflect the fact that the asset will generate benefits for the company over several accounting periods, not just in the accounting period in which it was purchased, all tangible non-current assets with a limited economic life are required to be **depreciated**. The concept of depreciation will be covered in more detail in Section 2.3.

Intangible Non-Current Assets

Intangible non-current assets are those assets that, although without physical substance, can be separately identified and are capable of being sold. Ownership of an intangible non-current asset confers rights known as intellectual property. These rights give a company a competitive advantage over its peers and commonly include brand names, patents, trademarks, capitalised development costs and purchased goodwill.

Purchased goodwill arises when the consideration, or price, paid by the acquiring company for the target exceeds the fair value of the target's separable, or individually identifiable, net assets. This is not necessarily the same as the book, or balance sheet, value of these net assets:

Purchased goodwill =

(price paid for company – fair value of separable net tangible and intangible assets)

Purchased goodwill is capitalised and included in the balance sheet and, once capitalised, cannot be revalued.

Investments

Non-current asset investments are long-term investments held in other companies. These investments might be equity investments or investments in debt instruments. They are recorded in the balance sheet at cost, less any impairment to their value.

2.2.2 Current Assets

Current assets are those assets purchased with the intention of resale or conversion into cash, usually within a 12-month period. They include stocks (or inventories) of finished goods and work in progress, the debtor balances that arise from the company providing its customers with credit (trade receivables), and any short-term investments held. Current assets also include cash balances held by the company and prepayments. Prepayments are simply when the company has prepaid an expense, as illustrated by the following example:

Example

XYZ plc draws up its balance sheet on 31 December each year. Just prior to the year end XYZ pays £25,000 to its landlord for the next three months' rental on its offices (to the end of March in the next calendar year).

This £25,000 is not an expense for the current year – it represents a prepayment towards the following year's expenses and is, therefore, shown as a prepayment within current assets in XYZ's balance sheet.

Current assets are listed in the balance sheet in ascending order of liquidity and appear in the balance sheet at the lower of cost or net realisable value (NRV).

2.3 Depreciation and Amortisation

Learning Objective

7.2.2 Understand the concept of depreciation and amortisation

Depreciation is applied to tangible, non-current assets such as plant and machinery. An annual depreciation charge is made in the year's income statement. The depreciation charge allocates the fall in the book value of the asset over its useful economic life. This requirement does not, however, apply to freehold land and non-current asset investments which, not having a limited economic life, are not usually depreciated.

To calculate the annual depreciation charge to be applied to a tangible asset, the difference between its cost and estimated disposal value, termed the **depreciable amount**, must first be established. This value is then written off, over the asset's useful economic life, by employing the most appropriate depreciation method. The most common depreciation method is the **straight line method**. The straight line method simply spreads the depreciable amount equally over the economic life of the asset. The straight line method is given by the following formula:

$$\text{Straight line depreciation} = \frac{(\text{cost} - \text{disposal value})}{\text{useful economic life in years}}$$

One thing to recognise about the annual depreciation charge is that it is an accounting book entry, or a non-cash charge. That is, no cash flows from the business as a result of making the charge: it is simply an accounting entry made against the income statement to reflect the estimated cost of resources used over an accounting period. The balance sheet value of the asset is given by its cost, less the accumulated depreciation to date, and is termed the **net book value (NBV)**. This NBV does not necessarily equal the market value of the asset.

Example

Depreciation

A machine purchased for £25,000 has an estimated useful economic life of six years and an estimated disposal value after six years of £1,000. Calculate the depreciation that should be charged to this asset and its NBV in years one to six, using the straight line depreciation method.

Solution

Straight depreciation

$$\text{Straight line depreciation} = \frac{(\text{cost} - \text{disposal value})}{\text{useful economic life (years)}}$$

$$= \frac{(£25,000 - £1,000)}{6} = £4,000 \text{ per annum}$$

Year	Opening net book value	Depreciation	Closing net book value
1	25,000	4,000	21,000
2	21,000	4,000	17,000
3	17,000	4,000	13,000
4	13,000	4,000	9,000
5	9,000	4,000	5,000
6	5,000	4,000	1,000

By reducing the book value of tangible non-current assets over their useful economic lives, depreciation matches the cost of the asset against the periods from which the company benefits from its use.

On occasion, tangible assets, such as land, are not depreciated but periodically revalued. This is done on the basis of providing the user of the accounts with a truer and fairer view of the assets, or capital, employed by the company. To preserve the accounting equation (total assets = equity and liabilities), the increase in the asset's value arising on revaluation is transferred to a **revaluation reserve**, which forms part of the equity.

Closely linked to the idea of depreciating the value of a tangible asset over its useful economic life is the potential need for intangible assets to be **amortised** over their useful economic lives. Amortisation, like depreciation, is simply a book entry whose impact is felt in the company's reported income and financial position but does not impact its cash position.

2.4 Equity

Learning Objective

7.2.3 Understand the difference between authorised and issued share capital, capital reserves and revenue reserves

---

Equity is referred to in a number of ways, such as shareholders' funds, owners' equity or capital. Equity usually consists of three sub-elements: **share capital, capital reserves** and **revenue reserves**. Additionally, when group accounts are presented, there may be **minority interests** within the group equity figure.

- **Share capital** – this is the nominal value of equity and preference share capital the company has in issue and has called up. This may differ from the amount of share capital the company is authorised to issue as contained in its constitutional documents – the company may have only called up some of its share capital and may not have issued all of the share capital that is authorised.
- **Capital reserves** – capital reserves include revaluation reserves and the share premium account. The revaluation reserve arises from the upward revaluation of non-current assets, and the share premium reserve arises when the company issues shares at a price above their nominal value. Capital reserves are not distributable to the company's shareholders in the form of dividends, as they form part of the company's capital base, although they can be converted into a bonus issue of ordinary shares.
- **Revenue reserves** – the major revenue reserve is the accumulated retained earnings of the company. This represents the accumulation of the company's distributable profits that have not been paid to the company's shareholders as dividends, but have been retained in the business. The retained earnings should not be confused with the amount of cash the company holds or with the income statement that shows how the retained, or undistributed, profit in a single accounting period was arrived at.
- **Minority interests** – as covered in Section 1.3 of this chapter, minority interests arise when a parent company controls one or more subsidiary companies, but does not own all of the share capital. The equity attributable to the remaining shareholders is the minority interests and this is reflected in the balance sheet within the equity section.

In total, equity is the sum of the called-up share capital, all of the capital reserves and the revenue reserves:

$$\text{Equity} = \text{share capital} + \text{reserves}$$

2.5 Liabilities

A liability is an obligation to transfer future economic benefits as a result of past transactions or events; more simply, it could be described as money owed to someone else. Liabilities are categorised according to whether they are to be paid within, or after more than, one year:

- **Non-current liabilities** – this comprises the company's borrowing not repayable within the next 12 months. This could include bond issues as well as longer-term bank borrowing. In addition, there is a separate sub-heading for those liabilities that have resulted from past events or transactions and for which there is an obligation to make a payment, but the exact amount or timing of the expenditure has yet to be established. These are commonly referred to as provisions. Such provisions may arise as a result of the company undergoing a restructuring, for example. Given the uncertainty surrounding the extent of such liabilities, companies are required to create a realistic and prudent estimate of the monetary amount of the obligation, once it is committed to taking a certain course of action.
- **Current liabilities** – this includes the amount the company owes to its suppliers, or trade payables, as a result of buying goods and/or services on credit, any bank overdraft, and any other payables such as tax, that are due within 12 months of the balance sheet date.

3.   The Income Statement

3.1   Purpose and Contents

The income statement summarises the company's income earned and expenditure incurred over the accounting period. The function of this financial statement is to detail how much profit has been earned and how the company's reported profit (or loss) was arrived at.

The amount of profit earned over the accounting period will impact the company's ability to pay dividends and how much can be retained to finance the growth of the business from internal resources.

Like the balance sheet, the format of the income statement is governed by the law and underpinned by the requirements of various accounting standards. The following table shows an income statement for A plc.

A plc income statement for the year end 31 December 2013			
	Notes	2013	2012
		£000	£000
Revenue		9500	8,750
Cost of sales		(7,000)	(6,600)
Gross profit		2,500	2,150
Distribution costs		(110)	(90)
Administrative expenses		(30)	(20)
Loss on disposal of plant		(260)	
Operating profit		2,100	2,040
Financial costs		(230)	(250)
Financial income		120	112
Profit before taxation		1,990	1,902
Taxation		(555)	(548)
Net income		1,435	1,354
Earnings per share (pence)		16.1p	15.9p

3.1.1 Revenue

The income statement starts with one of the most important things in any company's accounts: its sales revenues. In accounts, sales revenues are generally referred to as revenue, or sometimes turnover. It is simply everything that the company has sold during the year, regardless of whether it has received the cash or not. For a manufacturer, revenue is the sales of the products that it has made. For a company in the service industry, it is the consulting fees earned, or perhaps commissions earned on financial transactions.

3.1.2 Costs of Sales

The costs of sales are the costs to the company of generating the sales made in the financial year. These items are also sometimes known as the **cost of goods sold (COGS)**. They typically include the costs of the raw materials used to make a product and the costs of converting those raw materials into their finished state, including the wages of the staff making the products.

3.1.3 Gross Profit

Total sales, less the costs of those sales, results in the gross profit for the year.

3.1.4 Operating Profit

Operating profit is also referred to as **profit on operating activities**. It is the gross profit, less other operating expenses that the company has incurred. These other operating expenses might include cost incurred distributing products (distribution costs) and administrative expenses such as management salaries, auditors' fees and legal fees. Administrative expenses would also include depreciation and amortisation charges. Additional items may be separately disclosed before arriving at operating profit, such as the profit or loss made on selling a non-current asset. When a non-current asset, such as an item of machinery, is disposed of at a price significantly different from its balance sheet value, the profit or loss when compared to this NBV should be separately disclosed if material to the information conveyed by the accounts.

Operating profit is the profit before considering finance costs (interest) and any tax payable – so it can be described as **profit before interest and tax (PBIT)**.

3.1.5 Finance Costs/Finance Income

Finance costs are generally the interest that the company has incurred on its borrowings – that may be in the form of bonds or may be bank loans and overdrafts.

Finance income is typically the interest earned on surplus funds, such as from deposit accounts.

3.1.6 Profit Before Tax

This is the profit made by the company in the period, before considering any tax that may be payable on that profit.

3.1.7 Corporation Tax Payable

This is simply the corporation tax charge that the company has incurred for the period.

3.1.8 Net Income

Now that tax and financing costs have been deducted we have a vital figure: net income. It reflects all the income earned during the period, less all of the expenditures incurred. This net income is also the profit attributable to the shareholders of the company because, in theory, it could all be distributed to shareholders as dividends.

3.1.9 Earnings Per Share (EPS)

This is an important figure for readers of the financial statements as it displays the company's profit expressed on a per-share basis. This is always reflected at the bottom of the income statement, in pence. EPS is the amount of profit after tax that has been earned per ordinary share. EPS is calculated as follows:

$$\text{EPS} = \frac{\text{Net income for the financial year} - \text{Dividends on preferred shares}}{\text{Number of ordinary shares in issue}}$$

3.1.10 Dividends

Some, or all, of the profit for the financial year can be distributed as dividends. Dividends to any preference shareholders are paid out first, followed by dividends to ordinary shareholders at an amount set by the board and expressed as a number of pence per share. The dividends for most listed companies are paid in two instalments: an interim dividend paid after the half-year stage, and a final proposed dividend to be paid after the accounts have been approved. The dividends are shown in the accounts in a note that reconciles the movement in equity from one balance sheet to another.

A plc statement of changes in equity for the year ended 31 December 2013						
	Ord share capital	Pref share capital	Share premium account	Revaluation reserve	Retained earnings	Total
As at 1 January 2013	4,470	100		100	5,040	9,710
Gain on revaluation				80		80
Issue of shares	530		120			650
Net income for the year					1,435	1,435
Preference dividends paid					(5)	(5)
Ordinary dividends paid					(400)	(400)
As at 31 December 2013	5,000	100	120	180	6,070	11,470

3.2 Capital Versus Revenue Expenditure

Learning Objective

7.3.2 Understand the difference between capital and revenue expenditure

Money spent by a company will usually fall into one of two possible forms: capital expenditure or revenue expenditure.

Capital expenditure is money spent to buy non-current assets, such as plant, property and equipment. It is reflected on the balance sheet.

Revenue expenditure is money spent that immediately impacts the income statement. Examples of revenue expenditure include wages paid to staff, rent paid on property and professional fees, like audit fees.

4.   The Statement of Cash Flows

4.1   Purpose of the Statement of Cash Flows

Learning Objective

7.4.1   Know the purpose of the cash flow statement, its format as set out in IAS 7

The statement of cash flows or, as it was previously known, the cash flow statement, is basically a summary of all the payments and receipts that have occurred over the course of the year, the total reflecting the inflow (or outflow) of cash over the year.

A statement of cash flows (as it is now known in accordance with the IAS 1 Revised) is required by accounting standard IAS 7.

In what follows, the term cash flow statement will be used for familiarity and also to illustrate that the new title adopted by IAS 1 Revised is not mandatory.

The logic of adding a cash flow statement to a set of financial statements is that it enables the readers of the accounts to see clearly how cash has been generated and/or used over the course of the year. This is felt to provide easily understood information to the users of the accounts that supplements the performance figures provided by the income statement, and the statement of financial position given by the balance sheet.

IAS 7 cash flow statements require a company's cash flows to be broken down into particular headings, as illustrated in the following example:

A plc cash flow statement for the year ended 31 December 2013	
Operating activities	
Cash receipts from customers	4,528
Cash paid to suppliers and employees	−2,441
Cash generated from operations	2,527
Tax paid	--
Interest paid	−150
Net cash from operating activities	**4,464**
Investing activities	
Interest received	80
Dividends received	40
Purchase of fixed assets	−1,890
Proceeds on sale of investments	120
Net cash used in investing activities	**−1,650**
Financing activities	
Dividends paid	−435
Repayments of borrowings	−200
Proceeds on issue of shares	650
Net cash generated from financing activities	**15**
Net increase in cash and cash equivalents	2,829
Cash and cash equivalents at the beginning of the year	425
Cash and cash equivalents at the end of the year	3,254

Looking at the key cash flow statement headings in turn:

- **Operating activities** is the cash that has been generated from the trading activities of the company, excluding financing cost (interest).

- **Investing activities** details the investment income (dividends and interest) that has been received in the form of cash during the year and the cash paid to purchase new non-current assets, less the cash received from the sale of non-current assets during the year.
- **Financing activities** includes the cash spent during the year on paying dividends to shareholders, borrowing on a long-term basis or the cash raised from issuing shares, less the cash spent repaying debt or buying back shares.

The resultant total should explain the changes in cash (and cash equivalents) between the balance sheets. Many short-term investments are classified as cash equivalents, such as T-bills.

4.2   Profit Versus Cash

Learning Objective

7.4.2   Understand the difference between profit and cash and their impact on the long-term future of the business

Profit appears in the income statement and is the excess of revenues earned over the period, over the expenses incurred in that same period. Obviously, generating profits is necessary for the long-term survival of any business, although companies can (and many do) exhibit losses for a number of years. Without profit, that business is unlikely to survive indefinitely.

The extent to which a company has generated (or used up) cash is detailed in the cash flow statement. Cash is generated when cash received exceeds cash paid out, and cash is used up when the cash paid out exceeds the cash received. Cash is often described as the **lifeblood of the company**. Without it the company will not survive. If a company does not have the cash to pay a liability when it is due, there is a possibility of the company being forced to close down.

When comparing profit against cash, there are some key differences. Because profit is based on revenues earned, not cash received, there is a possibility that the two figures for a company could be very different. For example, a company may make sales on credit and, therefore, recognise the revenues at the point of sale in the income statement. The cash for those sales could be received significantly later.

Similarly, profit is based on expenditure incurred, not cash paid, and there can be significant differences between the two. A key example of the potential for difference is in the different treatments of the purchase of a non-current tangible asset, like a machine. In the income statement, the impact will be a gradual expense incurred each year for the depreciation of the machine. In the cash flow statement, the full cost will be paid in cash at the time of purchase.

Operating Cash Flow Statement for XYZ ltd for Year Ending 31 December 2013			
All figures are in £ Sterling			
Net income after Tax	240,000		
Other additions to Cash			
Depreciation and Amortisation	35,000		Depreciation is not a cash expense; it is added back into net income for calculating cash flow
Decrease in Accounts Receivable	17,000		If accounts receivable decreases more cash has entered the company from customers paying off their accounts – the amount by which accounts receivable has decreased is an addition to cash
Decrease in Inventory			A decrease in inventory signals that a company has spent less money to purchase more raw materials. The decrease in the value of inventory is an addition to cash
Decrease in Other Current Assets	19,000		Similar reasoning to above for other current assets
Increase in Accounts Payable	26,000		If accounts payable increases it suggests more cash has been retained by the company through not paying some bills – the amount by which accounts payable has increased is an addition to cash
Increase in Accrued Expenses			For example deferring payment of some salaries will add to cash
Increase in Other Current Liabilities			Similar reasoning to above for increase in taxes payable
Total Additions to Cash From Operations			
Subtractions from Cash			
Increase in Accounts Receivable			If accounts receivable increases less cash has entered the company from customers paying their accounts – the amount by which accounts receivable has increased is a subtraction of cash
Increase in Inventory	–33,000		An increase in inventory signals that a company has spent more money to purchase more raw materials. If the inventory was paid with cash, the increase in the value of inventory is a subtraction of cash

(Continued on following page)

Increase in Other Current Assets			Similar reasoning to above for other current assets
Decrease in Accounts Payable			If accounts payable decreases it suggests more cash has been used by the company to pay its bills – the amount by which accounts payable decreased is a subtraction from cash
Decrease in Accrued Expenses	−19,000		For example an increase in prepaid expenses results in a subtraction of cash
Decrease in Other Current Liabilities	−23,000		Similar reasoning to above for decrease in taxes payable
Total Subtractions from Cash from Operations		−75,000	
Total Operating Cash Flow		262,000	= net income after tax + total additions to cash from operations + total subtractions from cash from operations

4.3   Free Cash Flow

Learning Objective

7.4.3   Understand the purpose of free cash flow and the difference between enterprise cash flow and equity cash flow

There is no single definition of **free cash flow**. Logically, it perhaps should be drawn from the cash flow statement and represent the amount of cash that has been generated and that the company can choose what to do with. This might be the operating cash flow less the extent to which the company has to spend cash to maintain the operating capacity of the business. It is the latter figure that is difficult to isolate, and is likely to be a subjective judgement by the user of the accounts. The resultant figure might be adjusted further depending on whether the calculation is for free cash flow to the firm (enterprise cash flow), or just free cash flow to the shareholders (equity cash flow). This will be explored in more detail below.

Because of the difficulty in arriving at free cash flow from the cash flow statement, many users calculate a free cash flow figure from the income statement. This is generally arrived at by taking the net income from the income statement, adding back the charges for depreciation and amortisation and deducting capital expenditure. The capital expenditure will again be a judgement of the capital spend required to maintain the operating capacity of the business, with the use of income statement figures for operating cash flow presenting a smoother, potentially more representative figure for cash generation by removing the inconsistencies that payments in advance or in arrears can create.

As well as there being two potentially different sources for free cash flow (the cash flow statement or the income statement), there are further adjustments that might be made depending on whether the free cash flow is being calculated for the whole enterprise (the enterprise cash flow) or is being calculated for the equity holders only (the equity cash flow).

The enterprise cash flow is the free cash flow before considering payments made to any of the providers of finance to the firm. The providers of finance to the firm are both the lenders and the equity holders. The enterprise cash flow will, therefore, be the free cash flow before considering any financing costs.

In contrast the equity cash flow is the free cash flow to the shareholders, so it will be after any financing costs to the lenders, but before any dividend payments to the shareholders.

Cash Flow Statement for XYZ ltd for Year Ending 31 December 2013		
All figures are in £ Sterling		
Total Operating Cash Flow	262,000	= net income after tax + total additions to cash from operations + total subtractions from cash from operations
Investment/Capital Expenditures		
Additions to Cash From Investments		
Decrease in Fixed Assets	150,000	Sale of a building will lead to an addition to cash
Decrease in Notes Receivable	12,000	A reduction in notes receivable indicates that cash will have been received
Decrease in Securities, Investments		Securities will have been sold thereby raising cash
Decrease in Intangible, Non-Current Assets		Sale of a patent or copyright will lead to an addition of cash
Total Additions to Cash From Investments	162,000	
Subtractions from Cash for Investments		
Increase in Fixed Assets		Purchase of a building will lead to a subtraction from cash
Increase in Notes Receivable		An increase in notes receivable indicates that cash has not been received
Increase in Securities, Investments	–64,000	Securities will have been purchased thereby reducing cash
Increase in Intangible, Non-Current Assets	–250,000	Purchase of a copyright will lead to a reduction of cash
Total Subtractions from Cash for Investments	–314,000	

(Continued on following page)

Total Enterprise Cash Flow		110,000	= total operating cash flow + additions to cash from capital investments + subtractions from cash from capital investments
Financing Activities			
Additions to Cash From Financing			
Increase in Borrowings		50,000	Additional net borrowing will lead to an addition of cash
Increase Capital Stock			Additional net equity capital paid in will lead to an addition of cash
Total Additions to Cash From Financing		50,000	
Subtractions from Cash for Financing			
Increase in Borrowings			Net reduction in borrowing will lead to a subtraction of cash
Increase Capital Stock			Retirement of net equity capital paid in will lead to a subtraction of cash
Total Subtractions from Cash for Financing			
Total Equity Cash Flow		160,000	= total enterprise cash flow + additions to cash from financing + subtractions from cash from financing
Subtractions from Cash for Dividends			
Dividends Paid		−100,000	
Total Free Cash Flow		60,000	= total equity cash flow – dividends paid out
Cash at beginning of period		450,000	
Cash at end of period		510,000	

5. Financial Statement Analysis

The three principal financial statements and associated explanatory notes published by companies in their report and accounts furnish the user with a considerable amount of information. However, the needs of the user can be met more precisely by employing **ratio analysis**, as key relationships can be established and trends identified by consolidating this information into a more readily usable form. Ratios are commonly employed by analysts to assess the prospects for a particular company and, therefore, the investment potential of the shares of that company, as well as assisting other interested parties in assessing the company such as the board, suppliers, competitors and employees.

The purpose of ratio analysis is to:

1. assist in assessing business performance, by identifying meaningful relationships between numbers contained within company financial statements, that may not be immediately apparent. Although there are no statutory rules as to how ratios should be calculated, there should be logic in the numbers being related to each other;
2. summarise financial information into an easily understandable form;
3. identify trends, strengths and weaknesses by comparing the ratios to those of the same company in prior periods, other similar companies, sector averages and market averages.

However, ratio analysis does have its limitations:

1. As financial statements contain historic data, ratios are not predictive; indeed, occasionally, historic figures can be restated in later periods, making comparison difficult.
2. The use of alternative accounting methods and differences in international accounting practices makes it difficult to draw comparisons.
3. Significant judgement is needed when performing ratio analysis, which naturally leads to divergence.

The ratios required for the examination follow, first an explanation of key subsets of the ratios to meet the examiner's requirement that the candidate understands the ratios, followed by the formulae so that the candidate can also calculate the specified ratios.

5.1 Return on Capital Employed (ROCE) and Profitability Ratios

---

Learning Objective

7.5.1   Understand the following key ratios: profitability ratios (gross profit and operating profit margins); return on capital employed

---

5.1.1 ROCE and Profitability Ratios Explained

Profitability ratios look at the percentage return that the company generates relative to its revenues. The **gross profit** looks at the percentage of revenues that the company earns after considering the costs of sales. The **operating profit margin** looks at the percentage of revenues that the company earns after considering costs of sales and other operating costs (such as distribution costs and administrative expenses). Clearly, all other things being equal, a greater profit margin is preferable to a lesser profit margin.

Return on capital employed (ROCE) is widely seen as the best ratio for measuring overall management performance, in relation to the capital that has been paid into the business. It looks at the amount of return (profit) that is being generated as a percentage of the finance put into the business (the capital employed). The amount of capital employed is the equity plus the long-term debt. This is the money that the company holds from shareholders and debt providers, and it is from this money that the management should be able to generate profits.

5.1.2 ROCE and Profitability Ratios: Calculations

Effectively, the ROCE gives a yield for the entire company. It compares the money invested in the company with the generated return. This annual return can then be compared to other companies, or less risky investments.

The formula is:

$$\text{Return on Capital Employed (ROCE)} = \frac{\text{Operating profit}}{\text{Capital employed}} \times 100$$

where operating profit is the profit before financing and tax on the income statement, and capital employed is the total for equity on the balance sheet, plus the total for non-current liabilities from the balance sheet.

Using the example accounts for A plc encountered earlier:

$$\text{ROCE} = 2{,}100 / (12{,}280 + 2{,}000) \times 100 = 14.7\%$$

The figures for the profitability ratios are drawn from the income statement. The formulae for the profitability ratios are:

$$\text{Gross Profit Margin (\%)} = (\text{Gross Profit / Revenues}) \times 100$$

$$\text{Operating Profit Margin (\%)} = (\text{Operating Profit / Revenues}) \times 100$$

Using the example from A plc earlier:

$$\text{Gross Profit Margin (\%)} = (2,500 / 9,500) \times 100 = 26.3\%$$

$$\text{Operating Profit Margin (\%)} = (2,100 / 9,500) \times 100 = 22\%$$

5.2 Financial Gearing Ratios

Learning Objective

7.5.2 Understand the following financial gearing ratios: investors' debt to equity ratio; net debt to equity ratio; interest cover

5.2.1 Financial Gearing Ratios Explained

Financial gearing is a measure of **risk** within a company. Financial gearing is also called 'financial leverage', and the ratios are also referred to as 'financial leverage ratios'. It is determined by examining the amount of a company's financing that comes from debt, and the amount that comes from shareholders' funds or equity – the debt to equity ratio.

The higher the proportion of debt finance, the higher the risk that the company will not be able to meet its financing commitments. This is because interest on debt must be paid every year and the debt must be repaid at some point, whereas dividends on shares need only be paid in profitable years and share capital never has to be repaid. It is the inability to service and repay debt that brings about company failure. However, high levels of borrowing in some circumstances can be positive for the shareholders because, if the debt interest is fixed, what is left after paying debt interest is the entitlement of the equity holders so, in years when the firm earns substantial returns, all of the excess belongs to the equity holders.

Whether debt levels are excessive is a matter of judgement, but gearing ratios tend to look at the total debt compared to equity. Sometimes this ratio may be less useful because, as well as holding substantial amounts of debt, the company also holds substantial cash and short-term investments that could be used to repay the debt – it is in these circumstances when **net debt to equity** is used.

Another way to assess whether debt levels are excessive is to look at the extent to which profits are being made to cover the interest burden on that debt – the **interest cover**.

5.2.2   Financial Gearing Ratios: Calculations

Debt to Equity = Debt/Equity

Both figures for debt and equity are drawn from the balance sheet of a company. All non-current liabilities are generally considered to be **debt**, and the total of the equity portion of the balance sheet is considered to be equity. The ratio is either stated as a simple proportion: debt to equity is 0.6; or, as a percentage: debt is 60% of the equity.

Using the example of A plc:

$$\text{Debt to Equity} = 2{,}000 \, / \, 12{,}280 = 0.163 \text{ or } 16.3\%$$

Net Debt to Equity = (Debt less cash and short-term investments) / Equity

Net debt is simply the debt as in the debt-to-equity ratio, less the cash and short-term investments that are within the current assets on the balance sheet.

Using the example of A plc:

$$\text{Net Debt to Equity} = (2{,}000 - 860) \, / \, 12{,}280 = 0.093 \text{ or } 9.3\%$$

Interest Cover = Operating Profit/Interest Costs

Interest cover figures are drawn from the income statement. The operating profit is simply divided by the interest costs (the financing costs line on the income statement).

Using the example of A plc:

$$\text{Interest cover} = 2{,}100 \, / \, 230 = 9.13 \text{ times}$$

5.3   Investors' Ratios Explained

Learning Objective

7.5.3   Understand the following investors' ratios: earnings per share; diluted earnings per share; price earnings ratio (both historic and prospective); enterprise value to EBIT; enterprise value to EBITDA; net dividend yield; net dividend cover

Existing and potential investors look at a variety of ratios to assess whether or not a company is likely to be a good investment. These ratios look to establish how:

- expensive the shares are, in order to reach a conclusion on the likelihood of capital growth;
- much in dividends the shares pay, and how easily the company is able to bear the payment of those dividends, to reach a conclusion on the income those shares are likely to generate.

5.3.1 Earnings Per Share (EPS)

The earnings per share (EPS) ratio is one of the most useful and often-cited ratios used in the investment world. It is used universally and more or less has the same meaning in most jurisdictions, but is one ratio for which there are prescribed rules in the UK regarding its calculation. These are laid out in IAS 33, which essentially defines the EPS as follows:

$$\text{EPS} = \frac{\text{Net profit / loss attributable to ordinary shareholders}}{\text{Average weighted number of ordinary shares outstanding in a period}}$$

EPS is expressed in pence and reveals how much profit was made during the year that is available to be paid out to each share. As a figure for **profit per share**, it can be divided into the current share price to assess how many times the profit per share must be paid to buy a share – in effect, how expensive (or cheap) those shares are. This is the **price earnings ratio (PER)**.

Furthermore, investors are particularly interested in the earnings each share will generate in the future, rather than how much they have generated in the past. As a result, stockbrokers' research departments will endeavour to anticipate what the EPS will be – the **prospective EPS** – rather than what the EPS were in the last reported set of results – the **historic EPS**.

5.3.2 Diluted Earnings Per Share (EPS)

The purpose of publishing a separate figure for diluted EPS is to warn shareholders of potential future changes in the EPS figure as a result of events that actually may have, or theoretically could have, taken place.

EPS, as defined in Section 5.3.1, is potentially misleading if the company has substantial quantities of instruments in issue that are convertible into shares. These may be convertible bonds or share options issued to the senior management of the company. If the EPS is calculated in the usual way – by simply dividing the net income for the period by the number of issued shares – the users of the accounts are not incorporating the impact that convertible instruments may have – in particular their dilutive impact on the EPS. The issuance of more shares will mean a lower EPS. As a result, for companies with significant convertible instruments in issue, an adjusted figure for earnings per share is required to be disclosed that takes this into account. This ratio is called the **diluted EPS**.

The reason why the term **theoretically** is used in this context is because there is only a possibility – legally certain rights have been granted which could be exercised and require further issues of shares – and the prudent method of accounting is to assume, from the point of view of share dilution, the worst case scenario.

There are two possible factors that could cause share dilution and which need to be covered in the method of conservatively calculating a true and accurate picture of the EPS. A company may have either or both of the following kinds of securities outstanding:

- issued convertible loan stock or convertible preference shares;
- issued options or warrants.

Each of these circumstances may potentially result in more shares being issued, and thereby qualifying for a dividend in future years, which will have the material effect of diluting the current EPS.

The diluted EPS figure is considered of such importance to the reader of the accounts, and a potential investor, that its calculation and disclosure is required by IAS 33 – Earnings Per Share (Financial Reporting Standard (FRS 22) in the UK).

5.3.3 Price Earnings Ratio (P/E)

The price earnings (P/E) ratio is calculated as follows.

$$\text{Price/Earnings Ratio} = \frac{\text{Current market price per share}}{\text{Earnings per share}}$$

Let us suppose that the ordinary shares for a company are currently trading at £2.50 per share and that the EPS are 20p: the P/E ratio is £2.50/£0.20 = 12.5.

The P/E ratio informs as to after how many years of earnings the current earnings will equal the current share price, and in this case it is 12.5 years.

The price per share in the numerator is the market price of a single share of the stock. The EPS in the denominator of the formula can vary according to the type of P/E that is being offered for consideration.

Essentially, analysts will tend to look at two types of earnings for the denominator – backward-looking and forward-looking. The latter require forecasting, which can be notoriously unreliable and are often based on a company's own projections.

Trailing (P/E)

Also known as **P/E trailing twelve months (ttm)**, this is the version that has already been described in the formula – although it can be updated in between issuing a separate income statement. It is customary in the analyst community to take for earnings the net income of the company for the most recent 12-month period divided by the number of shares outstanding. This is the most common meaning of 'P/E' if no other qualifier is specified.

Forward P/E

This is also known as **P/E f** or estimated P/E, and is based on estimation of net earnings over the next 12 months. Estimates are typically derived as the mean of a select group of analysts. In times of rapid economic dislocation, such estimates become less relevant as the macro-environment changes (eg, new economic data is published and/or the basis of their forecasts becomes obsolete) more quickly than analysts adjust their forecasts.

Companies with losses (negative earnings) or no profit have an undefined P/E ratio (usually shown as **not applicable (N/A)**).

Uses of the P/E Ratio

By comparing price and EPS, one can analyse the market's stock valuation of a company and its shares, relative to the income the company is actually generating. Stocks with higher (and/or more certain) forecast earnings growth will usually have a higher P/E, and those expected to have lower (and/or riskier) earnings growth will, in most cases, have a lower P/E.

Investors can use the P/E ratio to compare the relative valuations of stocks. Too simplistically, one might claim that if one stock has a P/E twice that of another stock, all things being equal, it is a less attractive investment. Companies are rarely equal, however, and comparisons between industries, companies, and time periods can be very misleading.

P/E ratios are closely followed by the investment community and financial analysts. Indeed the P/E ratio of stock market indices or averages are often used to determine whether or not the overall market is considered to be expensive, is priced in line with historical norms, or is cheap. For example, in the US the S&P 500 index has a mean historical P/E ratio, over the last 50 years, of approximately 18, but has fluctuated rather considerably from that mean. When analysing the ratio it is customary to use the last 12 months of earnings of the constituent stocks of the index, and this is referred to as the trailing average.

At times during the recession in the early 1980s, the trailing P/E ratio for the S&P index reached below eight and, in the early part of 2000 just prior to the collapse of the dot com stocks, the P/E ratio reached above 40, measured on a trailing 12-month basis. In September 2011, the P/E ratio was approximately 15, somewhat below the level of 18 which, as mentioned, is the long-term historical norm. Forward-looking earnings are also often factored into the ratio, so some analysts are more interested in the forward ratio than the trailing ratio.

One factor which can influence the criterion used to assess whether the overall market is overpriced, fairly priced or underpriced is the interest rate environment as well as the annual rate of inflation. During periods when short-term interest rates are relatively low, and inflation is considered to be benign, a larger P/E ratio is supportable as there is less competition for equities coming from the income obtainable from fixed-income securities and vice versa.

Companies in different sectors of the economy will also tend to exhibit generically contrasting P/E ratios. This will itself be largely based upon the market's expectations as to future earnings growth in different sectors. For example, a relatively young technology company which has bright prospects will often be rewarded by investors with a relatively high P/E ratio as the earnings are expected to grow dynamically. On the other hand a mature utility company which has fairly predictable future earnings potential will tend to have a relatively lower P/E ratio based on more conservative growth estimations.

Another useful application of the P/E ratio is to consider the relationship between it on an individual company's security and the P/E ratio of the stock market average or of the sector average. Some investors will be attracted to companies with a low P/E ratio as it suggests that the company may be undervalued. Once again this needs to be placed into the context of which sector a possible acquisition candidate occupies; for example, a company interested in taking over a technology company will almost certainly have to pay an above-average market P/E multiple but will look for one that is still attractively priced within that sector of the market.

5.3.4 Enterprise Value (EV) to Earnings Before Interest and Tax (EBIT)

This ratio consists of two other metrics – enterprise value (EV), and EBIT (earnings before interest and tax).

EV is a measure of a company's value and is often used as an alternative to straightforward market capitalisation. A firm's EV is calculated as its market capitalisation plus all of its outstanding debt, minority interests and preferred shares, minus all of the cash and cash equivalents.

From a slightly different perspective, EV is the sum of the claims of all of a company's security-holders, which includes all of the debt-holders, preferred shareholders, minority shareholders, common equity holders, and others. EV is one of the fundamental metrics used in business valuation, financial modelling, accounting and portfolio analysis.

A simplified and intuitive way to understand EV is to envisage purchasing an entire business. If you settle with all the security-holders, you have essentially purchased the company at its EV.

EBIT is another fairly widely used indicator of a company's financial performance and is calculated in the following simple calculation:

EBIT = Revenue less expenses (excluding tax and interest)

Comparison of EV/EBIT with P/E Ratio

Price earnings ratios provide a measure of the expensiveness, or cheapness, of a particular company's shares. As an alternative, EV multiples look at the whole company, incorporating both the equity and the debt. Simplistically, the smaller the EV to the earnings, the cheaper the company is, which could highlight a buying opportunity for investors.

5.3.5 Enterprise Value (EV) to Earnings Before Interest Tax, Depreciation and Amortisation (EBITDA)

This ratio, once again, is used as a measure of the profitability of a business and also uses the EV as the numerator in the ratio.

EBITDA is essentially net income with interest, taxes, depreciation, and amortisation reversed and added back to become a variant of net income. EBITDA has been used by some in the financial world to compare profitability between companies because it eliminates the effects of financing and accounting decisions. However, it must be clearly understood that this is a non-GAAP measure. The criticism that is often made about the value is that it allows too much discretion as to what is (and is not) included in the calculation. This also means that companies often change the items included in their EBITDA calculation from one reporting period to the next.

EBITDA does not represent cash earnings: it may be a useful metric to evaluate profitability, but not cash flow. EBITDA also leaves out the cash required to fund working capital and the replacement of old equipment, which can be significant.

EBITDA = Revenue less expenses (excluding tax, interest, depreciation and amortisation)

5.3.6   Net Dividend Yield

The net dividend yield expresses the total dividends per share paid out over the last year as a percentage of the current share price.

A high yield may indicate that the share price is relatively low in comparison with the return it offers. This suggests that the market does not have confidence that the dividends paid in the past will continue to be paid in the future. Conversely, a low dividend yield indicates high market confidence in the company's ability to increase dividends.

5.3.7   Net Dividend Cover

The dividend cover can be used to assess how well a company covered its dividend payout with the profits it made. In other words, how easy was it for the company to pay these dividends?

Dividend cover compares the earnings of the company (net income in relation to the year's activity) with the dividends paid in the year. This also reveals the proportion of profits that were reinvested in the company. If dividend cover was two times, then half of the profits are paid out to shareholders and half are retained.

A dividend cover of less than one is known as an **uncovered dividend**, meaning the year's profits were not enough to cover the dividend.

5.4   Calculating Investors' Ratios

Learning Objective

7.5.4   Be able to calculate the following investors' ratios: earnings per share; price earnings ratio (both historic and prospective); net dividend yield; net dividend cover

5.4.1   Earnings Per Share (EPS)

To calculate the EPS, one simply divides the value of net income or earnings (which is the net income for the financial year) by the number of ordinary shares in issue.

$$\text{EPS} = \frac{\text{Net income for the financial year} - \text{Dividends on preferred shares}}{\text{Number of ordinary shares in issue}}$$

Note that if the company has preference shares in issue, the earnings are after the preference shareholders' dividend but before the ordinary shareholders' dividend. For a group of companies preparing **consolidated accounts**, the earning line will also be after any **minority interests**. Minority interests are the profits that belong to shareholders of any subsidiary companies that are not shareholders in the holding company.

The following illustration for an imaginary company, XYZ plc, shows how one can calculate the earnings per share.

Illustration ──

XYZ plc has net income or earnings of £898,000 for its most recent fiscal year and, at the time of preparing the EPS estimate, has five million outstanding ordinary shares.

The EPS is £898,000 / 5,000,000 shares = 18p per share.

5.4.2   Diluted Earnings Per Share (EPS)

The following illustration for the same imaginary company shows how one can calculate the diluted EPS.

Illustration ──

The debt financing of XYZ plc at the year-end 2013 includes £250,000 of 10% convertible loan stock, which was issued on 30 June 2013. The terms of conversion for every £100 nominal value of loan stock as of the following conversion dates are as follows:

*   31 December 2013 – conversion factor is 120.
*   31 December 2014 – conversion factor is 115.
*   31 December 2015 – conversion factor is 110.

Since the £250,000 of convertible loan stock is still in issue at year end 2013, the convertible stockholders have not taken the option of converting at a conversion factor of 120 shares.

XYZ plc Fully Diluted EPS Calculation			
Basic earnings as of 31 December 2013			
Dilution event	If convertible exercised interest saved for one half year	Period	898,000
		6/12	
	£250,000 @ 10%	12,500	
	Tax at 30%	−3,750	
			8,750
Earnings following dilution event			906,750

The best option that remains for them is to convert in 2014, at a rate of 115 shares. So, assuming the most dilutive possibility as required by IAS 33 rule, the maximum number of new ordinary shares that would be issued is [250,000 / 100] x 115 = 287,500 shares.

Number of shares pre-dilution		Period	5,000,000
	Conversion of 250,000 at a rate of 115 / 100	6/12	
		143,750	143,750
Fully diluted ordinary shares			5,143,750

The dilution is only assumed to occur for half a year, since the convertibles were only issued six months into 2013. In subsequent years, the dilution calculation will assume dilution for the whole year.

As shown above, pre-dilution, the EPS is £898,000 / 5,000,000 shares = 18p per share; fully diluted the EPS is £906,750 / 5,143,750 shares = 17.6p.

5.4.3 P/E Ratio

The **price/earnings ratio**, or **P/E**, is calculated by dividing the current market price of the ordinary shares by the EPS.

$$\text{P/E ratio} = \frac{\text{Current market price of ordinary shares}}{\text{Earnings per share}}$$

Historic P/E ratios use the last published EPS from the financial statements, whereas prospective P/E ratios use forecasts of the next EPS that the company is likely to deliver.

Illustration ————————————————————————————————————

Continuing with the illustration from above of XYZ plc, if the ordinary shares are currently trading at £1.60 each, and there is a forecast EPS for the next fiscal year for XYZ plc of 17p, the P/E ratios for the company will be as follows:

Historic P/E = 160 / 18 = 8.89 (this is based on the pre-diluted EPS of 18p.)
Prospective P/E = 160 / 17 = 9.41 (this is based on the forecast EPS of 17p.)

5.4.4 Net Dividend Yield

To calculate net dividend yield, simply divide the net dividend per share by the current share price and multiply it by 100.

$$\text{Net dividend yield} = \frac{\text{Net dividend}}{\text{Current share price}} \times 100$$

For XYZ plc, let us assume that the board of directors decides to distribute £400,000 to shareholders in the form of a dividend and retain the rest of net income on its balance sheet. The net dividend per share will be £400,000 divided by five million shares = 8p.

The net dividend yield will be:

$$\text{Net dividend yield} = 8 / 160 \times 100 = 5\%$$

5.4.5 Dividend Cover

To calculate the dividend cover for XYZ plc, take the company's EPS and divide it by the net dividends per share.

$$\text{Dividend cover} = \frac{\text{EPS}}{\text{Net dividends per share}}$$

Using the figures from above, the dividend cover for XYZ plc will be 18 / 8 = 2.25 times.

Chapter Eight
Risk and Reward

This syllabus area will provide approximately 9 of the 100 examination questions

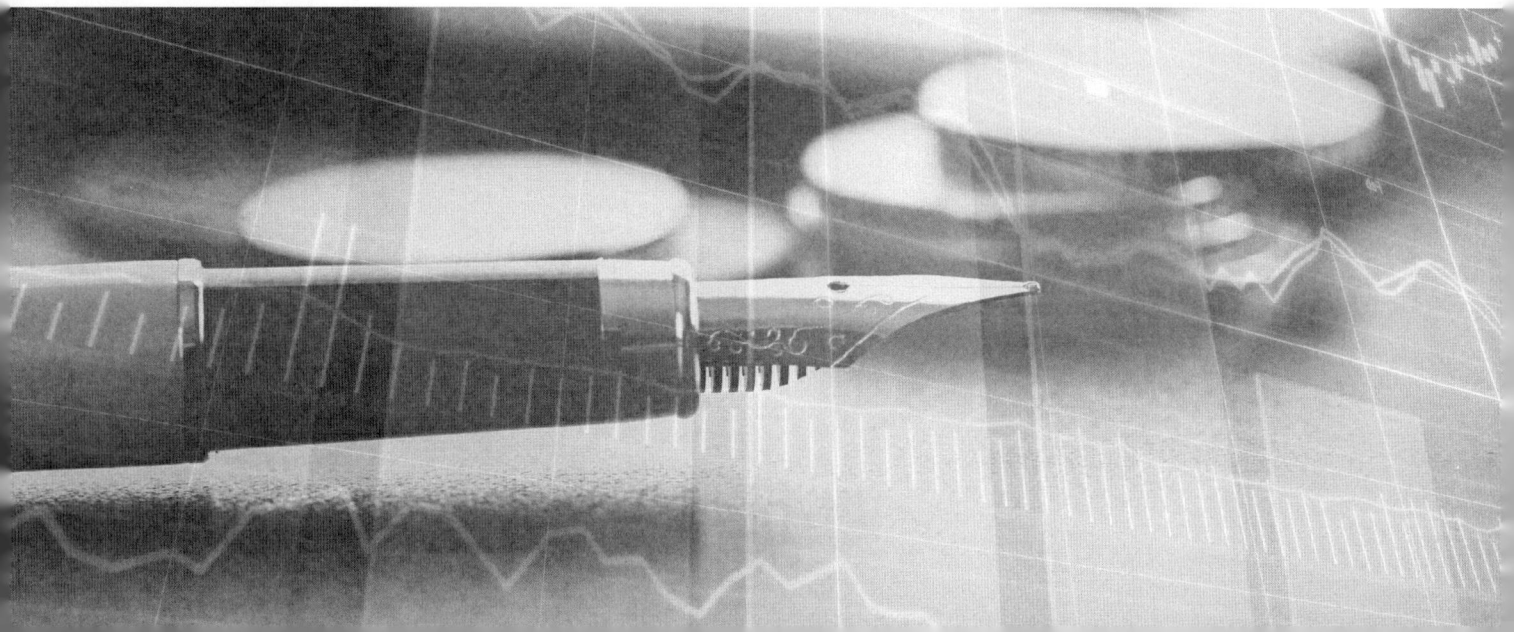

8

1. Investment Management

1.1 Risk and Reward

In general terms, the decisions which need to be made with respect to investment management are very much concerned with a balancing (or, as it is sometimes expressed, a trade-off) between the likely rewards or returns from the chosen investments and the risks associated with them and their manner of combination in a portfolio.

Let us consider the situation of a fund manager who is trying to put together an overall assessment of the business environment, based upon an expected returns analysis regarding the future growth of the economy. In the illustration below, which is consistent with the recent financial environment, the economic outlook is quite uncertain.

The table shows three different scenarios with their association probabilities and expected returns (ERs). The first row of the table considers that the economy will be in a recession with overall contraction. The fund manager gives that a probability of 20% and a return for that scenario of negative 10% for the assets under consideration. The second scenario is for a growth rate between just above zero up to 3% per annum (based upon GDP for example) and this is assumed to have a 50% probability with an associated annual return of 8%. The most upbeat scenario is for growth above 3% and the fund manager's assessment is that there is a 30% probability of this and an appealing 15% return for this scenario.

Future Growth of Economy	Probability P	Scenario Return SR	Probability * Scenario Return P*SR	Scenario Variance SV [SR–ER]2	Probability * Scenario Variance SV*P
Contraction < 0%	20%	−10.0%	−2.0%	0.027225	0.005445
> 0% Growth < 3%	50%	8.0%	4.0%	0.000225	0.0001125
Growth > 3%	30%	15.0%	4.5%	0.007225	0.0021675
	100%	Expected Return (ER)	6.5%	$\sigma2$	0.77%
		Standard Deviation $\sqrt{\sigma2}$		σ	8.79%

The overall ER from these scenarios is calculated by taking the probability of each and multiplying that by the SR and summing the results. Under the conditions in the table, the ER is 6.5%.

The manner in which the risks are associated with the different scenarios can be determined by calculating the variance. The variance measures the extent to which returns 'vary' from the average (or expected) return. As can be seen from the right-hand column of the table, the total of each variance can be calculated and, from this, we can derive the standard deviation. The standard deviation is the square root of variance, and is used as a statistical measure of risk that depicts the likely variation from expected return levels.

In essence the cornerstones of investment theory require calculations similar to the above in many instances. First what is the expected return, often based upon a probability study; and, just as important, what is the notion of the risk associated with achieving that return? From the point of view of investment management, the risk reflects the variability or deviation of the likely returns from the expected return and reflects the uncertainty of the likely outcomes.

1.1.1 Types of Risk

Risk arises from the uncertainty of outcomes. Each time an investor decides to purchase a security or invest in an opportunity, the outcome is uncertain in the same way that any future event is. The investor may incur a loss if the opportunity has been miscalculated, or they may not realise, fully or even partially, the expected return.

At the macro-level we may be concerned about the risks of market crashes, terrorist incidents that cause markets to plunge and other critical events. All of these contribute to the potential for profit from investment and speculation and the accompanying uneasiness that we all feel about the possibility of losses or adverse consequences from our investment or speculation activities. This is our general notion of risk.

There are a number of types of risk faced by investors that are difficult to avoid, and the main categories can be identified in overview under the following headings.

Market or Systematic Risk

This is the risk that the overall market in general, or the relevant part of the capital markets for investors wanting exposure to specific sectors, will rise or fall, as economic conditions and other market factors change. This may affect returns over a period of time, or it may have a more immediate impact if an investor buys at the top of the market or sells at the bottom.

Inflation Risk

Inflation will erode returns or purchasing power and even if the investor has taken account of inflation in their analysis the actual and expected inflation may be different from that assumed in calculating expected returns.

Interest Rate Risk

Changes in interest rates will affect prices; this is possibly a sub-category of market risk.

In addition, there are a number of risks, specific to particular companies or sectors, which can be avoided by diversification or by ignoring an investment altogether.

Exchange Rate Risk

Any investor who purchases securities which are denominated in a foreign currency may suffer (or benefit) from changes in the exchange rates between the home or base currency or the other currency. In addition one has to consider the risk that one's base or home currency may fall against other currencies, thereby diminishing one's purchasing power for global assets.

Default Risk

An investor may find that a company from which s/he has purchased a security could become insolvent due to a harsh operating environment, high levels of borrowing, poor management and other financial miscalculations. Fixed-income investors, who purchase the bonds of companies, have some access to alerts of possible credit defaults through the credit ratings agencies such as Moody's.

Liquidity Risk

The assumption that is usually made is that large capital markets such as the LSE provide liquidity for investors to sell a security easily with a narrow spread between the ask and the bid prices. During stressful periods this liquidity can diminish and it can become much harder to sell a security readily.

1.1.2 Quantifying Risk

How can we quantify the risk and expected return of any investment?

In order to assess the risk and expected returns from particular opportunities, an investor needs to conduct an analysis of the forecasts for the economy and the forecasts for particular companies and/or sectors and undertake a risk analysis of the possible outcomes, and their likelihood, which could adversely affect these forecasts. This can be summarised as both forward- and backward-looking:

- **Forward-looking** forecasts and probabilities assess the likelihood of each possible state of the world occurring and estimate the returns and values arising given that particular outcome.
- **Backward-looking** analyses tend to study historically observed returns and associated frequencies on the assumption that this past data will be representative of the future.

In both cases, assessing the likelihood or probability of certain outcomes becomes the central task and it is necessary to consider the probability of returns and their associated risks from a broad perspective.

Risk and reward are important aspects of investment decisions. Risk and potential reward are generally positively correlated: investments with a higher potential return generally carry a higher risk of loss. High-risk investments generally have potential for a higher reward, plus a greater possibility of loss. Low-risk investments generally have a lower reward, with a lower possibility of loss.

1.2 Equities

Learning Objective

8.1.1 Understand the risk and reward of investment in equities: risk profile; effect of longer term; can offer income and capital appreciation

Equities are shares in companies that give the investor an ownership stake in the company, alongside the attraction of limited liability. If the issuing company collapses, the shareholders' loss is simply the amount paid for the shares. As a part-owner of the company, the investor has the opportunity to share in the company's profits and vote at general meetings. Indeed, most investors are attracted to equities in the hope that the value of the shares increases (**capital appreciation**), and this may be combined with income in the form of regular, and perhaps increasing, **dividends**.

Risk Profile for Equities

Equity investments are generally considered to be risky, relative to other investments, such as bonds and money market instruments. Medium levels of risk are attached to larger, well-established company shares, and high levels of risk attached to smaller company shares and start-up company shares. However, equity investments offer the potential to deliver high returns if held long-term.

Equity Risk Premium

For equity investors there is an equity risk premium, which effectively is a higher rate of return that is required to entice investors to take on the risk of owning shares or equity, as opposed to holding a secured asset such as a bond. If one is seeking the most secure form of investment this will usually be available in the form of a government bond or short-term instrument. The risk-free rate is the rate on government bonds and short-term debts, because of the low chance that the government will default on its loans. An investment in stocks or equities has far more risk associated with it, as it is a non-secured asset and companies can suffer from adverse business conditions or go bankrupt, in which case shareholders often receive no residual value.

As an example, if the total return on a stock is 10% over a given period and the risk-free rate over the same period is 4%, the equity-risk premium is 6%.

1.3 Money Market Instruments

Learning Objective

8.1.2 Understand the risk and reward of investment in money market instruments: risk profile; use as short-term investment

For investment horizons that are very short (eg, the next six months rather than the next 20 years), there is the potential for investors to keep their funds in cash and place them on interest-earning deposit, or to invest in short-term money market instruments, like T-bills. These investments are low-risk, relatively secure and deliver income, but provide little scope for capital growth. For investors that do not want their money tied up for long periods, however, the predictable value and liquidity of these short-term investments is important.

Prices of money market instruments fluctuate and can, in moments of financial crisis, become quite erratic. Many investors will want to hold the shortest-term instruments such as T-bills during periods when the money markets are not functioning **normally**. During the financial crisis, which became especially acute in September and October of 2008, many institutions wanted to replace all of their other money market holdings with the shortest-duration T-bills. This can have the perverse consequence, on extreme occasions, of making such instruments, which are priced on a discount basis, yield a negative return or at a rate which is far below that which would normally be expected. The desire to move into such short-term paper during moments of crisis is referred to as a **flight to safety**.

While some institutional investors, such as pension funds, seek out longer-dated maturities in fixed income markets, there are many that prefer shorter and medium-term assets.

There is often a trade off and calculation to be made between the value of a long-term income stream from such instruments versus the greater volatility in the prevailing prices of longer-dated paper. Duration of bond portfolios is a special issue for pension funds, for example, which have to match their assets and liabilities.

1.4 Debt Instruments

Learning Objective

8.1.3 Understand the risk/reward of investments in debt (fixed interest, floating rate and index linked): compared to equities; effect of holding to maturity; can combine low risk and certain return; can provide a fixed income; inflation risk; interest rate risk; default risk

Bonds are fixed-interest loan instruments, predominantly issued by companies, governments, government agencies and supranationals like the World Bank, providing the issuer with debt finance. Their attractiveness to investors is driven by the fixed income that they offer from regular, pre-determined coupons, combined with the relative certainty of the principal amount to be repaid at redemption.

The coupons can be fixed (at a percentage of nominal value), they can float depending upon a published interest rate such as the LIBOR, or they can be tied to inflation by being index-linked (eg, to the CPI). The principal amount paid at maturity is generally the par or nominal value, although with index-linked bonds it will be uplifted for inflation. They are generally less risky than equities, but offer less potential for substantial returns. Indeed, for highly rated bonds like gilts when the risk of default is low, investors can be virtually certain of the yield that their investment will deliver, as long as they hold their bonds to maturity. If the bonds are sold before they reach maturity, however, there is a danger that their market value may be below their nominal value, bringing about a capital loss and the potential to impact the investor's yield adversely.

As explained in Section 1.1.1, **interest rate risk** is the risk that an interest rate movement brings about an adverse movement in the value of an investment. It is particularly acute when the investment is a fixed-interest bond and the interest rate rises. Because of the inverse relationship between bonds and interest rates, the value of the bond will fall. Interest rate risk is largely removed if the bond is floating rate, since the coupon will be reset in line with the higher market interest rate.

Inflation risk arises when inflation is more substantial than the investor expected, and the value of the investments held may fall. Generally, bonds will suffer because the fixed cash payments that they deliver are less valuable. Floating rate bonds will suffer less because the higher inflation will bring about a higher interest rate, but the real value of the principal at redemption will fall. Index-linked bonds will not suffer. The coupon and the principal are linked to a measure of inflation (increases in the RPI) so the investor will not lose out.

In contrast to debt instruments, equities and property cope reasonably well with unexpected inflation. Companies are able to increase their prices and deliver larger dividends, and the property market as a whole tends to reflect the inflationary increases.

Investors in bonds face **default risk**. This is the risk of the issuer defaulting on their payment obligations. The probability of default (often referred to as **credit risk**) is measured by various independent credit rating agencies; mainly Standard & Poor's (S&P), Moody's and Fitch Rating Services. These rating agencies divide issuers into two distinct classes: **investment grade** (alternatively referred to as **prime**) and **sub-investment grade** (alternatively referred to as **speculative**, **non-prime** or **junk**).

The three rating agencies apply similar criteria to assess whether the issuer will be able to service the required payments on the debt. The bonds are then categorised according to their reliability, payment history and current financial situation. As seen in Chapter 1, Section 4.4, **Triple A** is the best and the next best is **double A** (although the rating agencies can have lesser notches such as pluses and minuses).

Very few organisations, except some western governments and supranational agencies, have triple A ratings, but most large companies boast an investment grade rating. Issues of bonds categorised as sub-investment grade are alternatively known as **junk bonds** because of the high levels of credit risk.

If the rating agencies downgrade the issuer of a bond, potential investors will look to compensate for the increased risk by demanding a greater yield on the issuer's bonds. This will inevitably result in a lower price for the bond. Some issuers of bonds utilise **credit enhancements** to enable their bonds to be rated more highly by the credit rating agencies. Examples of credit enhancements are bonds guaranteed by another group company, or bonds with a fixed charge over particular assets.

1.5   Overseas Equities and Bonds

Learning Objective

8.1.4   Understand risk profile of investment in overseas shares and debt: country risk; exchange rate risk

To lessen the risk that a particular company, or issuer of a bond, delivers poor returns due to problems in the domestic economy, investors can invest in overseas companies' equities, or overseas bond issues. Like domestic equities and bonds, these overseas investments may offer the possibilities of income and capital appreciation.

However, the investor may be less knowledgeable about the overseas company/issuer and there may be particular idiosyncrasies in some overseas markets; for example, local custodians may not be required to give the holder access to corporate actions.

Currency (or Exchange Rate) Risk

These overseas investments are also higher-risk than their domestic equivalents because of the additional risk that is created by the possibility of exchange rates moving against the investor. For investments that are denominated in a currency other than sterling, an adverse exchange rate movement will create an adverse movement in the value of the investment. Clearly, this is particularly relevant for overseas investments. It can also be problematic if the investment is in a UK company that has substantial overseas business interests.

1.6   Types of Risk

Learning Objective

8.1.5   Understand the risks facing the investor: specific/unsystematic; market/systematic

Risk can be categorised in a number of different ways, but the overriding rule for investment is that the potential for spectacular return can only arise if the investor takes a large amount of risk: the **risk-return relationship**.

Market (or Systematic) Risk

As seen in Section 1.1.1, this is the risk that the whole market moves in a particular direction. It is typically applied to equities and brought about by economic and political factors. It cannot be diversified away. For example, political crises or general recessions will tend to bring about falls in the market value of all shares, although they may affect different company shares to different degrees.

Specific (or Unsystematic) Risk

This is the risk that something adverse impacts the value of a particular investment, but the adverse impact is not market-wide. An obvious example is a company's management making some sort of error – perhaps producing a defective product with resultant impact on profits and customer goodwill. Specific risk can be diversified away by holding many investments.

1.7   Correlation and Diversification

Learning Objective

8.1.6   Understand how to optimise the risk/reward relationship through the use of: correlation; diversification; use of different asset classes

Investors generally choose to avoid unnecessary risk in their portfolios by holding appropriate proportions of each class of investment. The more conservative investor will hold a greater proportion of low-risk bonds and money market instruments. These lower-risk investments are likely to give rise to lower, but more predictable, returns. The more adventurous investor will hold a greater proportion of medium- and high-risk equity investments, because higher risk means greater potential for higher returns. Essentially, the choice of investments is driven by the investor's attitude to risk and the fact that there is a trade-off between risk and return.

However, diversification can remove some of the general investment risk without having to remove all high-risk investments from a portfolio. This is done by combining securities that are not perfectly positively correlated into a portfolio, which will remove some of the unsystematic risk in that portfolio. Unsystematic risk affects certain sectors of the market, but not the market as a whole. So, by reducing the concentration in certain sectors (with diversification), the portfolio risk will be reduced with the addition of additional uncorrelated securities.

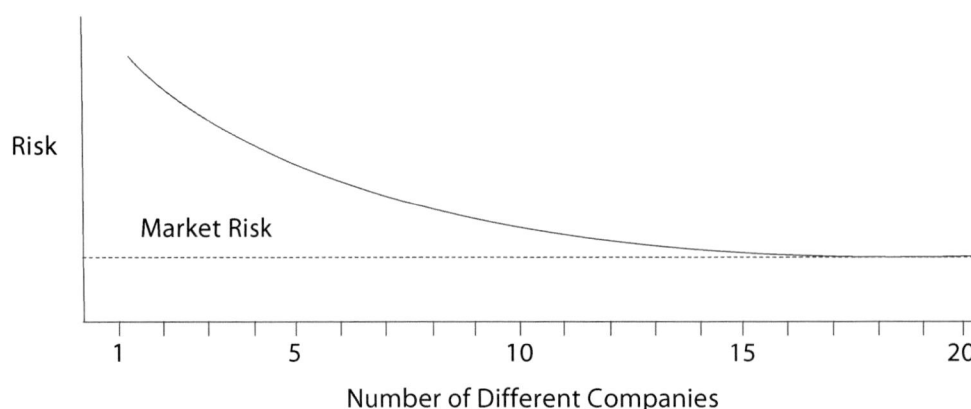

For example, an investor's portfolio might contain high-risk equity investments but as the portfolio diversifies, ie, as the investor includes a wider range of companies' shares, risk diminishes, because unexpected losses made on one investment are offset by unexpected gains on another.

1.7.1   Correlation

From an investment perspective the statistical notion of correlation is fundamental to portfolio theory. The very simplest idea is that, if one is seeking diversification in the holdings of a portfolio, one would like to have, say, two assets where there is a low degree of association between the movements in price and returns of each asset. The degree of association can also be expressed in terms of the extent to which directional changes in each asset's returns, or their co-movement, are related.

If assets A and B have a tendency to react to the same kinds of business conditions in a very simple and predictable manner they could be said to be **strongly correlated**. Let us assume that a certain kind of regular release of economic data (for example the monthly CPI data) is announced and company A's shares move up by 3% and company B's shares move up by 2.5% when the data is below expectations, and that the inverse pattern of price movement is seen when the data is above expectations. In such a case there is a strong correlation between the movements (or changes) in the performance returns of A and B and this is expressed as strong positive correlation.

1.7.2   Diversification

Diversification benefits are maximised by holding investments with uncorrelated returns (when the returns do not tend to move in the same direction and to the same degree). It is not necessary for the investments to be wholly negatively correlated, as combinations of investments that are positively correlated do still provide diversification benefits. It is only a combination of investments that are perfectly positively correlated that will offer no diversification benefits.

However, diversification cannot remove all of the risk. There are certain things, such as economic news, that tend to impact the whole market. The risk that can be removed is known as the specific or unsystematic risk, and the risk that cannot be diversified away is the market or systematic risk.

Diversification by Asset Class

This is achieved by holding a combination of different kinds of asset within a portfolio, possibly spread across cash, fixed-interest securities, equity investments, property-based investments, and other assets.

Cash can be useful as an emergency fund or for instantly accessible money. At times when the future for interest rates is uncertain, it may be wise to hold some cash in variable rate deposits, in the hope of a rate rise and some in fixed rate deposits as a hedge against a possible fall in the rate.

Fixed-interest securities, such as government bonds, National Savings & Investment (NS&I) certificates or guaranteed income bonds, give a secure income and known redemption value at a fixed future date.

Equities can be used to produce a potentially increasing dividend income and capital growth. For example, a share yielding 3% income plus capital growth of 6% gives an overall return of 9% compared with a building society deposit account yielding, say, 4%.

Collective investments such as unit trusts, investment trusts or unit-linked insurance products spread the risk still further. In this case the client is participating in a pool of shares. S/he may choose a fund investing in a number of different economies, thereby reducing risk still further. Pooled investments may be a sensible method of obtaining exposure to some of the less sophisticated world markets where there is a high risk in holding one company's shares.

The use of **property**, whether residential or commercial and other types of assets such as antiques, coins or stamps might help to spread risk further.

1.8   Hedging

Learning Objective

8.1.8   Know the role of hedging in the management of investment risk and how to achieve it: futures; options; CFDs

The risks that are inevitable when investing in shares, bonds and money market instruments can be largely removed by entering into **hedging**. Unfortunately, the hedging strategies will have a cost that inevitably impacts investment performance.

Hedging is the attempt to reduce risk, usually achieved by using derivatives, for example, options, futures and forwards. The objective is to buy or sell derivatives that reduce the exposure to market fluctuations that would take place in the portfolio. This is done by taking the opposite position of what is in the portfolio with the derivative. For example, buying put options (the right to sell) on investments held in the portfolio will enable the investor to remove the risk of a fall in value. However, the investor will have to pay a premium to buy the options.

Buying put options on investments held will enable the investor to remove the risk of a fall in value, but the investor will have to pay a premium to buy the options.

Futures, such as stock index futures, can be used to hedge against equity prices falling – but the future will remove any upside as well as downside.

Forwards, such as currency forwards, can be used to eliminate exchange rate risk – but, like futures, the upside potential will be lost in order to hedge against the downside risk.

1.8.1   Hedging with Futures Contracts

One of the most commonly used techniques for hedging a portfolio is through selling futures contracts to control the level of exposure that one has from ownership of equities. For example, a UK-based pension fund which has a large exposure to large-capitalisation equities traded on the LSE could use the FTSE 100 futures contract as a hedging instrument.

Calculating the number of futures contracts to sell for hedging purposes can be a formidable challenge. The simplest case is when the cash portfolio has similar characteristics to an available futures contract such as the FTSE 100. In such a case one simply divides the cash value of the portfolio by the nominal size of the futures contract and then sells that number of contracts. If the extent to which the cash portfolio moves in relation to the benchmark index, which is known as the portfolio's beta, can be measured with some precision, then the number of contracts sold needs to be pro-rated by the ratio between the portfolio's beta and the beta of the index which, since it is the benchmark reference, is given a beta value of one.

The use of futures has the advantages of lower cost, greater efficiency and less portfolio disruption. The shortcomings of selling futures contracts are as follows.

The exact risk characteristics, ie, the beta value of the portfolio, may not be emulated by the performance of any index or instrument which is available as a futures contract. For example, a portfolio which has a combination of small-capitalisation stocks and emerging market exchange-traded funds will be difficult to hedge by selling a broad-based futures contract on, say, the FTSE 100 index or the S&P 500.

Also, the key issue is one of knowing when to enter the futures hedge trade and when to exit the trade. If the short sale of an index future is not settled before the market has completed a correction and is starting to rise again, the continued ownership of a short position in an index futures position will offset the gains being made in the cash portfolio.

1.8.2 Hedging with Options

An alternative way of implementing a hedge strategy for a fund manager is to continue to hold the cash instruments, such as individual equities in the portfolio, but purchase put options on either those individual positions or on an index where the performance of an index closely matches the overall risk characteristics of the portfolio. This combination of being long a stock or index and long a put on that same stock or index provides a protection from losses which is the primary objective of the hedging exercise.

Being long a put option is thus motivated by a view that an asset's price will fall; it is a hedging move or can be used as an outright bearish strategy, which will enable the option buyer to benefit should the price of the underlying instrument or equity fall.

Example – Hedging with a Put Option

Assume that in December an investor holds 1,000 shares in XYZ plc and the current price is £1.10 or 110p and s/he has a bearish view of the price development in the intermediate term – let us assume six months forward in June. The investor can buy put options in XYZ plc with a strike of 110p, an expiry of June and a premium of 6p. This means that they have the right (but not the obligation) to sell the XYZ shares for 110p in June.

Model of Option Payoffs and Profits			Action	Buy	Put
Exercise Price	110.00	Premium Paid	6.00	Strategy	Long

Option Payoffs and Profits

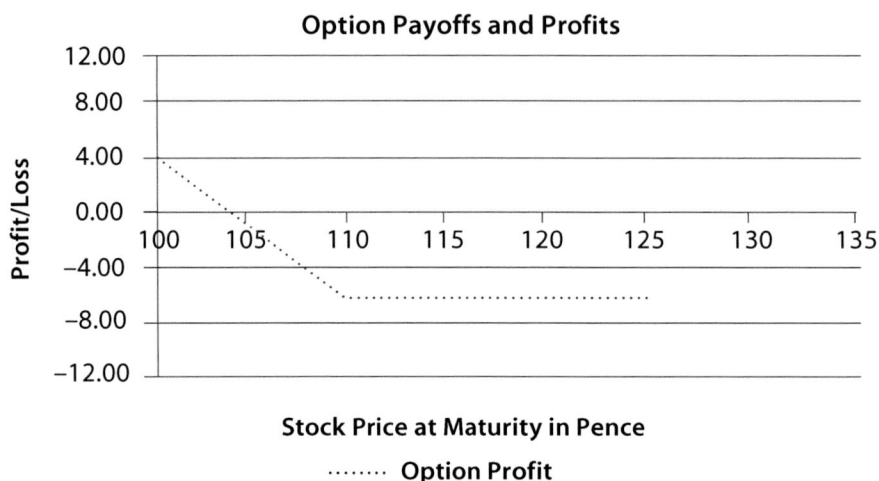

Stock Price at Maturity in Pence

········ Option Profit

Stock	95	100	105	110	115	120	125	130	135
Intrinsic Value	15.00	10.00	5.00	0.00	0.00	0.00	0.00	0.00	0.00
Profit/Loss	9.00	4.00	−1.00	−6.00	−6.00	−6.00	−6.00	−6.00	−6.00

The breakeven point for this option is calculated by deducting the premium from the exercise price, eg, 110p – 6p = 104p. The premium needs to be recovered before any profit or hedge protection is made.

However, the maximum profit will occur if the share price falls to zero, meaning that the shares can (theoretically) be bought for nothing and sold for 110p. With the premium of 6p deducted, the maximum profit will be 104p, the same as the breakeven point.

In a hedging exercise it must obviously be recalled that the profit seen from this option payoff diagram is only going to cover the losses which are incurred from holding the underlying shares of XYZ plc. But the option does provide the portfolio manager with protection all the way down to the worst case scenario of the shares going to zero.

The risks taken by the purchaser of a put option are limited to the premium paid and this is illustrated in the diagram as the extended horizontal line showing a return of minus six pence per share.

The motivation behind buying a put option will be to protect against a fall in the share price. The holder of a put obtains the right, but not the obligation, to sell at a fixed price. The value of this right will become increasingly valuable as the asset price falls. The greatest profit that will arise from buying a put will be achieved if the asset price falls to zero.

The purchase of put options is an added expense for a fund manager and, in the nature of all options contracts, the premium paid for the put option is known as a **wasting asset** as it is subject to decay as the expiration of the option period approaches. If a fund manager wishes to continue to protect a portfolio with put options, which have definite maturity dates, then a process of **rolling over** the options contracts can be employed. This will further add to the costs, and the least advantageous position from the point of view of the overall returns to the fund manager is the situation when portfolio insurance has been purchased through extended use of put options, the cash value of the portfolio continues to rise as the insurance is not required, and the cost of the premiums has to be charged against the earnings of the cash portfolio.

1.8.3   Hedging with Contracts for Differences (CFDs)

Contracts for differences (CFDs) were originally developed in the early 1990s and were initially used by institutional investors to hedge their exposure to stocks on the LSE in a cost-effective way.

CFDs are different from traditional cash-traded instruments (such as equities, bonds, commodities and currencies) in that they do not confer ownership of the underlying asset. Investors can take positions on the price of a great number of different instruments.

Along with futures and options, CFDs come under the FCA's definition of **derivatives**. It has been estimated that CFD trading in the UK now accounts for approximately 50% of all London equity trading.

The price of the CFD tracks the price of the underlying asset, and so the holder of a CFD benefits, or loses, from the price movement in the stock, bond, currency, commodity or index. But the CFD holder does not take ownership of the underlying asset.

CFDs are margin-traded, meaning that the investor does not have to deposit the full value of the underlying asset with the CFD provider. Thus, an investor or fund manager can use CFDs to buy exposure to market movements, using only a fraction of the capital they would require in the cash market. The investor then has a geared position relative to the capital deposited.

Since CFDs allow an investor to benefit from downward movements in an equity position or index, they are useful for hedging purposes. It enables the fund manager to retain a position in the cash instrument but have an equivalent derivative position which is equivalent to that of **short selling** the stock. This flexibility, and the possibility of margin trading, means that CFDs can be used flexibly either for hedging or speculation.

The costs of CFDs comprise a cost built into the spread of the CFD price, together with a funding charge. CFDs have the advantage that there is no stamp duty or SDRT to pay, although the holder will be liable to capital gains tax (CGT) on gains.

CFD contracts are subject to a daily financing charge, usually applied at a previously agreed rate linked to LIBOR. The parties to a CFD pay to finance long positions and may receive funding on short positions in lieu of deferring sale proceeds. The contracts are settled for the cash differential between the price of the opening and closing trades.

CFDs are subject to a commission charge on equities that is a percentage of the size of the position for each trade. Alternatively, an investor can opt to trade with a market maker, forgoing commissions at the expense of a larger bid/offer spread on the instrument.

Investors in CFDs are required to maintain a certain amount of margin as defined by the brokerage – usually ranging from 1% to 30%. One advantage to investors of not having to put up as collateral the full notional value of the CFD is that a given quantity of capital can control a larger position, amplifying the potential for profit or loss. On the other hand, a leveraged position in a volatile CFD can expose the buyer to a margin call in a downturn, which often leads to losing a substantial part of the assets.

As with many leveraged products, maximum exposure is not limited to the initial investment; it is possible to lose more than one put in.

Example

Suppose you wish to hedge 1,000 shares of GlaxoSmithKline (GSK) which are held in a portfolio and are currently trading at £12 each. To achieve this hedge with CFDs you could sell 1,000 shares locking in the current price, and then if the price declines the returns from the CFD position will be similar to those available if you had a short position in the stock.

In a normal non-margin broker account you need to have an initial cash deposit or balance of £12,000. Using CFDs, trading on a 5% margin, you will only need an initial deposit of £600. As the price decreases the returns from the CFD will compensate for the loss incurred on the actual long holding of the stock.

The easiest way to show the use of leverage in this case is to consider what will happen if the price declines to £10 per share:

Sell: 1,000 at £12 = £600 (5% deposit) + receive a credit to your account for £11,500 (95%)

Buy: 1,000 at £10 = £500 (5% deposit) + incur borrowing costs of £9,500 (95% in borrowed funds)

Profit = £2,100 which as a percentage of the margin amount of £600 is 350%

The fund manager has achieved the purpose of the hedge which was to protect the account from the loss of £2,000 resulting from the loss of £2 per share on the original 1,000 shares and through taking advantage of leverage has been able to achieve this with only a £600 outlay. Of course, if the shares had not fallen as expected, the investor would be subject to capital losses which would also be considerably magnified in relation to the initial margin amount used.

CFDs allow a trader to go short or long on any position using margin. There are always two types of margin with a CFD trade:

- **Initial margin** – normally between 5% and 30% for shares/stocks and 1% for indices and foreign exchange. In the case of GSK we saw that this would be 5% of the contract price.

- **Variable margin** – the CFD will be marked to the market at currently prevailing prices and if the position has moved beyond the amount taken as initial margin – eg, the position has moved adversely – the additional margin required to support the borrowing at 95% for GSK will have to be deposited or available in the current balance of the customer's cash account.

2.   Institutional Investment Advice

2.1   Institutional Client Profiles

Learning Objective

8.2.1   Know the differences between institutional client profiles including: pension funds; life and general insurance funds; hedge funds; regulated mutual funds; banks

---

2.1.1   Institutional Investors

There are a number of institutional investors, including pension funds, the providers of life assurance, the providers of general insurance and banks.

Pension funds are set up with the aim of providing retirement funds for the beneficiaries. They may be sponsored by an employer, be solely dependent on contributions from the workforce, or a combination of the two. Pension funds tend to be approved by tax authorities (such as HMRC in the UK), and can then accumulate income and capital gains tax-free. The money in the fund is invested by fund managers and, because pension funds have a relatively long investment horizon, they can take risks and have tended to invest heavily in equities.

Pension funds can be divided into two broad classes: those that define the benefits they will pay out (**defined benefit schemes** or **final salary schemes**), and those where the benefit is driven by the contributions made and the investment performance (**defined contribution schemes**).

Life assurance business arises from insurance contracts written by an insurance company on the life of an individual. They mainly comprise:

- **term assurance policies** which, in exchange for a regular premium, only pay out if the individual dies before the end of a set policy term;
- **whole of life policies** which simply pay out on death in exchange for regular premiums;
- **endowment policies** which are term assurance policies with a significant investment element that depends on the performance of the insurance company's fund;
- **single premium life assurance bonds** which are single premium endowments; again they have a significant investment element.

Like pension funds, because of the long-term nature of life assurance business, the funds tend to be willing to invest in higher-risk investments involving a heavy weighting in equity investments. Unlike pension funds, the income and the gains made within life assurance funds are subject to tax.

General insurance is when insurance is written by an insurance company against short-term personal and commercial risks, such as car or household contents insurance. Because of the short-term nature of the liabilities, the funds from the premiums tend to be invested in low-risk, liquid, short-term assets such as money market instruments. Like life assurance funds, general insurance funds are subject to tax on the income and gains within the fund.

If banks hold surplus cash at the end of each business day, they will place the funds on deposit with other banks (in the interbank market) and invest in eligible money market instruments (such as T-bills and CP) – relatively risk-free investments to cover the short-term nature of the banks' liabilities to depositors. An eligible money market instrument means that the BoE will accept it as collateral against loans. As with insurance companies, banks are taxed on income and gains they generate from their investments.

The following table provides a summary of the key distinctions and similarities across the institutional investors:

Institution	Investment horizon	Proportion of equity investments	Proportion of money market investments	Relative risk profile
Pension fund	Long-term	High	Low	High
Life assurance fund	Long-term	High	Low	High
General insurance fund	Short-term	Low	High	Low
Bank	Short-term	Low	High	Low

2.1.2 Regulated Mutual Funds

Diversification of shareholdings reduces risk, but for a private client with a relatively modest amount to invest this would be prohibitively expensive. One way of avoiding the high cost of investing in many different companies is to invest in a pooled fund where a fund manager handles the money of a group of investors. As a result, the portfolio is conveniently and cheaply diversified. There are four major vehicles that enable individuals to diversify collectively with others. They are unit trusts, investment trusts, OEICs and ETFs.

Questions on collective investment vehicles will refer to some schemes as being **regulated** and others as being **unregulated**. This refers to authorisation by the regulator – such as the FCA in the UK. Regulated schemes can be freely marketed; unregulated schemes cannot be **freely marketed**.

Certain schemes are also granted undertaking for collective investment in transferable securities (UCITS) status. UCITS status allows the scheme to be marketed across the EU.

An unauthorised collective investment scheme can still be marketed but with restrictions, eg, only to relatively large customers, more sophisticated investors or those who already hold such an investment.

2.1.3 Hedge Funds

Hedge funds are **unauthorised** investment vehicles that are free to invest in **high-risk** strategies, including highly geared **derivatives** and **arbitrage**, such as going long in some investments and short in others (a **long/short** strategy). Most hedge funds are offshore investments, with the fund domiciled in the most tax-efficient location.

Unlike most of the conventional collective investment vehicles (such as unit trusts, investment trusts, OEICs and ETFs) that are restricted to a long only investment strategy, hedge funds can be more flexible and take substantial short positions.

The term **hedge** fund comes from the fact that the unconventional nature of their investments means they can produce positive returns when the general market is suffering. For example, a long/short strategy will potentially generate positive returns regardless of the general market – it is described as a **market-neutral strategy**.

Because of their unauthorised nature, nothing prevents hedge funds from borrowing money and **gearing up** the returns for their shareholders. Indeed, many hedge funds have substantial amounts of borrowed funds and are highly geared.

Because they are not authorised, they cannot be freely marketed. This, combined with the requirement to invest substantial minimum amounts, means that hedge funds tend to be accessible only to institutional investors and high net worth individuals.

2.2 Active and Passive Investment Management Methodologies

Learning Objective

8.1.7 Know what are active and passive investment management methodologies and the advantages and disadvantages of each

2.2.1 Active Management

Active management (also called active investing) refers to a method of portfolio management where the manager's strategy is designed to outperform the returns available from an investment benchmark index. For example, an active portfolio manager focused on investing in UK equities will be seeking to realise returns superior to those available from a simple method/strategy of buying and holding all of the constituents of the FTSE 100.

It is worth pointing out that purchasing a simple derivative, such as a FTSE 100 futures contract, will not reflect the total returns available to an investor in the actual index, as it will only capture changes in the price level of the index and not dividend income. More complex derivative products can emulate the total returns without requiring an outright purchase of all 100 stocks in the index.

2.2.2 Passive Management

Passive managers are those that do not aspire to create a return in excess of a benchmark index. They often follow exactly the course just outlined and invest in an index fund or derivative that replicates as closely as possible the investment weighting and returns of a selected benchmark index such as the FTSE 100, or if they seek to match the returns of the US market they may invest in an instrument which exactly tracks the total returns of the S&P 500 index.

2.2.3 Management Strategy and the Efficient Markets Hypothesis (EMH)

The efficient markets hypothesis (EMH) is an investment theory stating that it is impossible to beat the market because stock market efficiency causes existing share prices to always incorporate and reflect all relevant information. According to the EMH, this means that stocks always trade at their **fair value** on stock exchanges, making it impossible for investors to either purchase undervalued stocks or sell stocks for inflated prices. As such, it should be impossible to outperform the overall market through expert stock selection, technical analysis or market timing, and the only way an investor can possibly obtain higher returns is by purchasing riskier investments.

Passive fund management is consistent with the idea that markets are efficient and that no mispricing exists. If the EMH is an accurate account of the way that capital markets work, then there is no benefit to be had from active trading. Such trading will simply incur dealing and management costs for no benefit. Investors who do not believe that they can identify active fund managers who they are confident can produce returns above the level of charges for active management will often elect to invest in passive funds or index trackers.

An active manager will try to achieve the desired goal of outperforming a designated benchmark by seeking out market inefficiencies and by purchasing securities that are undervalued, or by short selling securities that are overvalued. Either of these methods may be used alone or in combination. Depending on the goals of the specific investment portfolio, active fund management may also serve to create less volatility (or risk) than the benchmark index. The reduction of risk may be instead of, or in addition to, the goal of creating an investment return greater than the benchmark.

Active portfolio managers can use various strategies to construct their portfolios with a view to superior performance than that available from index tracking. For example, the manager could focus on selecting securities based on research and quantitative analysis focused on measures such as P/E ratios and price earnings growth (PEG) ratios, sector investments that attempt to anticipate long-term macro-economic trends (such as a focus on energy or housing stocks), and purchasing stocks of companies that are temporarily out of favour or selling at a discount to their intrinsic value. Certain actively managed funds will also pursue more specialised strategies such as merger arbitrage, option-writing, and other kinds of statistical arbitrage, involving more exotic securities, such as derivatives and convertible securities.

2.2.4   Performance

The effectiveness of an actively managed investment portfolio will clearly depend on the skill (or good fortune) of the manager and research staff. In reality, the majority of actively managed CISs rarely outperform their index counterparts over an extended period of time, assuming that they are benchmarked correctly. For example, research from the US shows that the Standard & Poor's Index Versus Active (SPIVA) quarterly scorecards demonstrate that only a minority of actively managed mutual funds have gains better than the S&P index benchmark. As the time period for comparison increases, the percentage of actively managed funds whose gains exceed the S&P benchmark declines further.

2.2.5   Advantages of Active Management

The primary attraction of active management is that it allows selection of a variety of investments instead of investing in the market as a whole. Investors may have a variety of reasons for not wanting to simply track an index. Investors may, for example, be sceptical of the EMH, or believe that some market segments are less efficient in creating profits than others. They may also want to reduce volatility by investing in less-risky, high-quality companies, rather than in the market as a whole, even at the cost of slightly lower returns. Conversely, some investors may want to take on additional risk in exchange for the opportunity of obtaining higher-than-market returns. Investments that are not highly correlated to the market are useful as a portfolio diversifier and may reduce overall portfolio volatility.

Some investors may also wish to follow a strategy that avoids or under-weights certain industries compared to the market as a whole, for instance, an employee of a high-technology growth company who receives company stock or stock options as a benefit might prefer not to have additional funds invested in the same industry.

2.2.6   Disadvantages of Active Management

The most obvious disadvantage of active management is that the fund manager may make bad investment choices or follow an unsound theory in managing the portfolio. The fees associated with active management are also higher than those associated with passive management, even if frequent trading is not present. Those who are considering investing in an actively managed fund should evaluate the fund's prospectus carefully.

Active fund management strategies that involve frequent trading generate higher transaction costs which diminish the fund's return. In addition, the short-term capital gains resulting from frequent trades often have an unfavourable income tax impact when such funds are held in a taxable account.

More specialised tracker funds can also be linked to the performance of securities in emerging markets, and specific industry sectors. Increasingly the proliferation of ETFs, allows investors to purchase shares in a fund which trades actively on a major exchange and which provides exposure to certain kinds of securities and where the minimal management fees are incorporated into the actual price of the shares of the ETF. The benefits to an investor purchasing such ETFs is that there is usually a high degree of liquidity, the asset values of the fund constituents as well as the price of the ETF shares are updated on a real-time basis, and the costs for the packaging of the securities is minimal.

When the assortment of assets of an actively managed fund becomes too large, it begins to take on index-like characteristics, because it must invest in an increasingly broad selection of securities which, in the limiting case, will tend to perform exactly in line with the overall market. In such a situation the fund becomes a pseudo-tracker, and an investor in such a fund is paying active management fees when the actual style is effectively passive. This last factor is why some fund managers close their funds to new investors after the fund reaches a certain size, so that they can avoid having to be so broadly diversified as to deviate from their original selection criteria underlying their active strategic focus.

2.2.7 Advantages of Passive Management

To a large extent, the advantages and disadvantages of a passive approach to portfolio management will tend to be the converse of the respective positions with respect to active management that were discussed in Sections 2.2.5 and 2.2.6.

Indeed, the most frequently cited advantage of a passive approach to asset management is that the performance of the fund is not dependent on the manager's ability to make investment choices which, it is contended by the active manager, will outperform the broad market, but which in fact may well prove not to be the case and will lead to a less rewarding performance than simply investing in a tracker fund.

Subscribers to the EMH will tend to favour the use of index trackers if they are seeking out a risk/reward ratio which is in accordance with the overall performance of the market. By investing in a fund which tracks a broad benchmark, such as the S&P 500 index or FTSE 100 index, the investor is only exposed to the systematic risk within the market and can avoid the risks (and potential rewards) of non-systematic risk.

Several research studies have provided evidence that the majority of actively managed large and mid-cap stock funds in the US have failed to outperform their passive index counterparts.

Investors in a passively managed fund, which most commonly takes the form of **index tracking**, in which the portfolio constituents are required to replicate the performance of a broad market index such as the FTSE 100 index, can also avoid incurring the fees associated with active management. A passive fund management strategy can avoid the frequent trading which is more likely under an active management approach, and transaction costs will be lower which, relatively speaking, will enhance the fund's return. Also, a strategy of buy-and-hold, which is typically the outcome of a passive strategy, is far less likely to incur frequent short-term capital gains resulting from the larger focus on short-term trading activities of active management, and to that extent will also be able to avoid the unfavourable income tax impact when such funds are held in a taxable account.

Another significant advantage of a passive management style is the fact that the total expense ratio will be considerably lower than for many actively managed funds, such as hedge funds which operate with fees charged for funds under management and also incentive fees. With regard to unit trusts and mutual funds, it is also the case that index tracker funds will have lower expense ratios and, somewhat ironically, they may not differ in their performance and fund composition to the actively managed funds. This can arise when the asset composition of an actively managed fund becomes so large that it begins to take on index-like characteristics. The largest funds have to invest in an increasingly diverse set of investments instead of those limited to the fund manager's specific asset selection acumen. In such cases, the actively managed fund, while it may not have set out with the intention, becomes, in effect, a closet index tracker. To avoid this situation, some large fund companies close their funds before they reach this point, but there is potential for a conflict of interest between the fund management and the unit-trust holders as closing the fund will result in a loss of income (management fees) for the fund managers.

Passive management has recently become more appealing to a broad range of investors because innovative investment products, introduced in recent years, now allow investors to invest in **sector trackers**. For example, specialised ETFs can be linked to the performance of securities in emerging markets, and specific industry sectors. Increasingly, the proliferation of ETFs allows investors to purchase shares in a fund which trades actively on a major exchange and which provides exposure to certain kinds of securities and where the minimal management fees are incorporated into the actual price of the shares of the ETF.

2.2.8   Disadvantages of Passive Management

Disadvantages of passive management include the fact that performance is always dictated by a benchmark or index, meaning that investors must be satisfied with market returns. In addition, the inherent lack of control dictated by being passive, thereby prevents defensive measures if it appears that a certain class of asset prices, specifically equities, may be heading for turbulent trading conditions and possible capital losses.

The investor in a passively managed fund should only expect to realise similar returns to those that are available from the broad market or sector index upon which the passively managed fund is based. So, while the investor's returns will be **acceptable** from a relative perspective, ie, they will be highly correlated with the broad market return, they may still be **unacceptable** from an absolute perspective in the sense that losses will arise if the broad market sustains such losses.

The main disadvantage of passive management is that it lacks the potential to generate alpha or above market returns. The investor in a passively managed fund forgoes the opportunity to have exposure to a variety of investments which could out-perform a broad benchmark index and which may have other desirable attributes providing diversification and lower correlation elements than simply investing in the market as a whole.

Investors may have a variety of reasons for not wanting to simply track an index. Those opposed to passive management may have serious reservations regarding the validity of the EMH and believe that some market segments are more efficient in creating profits than others. They may also want to reduce volatility by investing in less-risky, high-quality companies rather than in the market as a whole, even at the cost of slightly lower returns. Conversely, some investors may want to take on additional risk in exchange for the opportunity of obtaining higher-than-market returns, and such investors will be willing to seek out higher beta stocks (by definition a broad benchmark-based portfolio should have a beta of approximately one) in exchange for the possibility of above average potential gains (and losses). Investments that are not highly correlated to the market, eg, certain commodities such as gold, are useful as a portfolio diversifier and may reduce overall portfolio volatility.

Some investors may also wish to follow a strategy that avoids or under-weights certain industries compared to the market as a whole, as part of a deliberate diversification strategy. For example, someone employed in the financial services industry whose own compensation is closely tied to company stock or the stock options of his/her employer may prefer not to have any additional funds invested in the same sector.

2.2.9 Active Management with Manager Participation

Many funds do not have either the manager or directors with an equity stake in the fund that the manager is running. Another meaning sometimes given to active management is when the managers/directors have a vested interest in the success of the fund. Private equity is often real active management, since a privately owned company usually has just one owner that makes strategy decisions at the board level.

The advantage to an investor in a fund where the management is personally at risk by holding a stake in the fund under management, is that the manager's interests will be perfectly aligned with the investors' as s/he has what is known as **skin in the game**.

2.2.10 Smart Beta

Beta is a measure of the sensitivity of an investment's movements in relation to the overall market. The market has a beta of precisely one, and an index that tracks the market exactly would also have a beta of one. However, tracking a market capitalisation-weighted index has the inherent disadvantage of going overweight in those stocks that are overvalued, and underweight in those stocks that are undervalued. Smart beta is a potential solution to this.

Smart beta is a term for an investment strategy that does not use the traditional market capitalisation-weighting system, but instead uses alternative weighting systems, for example weighting constituents equally, or based on dividends paid, sales revenues or cash flow generation. Smart beta can be thought of as taking the key advantage of active investment management by introducing the possibility of outperformance, and combining it with the key advantages of passive index tracking by creating a well-diversified portfolio at a lower cost than active management.

2.2.11 Active Bond Strategies

Generally speaking, active strategies are used by those portfolio managers who believe the bond market is not perfectly efficient and therefore is subject to mispricing. If a bond is considered mispriced, then active management strategies can be employed to capitalise upon this perceived pricing anomaly.

Bond switching, or bond swapping, is used by those portfolio managers who believe they can outperform a buy-and-hold passive policy, by actively exchanging bonds perceived to be overpriced for those perceived to be underpriced.

Bond switching takes three forms:

- **Anomaly switching** – this involves moving between two bonds similar in all respects apart from the yield and price on which each trades. This pricing anomaly is exploited by switching away from the more to the less highly priced bond.
- **Policy switching** – when an interest rate cut is expected but not implied by the yield curve, low duration bonds are sold in favour of those with high durations. By pre-empting the rate cut, the holder can subsequently benefit from the greater price volatility of the latter bonds.
- **Inter-market spread switch** – when it is believed that the difference in the yield being offered between corporate bonds and comparable gilts, for example, is excessive given the perceived risk differential between these two markets, an inter-market spread switch will be undertaken from the gilt to the corporate bond market. Conversely, if an event that lowers the risk appetite of bond investors is expected to result in a flight to quality, gilts will be purchased in favour of corporate bonds.

Active management policies are also employed if it is believed the market's view on future interest rate movements, implied by the yield curve, are incorrect or have failed to be anticipated. This is known as market timing.

Riding the yield curve is an active bond strategy that does not involve seeking out price anomalies, but instead takes advantage of an upward-sloping yield curve.

Example

If a portfolio manager has a two-year investment horizon then a bond with a two-year maturity could be purchased and held until redemption. Alternatively, if the yield curve is upward-sloping and the manager expects it to remain upward-sloping without any intervening or anticipated interest rate rises over the next two years, a five-year bond could be purchased, and sold two years later when the bond has a remaining life of three years.

Assuming that the yield curve remains static over this period, the manager would benefit from selling the bond at a higher price than that at which it was purchased as its GRY falls.

2.2.12 Passive Bond Strategies

Passive bond strategies are employed either when the market is believed to be efficient, in which case a buy-and-hold strategy is used, or when a bond portfolio is constructed around meeting a future liability fixed in nominal terms.

Immunisation is a passive management technique employed by those bond portfolio managers with a known future liability to meet. An immunised bond portfolio is one that is insulated from the effect of future interest rate changes. Immunisation can be performed by using either of the following techniques.

- **Cash matching** involves constructing a bond portfolio whose coupon and redemption payment cash flows are synchronised to match those of the liabilities to be met.
- **Duration-based immunisation** involves constructing a bond portfolio with the same initial value as the present value of the liability it is designed to meet and the same duration as this liability. A portfolio that contains bonds that are closely aligned in this way is known as a **bullet portfolio**.

Alternatively, a **barbell strategy** can be adopted. If a bullet portfolio holds bonds with durations as close as possible to ten years to match a liability with ten-year duration, a barbell strategy may be to hold bonds with a durations of five and 15 years. Barbell portfolios necessarily require more frequent rebalancing than bullet portfolios.

Finally, a **ladder portfolio** is one constructed around equal amounts invested in bonds with different durations. So, for a liability with ten-year duration, an appropriate ladder strategy may be to hold equal amounts in bonds with one-year duration, two-year duration and so on right through to 20 years.

3. Market Data

3.1 Inflation and Interest Rate Expectations

Learning Objective

8.3.1 Understand the relationship between inflation and interest rate expectations

A major driver of bond prices is the prevailing interest rate and expectations of interest rates to come. Yields required by bond investors are a reflection of their interest rate expectations, eg, if interest rates are expected to rise, bond prices will fall, to bring the yields up to appropriate levels to reflect the interest rate increases and vice versa. To remain competitive, equities prices will also suffer.

The interest rate itself is heavily impacted by inflationary expectations. Simplistically, if inflation is expected to be at 4% per annum, the interest rate will have to be greater than this in order to provide the investor with any real return. The interest rate might stand at 7% per annum.

If economic news suggests that inflation is likely to increase further, to, say, 6%, then the interest rate will increase too, perhaps up to 9%.

The reverse is true if inflation is expected to fall.

Technically, the interest rate referred to in the preceding paragraphs is the **nominal interest rate**. The nominal rate is the interest rate including inflation. The interest rate excluding inflation is generally referred to as the **real interest rate**.

3.2 Interest Rates and Securities Prices

Learning Objective

8.3.2 Understand how interest rates impact securities pricing

As explained in above, when interest rates rise, or are expected to rise, securities prices tend to fall. Bonds fall in price to bring about a more competitive yield, and equity prices fall to remain competitive with bonds and because companies may now face increased costs on their borrowing, reducing profits. Consumers are also likely to reduce expenditure because of increased costs on their borrowing (such as mortgages) which will adversely impact company sales.

In contrast, when interest rates fall, or are expected to fall, securities prices tend to rise. Bonds rise in price to reduce the yield, in line with the fall in interest rates that is expected. Other investments, such as equities, will also rise in price, since cheaper interest rates will reduce the costs of borrowing for companies and therefore be likely to increase their profits.

4. Regulatory Information and Financial Communications

4.1 Main Sources

Learning Objective

8.2.2 Know the main sources of regulatory information and financial communications within UK equity: PIPs; RNS; SIPs; Bloomberg; Reuters; analyst research; websites: FCA, PRA, LSE, EU (Europa, ESMA)

Companies that have their shares traded on the LSE need to keep market participants posted on any price-sensitive information that may arise. For example, if a company has won a significant, new contract or simply announced its most recent set of results, it needs to inform the market participants in an orderly manner. This is a requirement of the EU's Transparency Directive, and UK-listed companies typically satisfy this by notifying one of the FCA's primary information providers (PIPs).

RISs are also referred to as primary information providers (PIPs). PIPs simply offer a service that receives regulatory information from listed companies, processes that information and disseminates it by circulating it to secondary information providers (SIPs). The SIPs then disseminate the information to the wider financial community, such as stockbrokers and research analysts.

The FCA maintains a list of approved PIPs, but does not specifically recommend any one of them. At the time of writing, the list includes, among others, the LSE's Regulatory News Service (RNS) and PR Newswire Disclose provided by PR Newswire.

The information that reaches the financial community via the PIPs and SIPs is used to inform and update research reports written by research analysts that comment on the likely future movements in the companies' share prices.

Obviously, this is not the only source of information that may impact securities' prices and trading generally. Other websites, such as those of the regulators (the FCA and the Prudential Regulation Authority (PRA)), the LSE and EU sites like Europa and ESMA, will be of interest to financial services firms and investors alike.

Glossary and Abbreviations

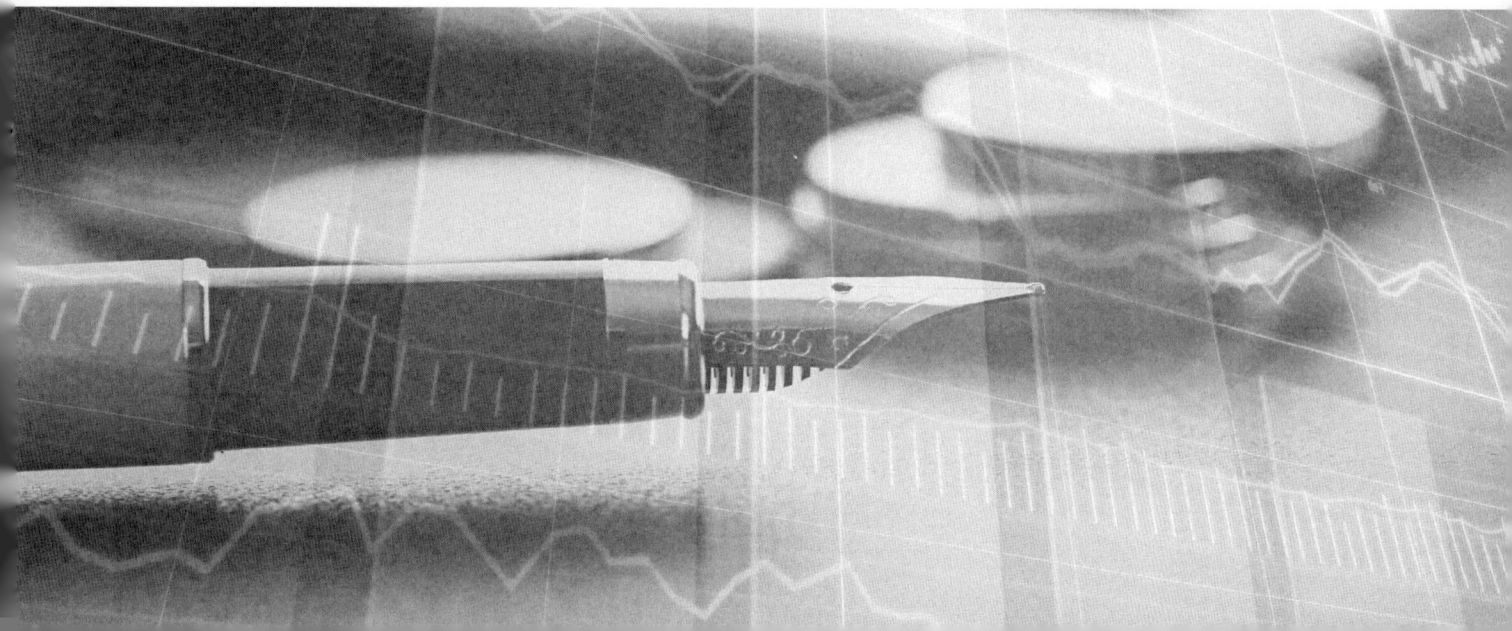

Active Management

A type of investment approach employed to generate returns in excess of an investment benchmark index. Active management is employed to exploit pricing anomalies in those securities markets that are believed to be subject to mispricing by utilising fundamental analysis and/or technical analysis to assist in the forecasting of future events and the timing of purchases and sales of securities.

Alpha

The return from a security or a portfolio in excess of a risk-adjusted benchmark return.

American Depositary Receipt (ADR)

An ADR is a security that represents securities of a non-US company that trades in the US financial markets.

Alternative Investment Market (AIM)

The London Stock Exchange's (LSE) market for smaller UK public limited companies (PLCs). AIM has less demanding admission requirements and places less onerous continuing obligation requirements upon those companies admitted to the market than those applying for a full list on the LSE.

Amortisation

The depreciation charge applied in company accounts against capitalised intangible assets.

Annual General Meeting (AGM)

The annual meeting of directors and ordinary shareholders of a company. All companies are obliged to hold an AGM at which the shareholders receive the company's report and accounts and have the opportunity to vote on the appointment of the company's directors and auditors and the payment of a final dividend recommended by the directors. Also referred to as an Annual General Assembly in some jurisdictions.

Arbitrage

The process of deriving a risk-free profit by simultaneously buying and selling the same asset in two related markets where a pricing anomaly exists.

Asset Allocation

The process of deciding on the division of a portfolio's assets between asset classes and geographically before deciding upon which particular securities to buy.

Auction

System used to issue securities where the successful applicants pay the price that they bid. Examples of its use include the UK Debt Management Office when it issues gilts. Auctions are also used by the London Stock Exchange to establish prices, such as opening and closing options on SETS.

Authorisation

Required status in the UK for firms that want to provide certain financial services – examples include collective investment vehicles that want to advertise their fund to retail investors.

Authorised Corporate Director (ACD)

Fund manager for an open-ended investment company (OEIC).

Bank of England

The UK's central bank.

Base Currency

The currency against which the value of a quoted currency is expressed. The base currency is currency X for the X/Y exchange rate.

Bear Market

A negative move in a securities market, conventionally defined as a 20%+ decline. The duration of the market move is immaterial.

Bearer Securities

Those whose ownership is evidenced by the mere possession of a certificate. Ownership can, therefore, pass from hand to hand without any formalities.

Beneficiaries

The beneficial owners of trust property.

Beta

The relationship between the returns on a stock and returns on the market. Beta is a measure of the systematic risk of a security or a portfolio in comparison to the market as a whole.

Bonus Issue

The free issue of new ordinary shares to a company's ordinary shareholders, in proportion to their existing shareholdings through the conversion, or capitalisation, of the company's reserves. By proportionately reducing the market value of each existing share, a bonus issue makes the shares more marketable. Also known as a capitalisation issue or scrip issue.

Broker-Dealer (UK)

A London Stock Exchange (LSE) member firm that can act in a dual capacity both as a broker acting on behalf of clients and as a dealer dealing in securities on their own account.

Bull Market

A rising securities market. The duration of the market move is immaterial.

Central Bank

Central banks typically have responsibility for setting a country's or a region's short-term interest rate, controlling the money supply, acting as banker and lender of last resort to the banking system and managing the national debt.

Circuit Breaker

An automated suspension of trading on an exchange when prices move by more than a predetermined amount to enable market participants to reflect and prevent panic buying or selling.

Clean Price

The quoted price of a bond. The clean price excludes accrued interest to be added or to be deducted, as appropriate.

Closed-Ended

Organisations such as companies which are a fixed size as determined by their share capital. Commonly used to distinguish investment trusts (closed-ended) from unit trusts and OEICs (open-ended).

Closing

Reversing an original position by, for example, selling what you have previously bought.

Commercial Paper (CP)

Money market instrument issued by large corporates.

Commission

Charges for acting as agent or broker.

Commodity

Items including sugar, wheat, oil and copper. Derivatives of commodities are traded on exchanges (eg, oil futures on ICE Futures).

Consumer Prices Index (CPI)

Index that measures the movement of prices faced by a typical consumer.

Contract

For derivatives, a contract is the minimum, standard unit of trading.

Convertible Bond

A bond which is convertible, usually at the investor's choice, into a certain number of the issuing company's shares.

Coupon

The regular amount of interest paid on a bond.

CREST

Electronic settlement system used to settle transactions for shares, gilts and corporate bonds, particularly on behalf of the London Stock Exchange.

Cum-Dividend

The way a financial instrument is described when the buyer will be entitled to the next dividend (on a share) or coupon (on a bond).

Debt Management Office (DMO)

Agency responsible for issuing gilts on behalf of the UK Treasury.

Dematerialised

System where securities are held electronically without certificates.

Derivatives

Instruments where the price or value is derived from another underlying asset. Examples include options, futures and swaps.

Dirty Price

The price of a bond inclusive of accrued interest or exclusive of interest to be deducted, as appropriate.

Diversification

Investment strategy that involves spreading risk by investing in a range of investments.

Dividend

Distribution of profits by a company to shareholders.

Dividend yield

Most recent dividend as a percentage of current share price.

Dow Jones Industrial Average (DJIA)

Major share index in the USA, based on the prices of 30 major US listed company shares.

Equities

Another name for shares.

The European Securities and Markets Authority (ESMA)

European Union financial regulatory institution and European Supervisory Authority located in Paris.

Eurobond

An interest-bearing security issued internationally. More strictly a eurobond is an international bond issue denominated in a currency different from that of the financial centre(s) in which the bonds are issued. Most eurobonds are issued in bearer form through bank syndicates.

Euronext

European stock exchange network formed by the merger of the Paris, Brussels, Amsterdam and Lisbon exchanges and which merged with the New York Stock Exchange to form NYSE Euronext. NYSE Euronext was subsequently acquired by the IntercontinentalExchange (ICE) Group.

Exchange

Marketplace for trading investments.

Exchange Rate

The rate at which one currency can be exchanged for another.

Ex-Dividend (xd)

The period during which the purchase of shares or bonds (on which a dividend or coupon payment has been declared) does not entitle the new holder to this next dividend or interest payment.

Exercise an Option

Take up the right to buy or sell the underlying asset in an option.

Exercise Price

The price at which the right conferred by a warrant or an option can be exercised by the holder against the writer.

Financial Conduct Authority (FCA)

One of the two regulators of the financial services sector in the UK.

Fiscal Years

These are the periods for reporting, alternatively referred to as financial years. The term is particularly used by the tax authorities for periods of assessment for tax purposes.

Fixed Interest Security

A tradeable negotiable instrument, issued by a borrower for a fixed term, during which a regular and predetermined fixed rate of interest based upon a nominal value is paid to the holder until it is redeemed and the principal is repaid.

Floating Rate Notes (FRNs)

Debt securities issued with a coupon periodically referenced to a benchmark interest rate such as Libor.

Forex

Abbreviation for foreign exchange.

Forward

A derivatives contract that creates a legally binding obligation between two parties for one to buy and the other to sell a pre-specified amount of an asset at a pre-specified price on a pre-specified future date. Forward contracts are commonly entered into in the foreign exchange market. As individually negotiated contracts, forwards are not traded on a derivatives exchange.

Forward Exchange Rate

An exchange rate set today, embodied in a forward contract, that will apply to a foreign exchange transaction at a pre-specified point in the future.

FTSE 100

Main UK share index of the 100 largest listed company shares measured by market capitalisation. Also referred to as the 'Footsie'.

FTSE All Share Index

Index comprising more than 90% of UK listed shares by value.

Fundamental Analysis

The calculation and interpretation of yields, ratios and discounted cash flows (DCFs) that seek to establish the intrinsic value of a security or the correct valuation of the broader market.

Fund Manager

Firm or person that makes investment decisions on behalf of clients.

Future

An agreement to buy or sell an item at a future date, at a price agreed today. Differs from a forward in that it is a standardised contract traded on an exchange.

Gilt-Edged Security (Gilt)

UK government bond.

Gross Domestic Product (GDP)

A measure of a country's output.

Gross Redemption Yield (GRY)

The annual compound return from holding a bond to maturity taking into account both interest payments and any capital gain or loss at maturity. Also referred to as the yield to maturity (YTM). The GRY or YTM is the internal rate of return on the bond based on its trading price.

Harmonised Index of Consumer Prices (HICP)

The way the consumer prices index in the EU was originally described.

Hedging

A technique employed to reduce the impact of adverse price movements on financial assets held.

Index (movement)

A single number that summarises the collective movement of certain variables at a point in time in relation to their average value on a base date or a single variable in relation to its base date value. For example, a stock market index such as the FTSE 100.

Index-Linked Gilts

Gilts whose principal and interest payments are linked to the retail prices index (RPI).

Inflation

A persistent increase in the general level of prices. Usually established by reference to consumer prices and the CPI.

Initial Public Offering (IPO)

A new issue of ordinary shares that sees the company gain a stock market listing for the first time, whether made by an offer for sale, an offer for subscription or a placing.

Insider Dealing/Trading

Criminal offence by people in possession of unpublished price-sensitive information from an inside source who deal, advise others to deal or pass the information on.

IntercontinentalExchange (ICE)

IntercontinentalExchange traditionally operated regulated global futures exchanges and over-the-counter (OTC) markets for agricultural, energy, equity index and currency contracts, as well as credit derivatives. It has recently acquired the NYSE Euronext group of exchanges that includes the traditional stock exchanges in New York (the NYSE), Paris, Brussels, Amsterdam and Lisbon, as well as the London-based derivatives exchange, Liffe.

Introduction

In the context of a listing or IPO, an introduction is a company applying for, and gaining a listing for, its securities on a stock market, without raising any funds.

Investment Bank

Firms that specialise in advising companies on M&A (mergers and acquisitions), and corporate finance matters such as raising debt and equity. The larger investment banks are also heavily involved in trading financial instruments.

Investment Company with Variable Capital (ICVC)

Alternative term for an OEIC.

Investment Trust

Despite the name, an investment trust is a company, not a trust, which invests in a diversified range of investments.

Limit Order

An order placed on a market (such as the London Stock Exchange's SETS system) which specifies the highest price it will pay (for a buy order) or the lowest price it will accept (for a sell order).

Liquidity

Ease with which an item can be traded on the market. Liquid markets are also described as 'deep'.

Liquidity Preference Theory

The proposition that investors have a natural preference for short-term investments and therefore demand a liquidity premium in the form of a higher return the longer the term of the investment.

Liquidity Risk

The risk that an item, such as a financial instrument, may be difficult to sell at a reasonable price.

Listing

Companies whose securities are listed are available to be traded on an exchange, such as the London Stock Exchange.

London Interbank Offered Rate (LIBOR)

Benchmark money market interest rates published for a number of different currencies over a range of periods. LIBOR, which is the rate at which funds in a particular currency and for a particular maturity, are available to one bank from other banks. LIBORs are gathered and published on a daily basis.

London Stock Exchange (LSE)

The main UK market for securities.

Long Position

The position following the purchase of a security or buying a derivative.

Market

All exchanges are markets – electronic or physical meeting places where assets are bought or sold.

Market Capitalisation

The total market value of a company's shares or other securities in issue. Market capitalisation is calculated by multiplying the number of shares or other securities a company has in issue by the market price of those shares or securities.

Market Maker

A stock exchange member firm registered to quote prices and trade shares throughout the trading day (such as the LSE's mandatory quote period).

Market Segmentation

The proposition that each bond market can be divided up into distinct segments based upon term to maturity, with each segment operating as if it is a separate bond market operating independently of interest rate expectations.

Maturity

Date when the principal on a bond is repaid.

Monetary Policy Committee (MPC)

Committee run by the Bank of England that sets UK interest rates.

Multilateral Trading Facilities (MTFs)

Systems that bring together multiple parties that are interested in buying and selling financial instruments including shares, bonds and derivatives.

NASDAQ

The second-largest stock exchange in the US. NASDAQ lists certain US and international stocks and provides a screen-based quote-driven secondary market that links buyers and sellers worldwide. NASDAQ tends to specialise in the shares of technology companies.

NASDAQ Composite

NASDAQ stock index.

Nikkei 225

The main Japanese share index.

Nominal Value

The amount on a bond that will be repaid on maturity. Also known as face or par value. Also applied to shares in some jurisdictions and representing the minimum that the shares are issued for.

Nominee

A nominee is the party holding legal ownership of securities, such as shares, on behalf of another beneficial owner.

NYSE Liffe

The UK's principal derivatives exchange for trading financial and soft commodity derivatives products. Owned by NYSE Euronext.

Offer Price

Bond and share prices are quoted as bid and offer. The offer is the higher of the two prices and is the one that would be paid by a buyer.

Open

Initiating a transaction, for example an opening purchase or sale of a future. Futures are normally reversed by a closing transaction at a later date.

Open-Ended

Type of investment, such as OEICs or unit trusts, which can expand without limit.

Open-Ended Investment Company (OEIC)

Collective investment vehicle similar to a unit trust. Alternatively described as an ICVC (investment company with variable capital).

Opening

Undertaking a transaction which creates an initial long or short position.

Option

A derivative giving the buyer the right, but not the obligation, to buy or sell an asset in the future.

Over-the-Counter (OTC) Derivatives

Derivatives that are not traded on a derivatives exchange.

Passive Management

In contrast to active management, passive management is an investment approach that does not aspire to create a return in excess of a benchmark index. The approach often involves tracking the benchmark index.

Pre-Emption Rights

The rights accorded to ordinary shareholders to subscribe for new ordinary shares issued by the company in proportion to their current shareholding.

Preference Share

Shares which usually pay fixed dividends but do not have voting rights. Preference shares have preference over ordinary shares in relation to the payment of dividends and in default situations.

Premium

An excess amount being paid, such as the excess paid for a convertible bond over the market value of the underlying shares it can be converted into. The term is also used for the amount of cash paid by the holder of an option or warrant to the writer in exchange for conferring a right.

Pricing Off

The term 'pricing off' simply means that the price or value of one thing, such as a corporate bond, is determined from the price or value of another, such as a government bond.

Primary Market

Also known as the new issues market, the primary market is where securities are issued for the first time, for example an IPO.

Prospectus

A detailed document about a company that is issuing securities. If it relates to an initial public offer, it will include all of the information to enable prospective investors to decide on the merit of the company's shares.

Proxy

Appointee who votes on a shareholder's behalf at company meetings.

Prudential Regulation Authority (PRA)

One of the two regulators of the financial services sector in the UK.

Quote-Driven

Dealing system driven by market makers quote buying and selling prices.

Real Estate Investment Trust (REIT)

An investment trust that specialises in investing in commercial property.

Redeemable Security

A security issued with a known maturity, or redemption, date.

Redemption

The repayment of principal to the holder of a redeemable security.

Registrar

The official who maintains the share register on behalf of a company.

Repo

The sale and repurchase of securities between two parties: both the sale and the repurchase agreement are made at the same time, with the purchase price and date fixed in advance.

Resolution

Proposal on which shareholders vote.

Retail Prices Index (RPI)

Index that measures the movement of prices faced by retail consumers in the UK.

Rights Issue

The issue of new ordinary shares to a company's shareholders in proportion to each shareholder's existing holding. The issue is made in accordance with the shareholders' pre-emptive rights and the new shares are usually offered at a discounted price to that prevailing in the market. This means that the rights have a value, and can be traded 'nil paid'.

RPIX

UK index that shows the underlying rate of inflation, excluding the impact of mortgage payments.

Scrip Issue

Another term for a bonus or capitalisation issue.

Secondary Market

Marketplace for trading in existing securities.

Share Buyback

The purchase and typically the cancellation by a company of a proportion of its ordinary shares.

Share Capital

The nominal value of a company's equity or ordinary shares. A company's authorised share capital is the nominal value of equity the company may issue, while the issued share capital is that which the company has issued. The term share capital is often extended to include a company's preference shares.

Share Split/Stock Split

A method by which a company can reduce the market price of its shares to make them more marketable without capitalising its reserves. A share split simply entails the company reducing the nominal value of each of its shares in issue while maintaining the overall nominal value of its share capital. A share split should have the same impact on a company's share price as a bonus issue.

Short Position

The position following the sale of a security not owned or selling a derivative.

Special Purpose Vehicle (SPV)

Bankruptcy remote, off balance sheet vehicle set up for a particular purpose such as buying assets from the originator and issuing asset-backed securities.

Special Resolution

Proposal put to shareholders requiring 75% of the votes cast in order to be accepted.

Spread

The difference between a buying (bid) and selling (ask or offer) price.

Stock Exchange Electronic Trading System (SETS)

The LSE's electronic order-driven trading system for the UK's largest listed companies.

Stock Exchange Electronic Trading System – Quotes and Crosses (SETSqx)

The LSE's electronic order-driven trading system for the UK's less liquid securities. A hybrid system combining order-driven trading with the potential for two-way quotes from market makers.

Super-Equivalence

The ability of member states in the European Union to exceed the requirements of an EU directive. An example is the UK retaining a 3% disclosure requirement when the EU Transparency Directive only requires disclosure at 5%.

Swap

An over-the-counter (OTC) derivative whereby two parties exchange a series of periodic payments based on a notional principal amount over an agreed term. Swaps can take a number of forms including interest rate swaps, currency swaps, credit default swaps and equity swaps.

T+2

The two-day rolling settlement period over which all equity deals executed on the London Stock Exchange's (LSE) SETS are settled.

Takeover

When one company buys more than 50% of the shares of another (UK).

Treasury Bills

Short-term (often three months) borrowings of the government. Issued at a discount to the nominal value at which they will mature. Traded in the money market.

Two-Way Price

Prices quoted by a market maker at which they are willing to buy (bid) and sell (offer).

Underlying

Asset from which a derivative is derived.

Undertakings for Collective Investments in Transferable Securities (UCITS) Directive

An EU directive originally introduced in 1985 but since revised to enable collective investment schemes (CISs) authorised in one EU member state to be freely marketed throughout the EU, subject to the marketing rules of the host state(s) and certain fund structure rules being complied with.

Underwriting

When financial institutions, such as banks, insurers and asset managers, agree to buy securities being issued (for example in an IPO) if demand is otherwise insufficient.

Unit Trust

A vehicle whereby money from investors is pooled together and invested collectively on their behalf. Unit trusts are open-ended vehicles.

Xetra Dax

German shares index, comprising 30 shares.

Yield

Income from an investment expressed as a percentage of the current price.

Yield Curve

The depiction of the relationship between the yields and the maturity of bonds of the same type.

Zero Coupon Bonds (ZCBs)

Bonds issued at a discount to their nominal value that do not pay a coupon but which are redeemed at par on a pre-specified future date.

ABS
Asset-Backed Security

ACD
Authorised Corporate Director

ADR
American Depositary Receipt

AESP
Automatic Execution Suspension Period

AGM
Annual General Meeting

AIM
Alternative Investment Market

ARCA
Archipelago Exchange (previously known as ArcaEx)

ATS
Alternative Trading System

AUT
Authorised Unit Trust

B2B
Business to Business

B2C
Business to Client

BBA
British Bankers' Association

BBT
Bloomberg Bond Trader

BIS
Bank for International Settlements

Bobl
Bundesobligationen

BoE
Bank of England

BoJ
Bank of Japan

BP
British Petroleum

BTAN
Bons du Trésor à Taux Fixe et à Intérêts Annuels

BTF
Bons du Trésor à Taux Fixe et à Intérêts Précomptés

CAC
Cotation Assistée en Continu

CAD
Cash Against Delivery

CBO
Collateralised Bond Obligation

CBOT
Chicago Board of Trade

CC
Competition Commission

CCP
Central Counterparty

CDS
Credit Default Swap

CET
Central European Time

CFD
Contract for Difference

CFTC
Commodity Futures Trading Commission

CGT
Capital Gains Tax

CHAPS
Clearing House Automated Payment System

CHF
Swiss Franc

CIS
Collective Investment Scheme

CLO
Collateralised Loan Obligation

CLS
Continuous Linked Settlement

CMB
Cash Management Bill

CME
Chicago Mercantile Exchange

CP
Commercial Paper

CPI
Consumer Prices Index

CSD
Central Securities Depository

DAX
Deutscher Aktien IndeX

DIS
Discount

DJIA
Dow Jones Industrial Average

DMO
Debt Management Office

DTCC
Depository Trust Clearing Corporation

DTR
Disclosure and Transparency Rules

DVP
Delivery Versus Payment

EAFE
Europe, Australasia and Far East

EBIT
Earnings Before Interest and Tax

EBITDA
Earnings Before Interest and Tax, Depreciation
and Amortisation

EC
European Commission

ECB
European Central Bank

ECN
Electronic Communication Network

EDGAR
Electronic Data Gathering And Retrieval System

EEA
European Economic Area

EGM
Extraordinary General Meeting

EMH
Efficient Markets Hypothesis

EMU
European Monetary Union

EPS
Earnings Per Share

ER
Expected Return

ERISA
Employee Retirement Income Security Act

ESMA
European Securities and Markets Authority

ETC
Exchange-Traded Commodity

ETF
Exchange-Traded Fund

ETP
Exchange-Traded Product

EU
European Union

EUR
Euro

EV
Enterprise Value

EVA
Economic Value Added

Fannie Mae
Federal National Mortgage Association

FCA
Financial Conduct Authority

FIFO
First In, First Out

Freddie Mac
Federal Home Loan Mortgage Corporation

FRS
Financial Reporting Standard

FSAP
Financial Services Action Plan

FSCS
Financial Services Compensation Scheme

FSMA
Financial Services and Markets Act

FTSE
Financial Times Stock Exchange

FX
Foreign Exchange

GAAP
Generally Accepted Accounting Principles

GBP
Great Britain Pound

GDP
Gross Domestic Product

GDR
Global Depositary Receipt

GE
General Electric

GEMM
Gilt-Edged Market Maker

Ginnie Mae
Government National Mortgage Association

GMAC
General Motors Acceptance Corporation

GMSLA
Global Master Securities Lending Agreement

GRY
Gross Redemption Yield

GSK
GlaxoSmithKline

GUI
Graphical User Interface

HFT
High Frequency Trading

HICP
Harmonised Index of Consumer Prices

HMRC
Her Majesty's Revenue & Customs

HSBC
Hong Kong and Shanghai Banking Corporation

IASB
International Accounting Standards Board

ICE
Intercontinental Exchange

ICMA
International Capital Market Association
(formally known as the International Securities
Market Association (ISMA))

ICVC
Investment Company with Variable Capital

IDB
Inter-Dealer Broker

IHT
Inheritance Tax

Inc
Incorporated

IOB
International Order Book

IOU
I Owe You

IPA
Individual Pension Account

IPO
Initial Public Offering

IRR
Internal Rate of Return

ISA
Individual Savings Account

ISDA
International Swaps and Derivatives Association

ITG
Investment Technology Group

IV
Intrinsic Value

JASDEC
Japan Securities Depository Centre

JGB
Japanese Government Bond

JPY
Japanese Yen

KFI
Key Features Information

LCH
London Clearing House

LIBOR
London Inter-Bank Offered Rate

LIFO
Last In, First Out

LLC
Limited Liability Company

LSE
London Stock Exchange

MBS
Mortgage-Backed Security

MiFID
Markets in Financial Instruments Directive

MPC
Monetary Policy Committee

MQP
Mandatory Quote Period

MQS
Minimum Quote Size

MSCI
Index provider once known as Morgan Stanley Capital International

MTF
Multilateral Trading Facility

MTN
Medium-Term Note

MTS
Message Transfer System

N/A
Not Applicable

NASDAQ
The US exchange that was once referred to as the National Association of Securities Dealers Automated Quotations

NAV
Net Asset Value

NBV
Net Book Value

NED
Non-Executive Director

NFP
Non-Farms Payroll

NMPI
Non-Mainstream Pooled Investment

NMS
Normal Market Size

NPV
Net Present Value

NRV
Net Realisable Value

NRY
Net Redemption Yield

NS&I
National Savings & Investment

NYMEX
New York Mercantile Exchange

NYSE
New York Stock Exchange

OAT
Obligations Assimilables du Trésor

OEIC
Open-Ended Investment Company

OFT
Office of Fair Trading

ONS
Office for National Statistics

OTC
Over-the-Counter

P&L
Profit and Loss

PAT
Profit After Tax

PAYE
Pay As You Earn

PBIT
Profit Before Interest and Tax

PD
Prospectus Directive

P/E
Price/Earnings Ratio

PEG
Price Earnings to Growth

PEP
Personal Equity Plan

PIK
Payment In Kind notes

PIP
Primary Information Provider

POTAM/PTM
Panel On Takeovers And Mergers

PPI
Producer Prices Index

PPP
Purchasing Power Parity

PR
Public Relations

PRA
Prudential Regulation Authority

PSBR
Public Sector Borrowing Requirement

PSNCR
Public Sector Net Cash Requirement

PVP
Payment Versus Payment

PwC
PricewaterhouseCoopers

QI
Qualified Investor

RCH
Recognised Clearing House

REIT
Real Estate Investment Trust

RFQ
Request for Quote

RIE
Recognised Investment Exchange

RIS
Regulatory Information Service (the old name for a Primary Information Provider (PIP))

RNS
Regulatory News Service

ROCE
Return On Capital Employed

RPI
Retail Prices Index

RPIX
RPI, excluding mortgage interest payments

RPIY

RPI, excluding mortgage interest payments and indirect taxes

RUR

Register Update Request

Sallie Mae

Student Loan Marketing Association

S&P

Standard & Poor's

SAR

Substantial Acquisition Rule

SBLI

Stock Borrowing and Lending Intermediary

SDRT

Stamp Duty Reserve Tax

SEAQ

Stock Exchange Automated Quotation system

SEC

Securities and Exchange Commission

SEDOL

Stock Exchange Daily Official List

SETS

Stock Exchange Electronic Trading Service

SETSqx

Stock Exchange Electronic Trading Service quotes and crosses

SIP

Secondary Information Provider

SIPP

Self-Invested Personal Pension Scheme

SIV

Structured Investment Vehicle

SME

Small and Medium (Sized) Enterprises

SPIVA

Standard & Poor's Index Versus Active

SPV

Special Purpose Vehicle

SR

Scenario Return

SRO

Self Regulating Organisation

SSAP

Statement of Standard Accounting Practice

STP

Straight-Through Processing

STRIPS

Separate Trading of Registered Interest and Principal of Securities

SV

Scenario Variance

T

Treasury (as in T-bonds, T-bills, T-notes)

TARGET

Trans-European Automated Real-time Gross Settlement Express Transfer

TIPS

Treasury Inflation Protected Securities

TSE

Tokyo Stock Exchange

TTM

Trailing Twelve Month

TV

Time Value

UBS

Union Bank of Switzerland

UCIS

Unregulated Collective Investment Scheme

UCITS

Undertaking for Collective Investment in Transferable Securities

UKLA

United Kingdom Listing Authority

USD

United States Dollar

VWAP

Volume Weighted Average Price

WACC

Weighted Average Cost of Capital

WHT

Withholding Tax

YTM

Yield to Maturity

ZCB

Zero Coupon Bond

Syllabus Learning Map

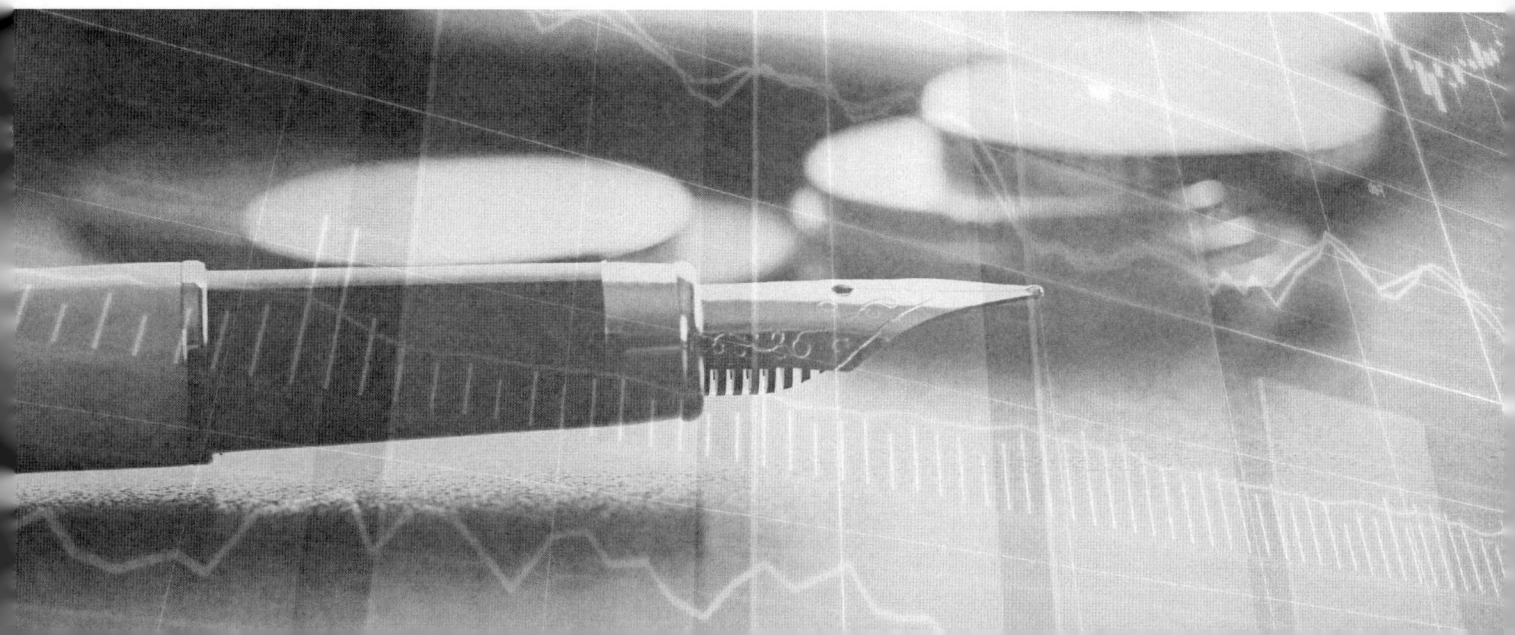

Syllabus Unit/ Element		Chapter/ Section
Element 1	**Asset Classes**	**Chapter 1**
1.1	**Shares** On completion, the candidate should:	
1.1.1	know the principal features and characteristics of ordinary shares and non-voting shares: • 'A' ordinary shares • redeemable shares • partly paid shares and calls • ranking for dividends • ranking in a liquidation • voting rights • purpose of non-voting shares	1
1.1.2	understand the differences and principal characteristics of the following classes of preference shares: • cumulative • participating • redeemable • convertible	1.2
1.1.3	understand the purpose and use of dividends from the point of view of the investor and the treatment of the tax credit	1.3
1.1.4	understand how different indices are created and their purpose: • types of index • purpose of weighted indices • purpose of unweighted indices • sector versus national indices • price return, total return and net total return indices	1.4
1.1.5	know the implications of free-float on market capitalisation	1.5
1.2	**Debt Instruments** On completion, the candidate should:	
1.2.1	know the principal features and characteristics of debt instruments	2
1.2.2	• understand the uses and limitations of the following: • flat yield • gross redemption yield (using internal rate of return) • net redemption yield • modified duration in the calculation of price change	2.2
1.2.3	be able to calculate: • simple interest income on corporate debt • conversion premiums on convertible bonds • flat yield • accrued interest (given details of the day count conventions)	2.3

Syllabus Unit/ Element		Chapter/ Section

1.2.4	understand the concept of spreads:
	• be able to convert spread over a government benchmark to a LIBOR-based spread:
	   ○ spread over government bond benchmark
	   ○ spread over/under LIBOR
	   ○ spread over/under swap
		2.4

1.2.5	understand the role of the yield curve and the relationship between price and yield with reference to the yield curve (normal and inverted)	2.5
1.2.6	be able to calculate the present value of a bond (maximum two years) with annual coupon and interest income	2.6
1.3	**Government Debt** On completion, the candidate should:	
1.3.1	know the principal features and characteristics of the following classes of government debt: • short-, medium-, long-dated • dual-dated • undated	3.1
1.3.2	understand the following features and characteristics of government debt: • redemption price • interest payable • accrued interest • effect of changes in interest rates	3.2
1.3.3	understand the following features and characteristics of index-linked debt: • inflation – effects and measurement – RPI and CPI • index-linking • effect of the index on price, interest and redemption • return during a period of zero inflation	3.3
1.3.4	know the basic purpose and characteristics of the strip market: • result of stripping a bond • zero coupon securities	3.4
1.3.5	know the features and characteristics of French, German, Japanese and US bonds: • settlement periods • coupons • terms and maturities	3.5
1.4	**Corporate Debt** On completion, the candidate should:	
1.4.1	understand the principal features and uses of secured debt: • fixed charges and floating charges • asset-backed securities • mortgage-backed securities • covered bonds • securitisation process • role of the trustee	4.1

Syllabus Unit/ Element		Chapter/ Section
1.4.2	understand the principal features and uses of unsecured debt: • subordinated • guaranteed • convertible bonds	4.2
1.4.3	understand the principal features and uses of credit ratings: • rating agencies • impact on price • uses and risks of credit enhancements • difference between investment grade and sub-investment grade bonds	4.4
1.4.4	understand the seniority of debt and how they rank in default: • senior • subordinated • mezzanine • payment in kind notes (PIK)	4.3
1.4.5	know the principal features and uses of commercial paper: • issuers, including CP programmes • investors • discount security • unsecured • asset-backed • rating • normal life • method of issuance • role of dealer	4.5
1.5	**Money Markets** On completion, the candidate should:	
1.5.1	understand the features and characteristics of Treasury bills: • issuer • purpose of issue • minimum denomination • normal life • no coupon and redemption at par	5.1
1.5.2	understand the basic purpose and characteristics of the repo markets: • repo • reverse repo • documentation • benefits of the repo market	5.2

Syllabus Unit/ Element		Chapter/ Section
1.6	**Eurobonds** On completion, the candidate should:	
1.6.1	understand the principal features and uses of eurobonds: • issued through syndicates of international banks • bearer • immobilised in depositories • accrued interest • ex-interest date • interest payments	6
1.7	**Other Securities** On completion, the candidate should:	
1.7.1	know the principal features and characteristics of Depositary Receipts: • American depositary receipts • global depositary receipts • means of creation including pre-release facility • registration • rights attached • dividends • transfer to underlying shares	7.1
1.7.2	know the rights, uses and differences between warrants and covered warrants: • benefit to the issuing company and purpose • issuer • right to subscribe for capital • effect on price of maturity and the underlying security • detachability • exercise and expiry • the calculation of the conversion premium (discount) on a warrant (warrant price + exercise price minus the share price)	7.2
1.8	**Foreign Exchange** On completion, the candidate should:	
1.8.1	know the principal features and uses of spot, forward and cross rates: • quotation as bid-offer spreads • forwards quoted as bid-offer margins against the spot • quotation of cross rates	8.1
1.8.2	be able to calculate spot and forward settlement prices using: • adding or subtracting forward adjustments • interest rate parity	8.2
1.8.3	understand the factors that affect foreign exchange rates	8.3

Syllabus Unit/ Element		Chapter/ Section
1.9	**Prime Brokerage and Equity Finance** On completion, the candidate should:	
1.9.1	know the main services provided by an equity and fixed Income prime broker, including: • securities lending and borrowing • leverage trade execution • cash management • core settlement • custody • rehypothecation	9.1
1.9.2	know the use of the main sources of equity and fixed income financing: • stock borrowing and lending • repurchase agreements • collateralised borrowing • tri-party repos • synthetic financing	9.2
1.9.3	know the uses of, requirements and implications of stock lending: • what is stock lending • purpose for the borrower • purpose for the lender • function of market makers and stock borrowing and lending intermediaries • effect on the lender's rights • lender retains the right to sell • collateral	9.3
1.10	**Collective Investments** On completion, the candidate should:	
1.10.1	know the key features, risks, charges, valuation and yield characteristics of unit trusts and OEICs/ICVCs	10
1.10.2	know the key features, risks, charges, valuation and yield characteristics of investment trusts	10
1.10.3	know the key features, risks, charges, valuation and yield characteristics of the main types of exchange-traded products	10
1.10.4	know the key features, risks, charges, valuation and yield characteristics of the main types of non-mainstream pooled investments (including UCIS)	10

Syllabus Unit/ Element		Chapter/ Section
Element 2	**The Primary and Secondary Markets**	**Chapter 2**
2.1	**Principal Characteristics** On completion, the candidate should:	
2.1.1	know the principal characteristics of, and the differences between, the primary and secondary markets. In particular: • the role of the listing authority • users of the primary market • users of the secondary market • uses of primary and secondary markets	1
2.2	**Trading Venues** On completion, the candidate should:	
2.2.1	understand the purpose, role and main features of stock exchanges. In particular: • scope • provision of liquidity • price formation • brokers versus dealers	2
2.2.2	understand the purpose, role and main features of alternative trading venues: • off-exchange trades • dark pools • OTC • private transactions • multilateral trading facilities	2
2.3	**London Stock Exchange** On completion, the candidate should:	
2.3.1	• know the regulatory framework for the LSE: • Companies Act • FCA • Exchange Rule Book	3
2.3.2	know the admissions criteria for listing: • trading record • amount raised • percentage in public hands • market capitalisation	3.1
2.4	**AIM** On completion, the candidate should:	
2.4.1	know the admissions criteria: • appointment and role of a nominated advisor • appointment and role of a broker • transferability of shares • no minimum shares in public hands • no trading record required • no shareholder approval needed • no minimum market capitalisation	3.1

Syllabus Unit/ Element		Chapter/ Section
2.4.2	know the regulatory framework for AIM: • London Stock Exchange • AIM Rules • Companies Act • FCA	3.1
2.5	**Methods of Trading and Participants** On completion, the candidate should:	
2.5.1	understand the differences between quote-driven and order-driven markets and how they operate	4.1
2.5.2	know the functions and obligations of: • market makers • broker-dealers • inter-dealer brokers	4.2
2.5.3	understand high frequency trading: • reasons • consequences for the market (eg, flash crashes) • types of company that pursue this strategy	4.3
2.6	**Government Bonds** On completion, the candidate should:	
2.6.1	understand the basic characteristics and purpose of government bond markets in the UK, US, Japan, France and Germany: • ratings and the concept of 'risk free' • currency, credit and inflation risks • inflation indexed bonds	5
2.7	**Corporate Bond Markets** On completion, the candidate should:	
2.7.1	understand the characteristics of corporate bond markets: • decentralised dealer markets and dealer provision of liquidity • the impact of default risk on prices • the differences between bond and equity markets • dealers rather than market makers • bond pools of liquidity versus centralised equity exchange • relevance of the retail bond market	6.1

Element 3	Dealing	Chapter 3
3.1	**London Stock Exchange (LSE) – UK Equity** On completion, the candidate should:	
3.1.1	understand the rules, procedures and requirements applying to dealing through the Stock Exchange Electronic Trading System (SETS) in the following areas: • order book features • order management • limitations and benefits of trading through SETS	1.1

Syllabus Unit/ Element		Chapter/ Section
3.1.2	understand the following order types and their differences: • market • limit • fill or kill • execute and eliminate • iceberg • multiple fills	1.2
3.1.3	understand the operation and purpose of the LSE's central counterparty: • LCH.Clearnet Limited • x-clear • benefits and limitations	1.3
3.1.4	know the LSE's right to call for a halt in trading in any listed security: • for any reason • length of trading halt	1.4
3.1.5	know the features and requirements of SETSqx dealing: • SETSqx as a hybrid trading system • relative illiquidity • securities covered • normal market size (NMS) • minimum number of market makers	1.5
3.2	**London Stock Exchange International Equity Market** On completion, the candidate should:	
3.2.1	understand the rules, procedures and requirements applying to dealing through the International Order Book (IOB) in the following areas: • securities covered • minimum and maximum trading sizes • who can access the IOB	2.1
3.3	**Other Equity Markets** On completion, the candidate should:	
3.3.1	Know how trading on the NYSE compares with trading on the LSE	3.1
3.4	**Government Bonds** On completion, the candidate should:	
3.4.1	know the functions, obligations and benefits of the following in relation to government bonds with respect to the UK, US, Japan, France and Germany: • primary dealers • broker-dealers • inter-dealer brokers • government issuing authority such as the UK Debt Management Office	4

Syllabus Unit/ Element		Chapter/ Section
3.5	**Dealing Methods** On completion, the candidate should:	
3.5.1	know the different trading methods for bonds: • OTC inter-dealer voice trading • inter-dealer electronic market • OTC customer to dealer voice trading • customer to dealer electronic market • on-exchange trading	5.1
3.5.2	understand the different trends between trading methods: • characteristics of electronic trading • OTC • exchange-traded • price driven via inter-dealer brokers (IDBs) – dealer to dealer • request for quote (RFQ) – customer to dealer	5.2
3.5.3	know the factors that influence bond pricing: • issuer factors • yield to maturity • seniority • structure • technical factors • credit rating • market factors • benchmark bonds • liquidity premiums for highly traded bond issues • indicative pricing versus firm two-way quotes • availability of a liquid repo market and the difficulty in offering illiquid bonds • inability to borrow or cover shorts	5.3
3.5.4	know the different quotation methods (ie, yield, spread, price) and the circumstances in which they are used	5.4
3.5.5	understand the basic mechanisms by which bond prices are driven by bond future prices	5.5

Element 4	Offers and Capital Adjustments	Chapter 4
4.1	**Participants Involved** On completion, the candidate should:	
4.1.1	understand the role of the syndicate group: • different roles within a syndicate • bookrunner • co-lead • co-manager • marketing and bookbuilding	1.2
4.1.2	know the role of advisors: • listing agent • corporate broker	1.1

Syllabus Unit/ Element		Chapter/ Section
4.1.3	know the issuer's obligations: • corporate governance • reporting	1.1
4.1.4	understand the purpose and practice of underwriting, rights and responsibilities of the underwriter: • benefits to the issuing company • risks and rewards to the underwriter	1.3
4.1.5	understand stabilisation and its purpose: • governing principles and regulation with regard to stabilisation activity • who is involved in stabilisation • what does stabilisation achieve • benefits to the issuing company and investors	1.4
4.2	**Types of Offer** On completion, the candidate should:	
4.2.1	understand the use of an initial public offering: • why would a company choose an IPO • structure of IPO – base deal plus greenshoe • stages of an IPO • underwritten versus best efforts	1.5
4.2.2	understand the use of follow-on offerings: • why would a company choose a follow-on offering • structure of follow-on – base deal plus greenshoe • stages of follow-on offering • underwritten versus best efforts	1.6
4.2.3	understand the use of open offers and offers for subscription: • why would a company choose an open offer • structure of offer • stages of offer • tenders, strike price, who is involved in the offer process	1.7
4.2.4	understand the use of offers for sale: • why would a company choose an offer for sale • structure of an offer for sale • stages of an offer for sale • tenders, strike price, who may receive an allotment, who is involved in the offer process	1.8
4.2.5	understand the basic process and uses of selective marketing and placing: • advantages to the issuing company • what is a placing • what is selective marketing • how is a placing achieved • how is selective marketing achieved	1.9

Syllabus Unit/ Element		Chapter/ Section
4.2.6	understand the use of introductions: • why would a company undertake an introduction • structure of an introduction • stages of an introduction	1.10
4.2.7	understand the use of exchangeable/convertible bond offerings: • the difference between exchangeable and convertible bonds • structure of offering – base deal plus greenshoe • stages of offering • underwritten versus best efforts	1.11
4.3	**Bond Offerings** On completion, the candidate should:	
4.3.1	know the different types of issuer: • supranationals • governments • agency • municipal • corporate • financial institutions and special purpose vehicles	2.1
4.3.2	know the methods of issuance: • scheduled funding programmes and opportunistic issuance, eg, medium-term notes (MTN) • auction/tender • reverse inquiry (under MTN)	2.2
4.3.3	understand the role of the origination team including: • pitching • indicative bid • mandate announcement • credit rating • roadshow • listing • syndication	2.3
4.4	**Corporate Actions** On completion, the candidate should:	
4.4.1	understand the use of rights issues: • reasons for a rights issue • structure of rights issue • stages of rights issue • pre-emptive rights • trading nil paid	3.1
4.4.2	be able to calculate the impact of a rights issue on the share price	3.1.3
4.4.3	understand the use of scrip (also known as bonus or capitalisation) issues and why a company will undertake a scrip issue	3.2
4.4.4	be able to calculate the impact of a scrip issue on the share price	3.2.1

Syllabus Unit/ Element		Chapter/ Section
4.4.5	be able to calculate the maximum nil paid rights to be sold to take up the balance at nil cost	3.1.5
4.4.6	be able to calculate the value of nil paid rights	3.1.4
4.4.7	understand the difference between a stock split and a scrip issue	3.3
4.5	**Share Capital and Changes to Share Ownership** On completion, the candidate should:	
4.5.1	understand why share buybacks are undertaken: • governing regulation • resolution at AGM • limits on percentage of shares and price • use of company's own money • key aspects of share buybacks – criteria to comply with • different structures regarding block trades • accelerated bookbuild – best efforts basis • accelerated bookbuild – back stop price • bought deal	4.1
4.5.2	understand how and why stake building is used: • strategic versus acquisition • direct versus indirect • direct – outright purchase, ie, dawn raid • indirect – CFDs • disclosure thresholds, including mandatory takeover threshold	4.2

Element 5	Clearing and Settlement	Chapter 5
5.1	**Activities** On completion, the candidate should:	
5.1.1	understand the main stages of clearing and settlement	1

5.1.2	know the principal details of settlement in the UK, France, Germany, the US and Japan:
	• DVP
	• free delivery
	• potential for financial transaction taxes
	• trade confirmation
	• settlement periods
	• instruments settled
	• settlement systems:
	   ○ Euroclear UK & Ireland
	   ○ LCH.Clearnet
	   ○ Clearstream
	   ○ DTCC
	   ○ Jasdec
		1

Syllabus Unit/ Element		Chapter/ Section
5.1.3	know the concept of custody and the roles of the different types of custodian: • global • regional • local • sub-custodian	2
5.1.4	understand the implications of registered title: • registered title versus unregistered (bearer) • legal title • beneficial interest • voting rights • right to participate in corporate actions	3
5.1.5	understand the basics of designated and pooled nominee accounts and their uses, and the concept of corporate nominees: • designated nominee accounts • pooled nominee accounts • details in share register • function of corporate nominees • legal ownership • beneficial ownership • effect on shareholder rights of using a nominee	4
5.1.6	know which securities may be subject to UK stamp duty/SDRT and which transactions are exempt from UK stamp duty	5
5.1.7	understand the concepts, requirements, benefits and disadvantages of deals executed cum, ex, special cum and special ex: • timetable • effect of deals on the underlying right • effect on the share price before and after a dividend • the meaning of 'books closed', 'ex-div' and 'cum div', cum and ex-rights • effect of late registration • benefits that may be achieved • disadvantages/risks • when dealing is permitted	6
5.1.8	understand what continuous linked settlement (CLS) is and its purpose: • the settlement of currencies across time zones • receiving and matching instructions • advantages • how it reduces settlement risk	7

Syllabus Unit/ Element		Chapter/ Section
Element 6	**Special Regulatory Requirements**	**Chapter 6**
6.1	**Takeovers and Mergers** On completion, the candidate should:	
6.1.1	know the implications of the EU Takeover Directive: • that some countries continue with their own rules as minimum standards and that takeover rules vary between states • application to all EU companies trading on an EU regulated market • requirements for a designated supervisory authority and scope for shared supervision • general principles of the Directive (Art. 3) • consequences of a mandatory bid and different mandatory bid thresholds • publication of information on the bid (Articles 6 and 10)	1
6.1.2	know the legal nature and purpose of the UK Takeover Code (Section 2 of the Introduction): • the six General Principles • the definitions of: ○ 'acting in concert' ○ 'dealings' ○ 'interest in shares' ○ 'relevant securities'	2
6.2	**Disclosure of Interests** On completion, the candidate should:	
6.2.1	understand the principles behind disclosure of interest rules and why they are required	3.1
6.2.2	know the following disclosure of interest rules: • EU under the Transparency Directive: ○ the disclosure thresholds ○ to whom disclosure has to be made and within what time scale ○ differing implementation of the Transparency Directive across EEA countries • US Securities and Exchange Commission: ○ the disclosure thresholds ○ to whom disclosure has to be made and within what time scale • UK under the Companies Act 2006, Section 793, in relation to company investigations	3.2
6.3	**Transaction and Trade Reporting** On completion, the candidate should:	
6.3.1	understand the definition of a reportable transaction (FCA and LSE)	4.1

Syllabus Unit/ Element		Chapter/ Section
6.3.2	understand the role and purpose of reporting: • transaction • trade	4.2
6.3.3	know which party to a trade is responsible for reporting including trades carried out by overseas branches	4.3
6.3.4	know the reporting channels and systems	4.3

Element 7	Accounting Analysis	Chapter 7
7.1	**Basic principles** On completion, the candidate should:	
7.1.1	understand the purpose of financial statements	1.1
7.1.2	understand the requirements for companies and groups to prepare accounts in accordance with applicable accounting standards and the difficulties encountered when comparing companies using different standards: • accounting principles • International Financial Reporting Standards (IFRS) • International Accounting Standards (IAS) • UK GAAP	1.2
7.1.3	understand the differences between group accounts and company accounts and why companies are required to prepare group accounts. (Candidates should understand the concept of goodwill and minority interests but will not be required to calculate them.)	1.3
7.2	**Statements of Financial Position** On completion, the candidate should:	
7.2.1	know the purpose of the balance sheet, its format and main contents	2.1
7.2.2	understand the concept of depreciation and amortisation	2.3
7.2.3	understand the difference between authorised and issued share capital, capital reserves and revenue reserves	2.4
7.2.4	know how loans and indebtedness are included within a balance sheet	2.5
7.3	**Income Statement** On completion, the candidate should:	
7.3.1	know the purpose of the income statement, its format and main contents	3.1
7.3.2	understand the difference between capital and revenue expenditure	3.2
7.4	**Cash Flow Statement** On completion, the candidate should:	
7.4.1	know the purpose of the cash flow statement, its format as set out in IAS 7	4.1
7.4.2	understand the difference between profit and cash and their impact on the long-term future of the business	4.2
7.4.3	understand the purpose of free cash flow and the difference between enterprise cash flow and equity cash flow	4.3

Syllabus Unit/ Element		Chapter/ Section
7.5	**Financial Statements Analysis** On completion, the candidate should:	
7.5.1	understand the following key ratios: • profitability ratios (gross profit and operating profit margins) • return on capital employed	5.1
7.5.2	understand the following financial gearing ratios: • investors' debt to equity ratio • net debt to equity ratio • interest cover	5.2
7.5.3	understand the following investors' ratios: • earnings per share • diluted earnings per share • price earnings ratio (both historic and prospective) • enterprise value to EBIT • enterprise value to EBITDA • net dividend yield • net dividend cover	5.3
7.5.4	be able to calculate the following investors' ratios: • earnings per share • price earnings ratio (both historic and prospective) • net dividend yield • net dividend cover	5.4

Element 8	Risk and Reward	Chapter 8
8.1	**Investment Management** On completion, the candidate should:	
8.1.1	understand the risk and reward of investment in equities: • risk profile • effect of longer term • can offer income and capital appreciation	1.2
8.1.2	understand the risk and reward of investment in money market instruments: • risk profile • use as short-term investment	1.3
8.1.3	understand the risk/reward of investments in debt (fixed interest, floating rate and index linked): • compared to equities • effect of holding to maturity • can combine low risk and certain return • can provide a fixed income • inflation risk • interest rate risk • default risk	1.4

Syllabus Unit/ Element		Chapter/ Section
8.1.4	understand risk profile of investment in overseas shares and debt: • country risk • exchange rate risk	1.5
8.1.5	understand the risks facing the investor: • specific/unsystematic • market/systematic	1.6
8.1.6	understand how to optimise the risk/reward relationship through the use of: • correlation • diversification • use of different asset classes	1.7
8.1.7	know what are active and passive investment management methodologies and the advantages and disadvantages of each	2.2
8.1.8	know the role of hedging in the management of investment risk and how to achieve it: • futures • options • CFDs	1.8
8.2	**Institutional Investment Advice** On completion, the candidate should:	
8.2.1	know the differences between institutional client profiles including: • pension funds • life and general insurance funds • hedge funds • regulated mutual funds • banks	2.1
8.2.2	know the main sources of regulatory information and financial communications within UK equity: • PIPs • RNS • SIPs • Bloomberg • Reuters • analyst research • websites: FCA, PRA, LSE, EU (Europa, ESMA)	4.1
8.3	**Market Data** On completion, the candidate should:	
8.3.1	understand the relationship between inflation and interest rate expectations	3.1
8.3.2	understand how interest rates impact securities pricing	3.2

Examination Specification

Each examination paper is constructed from a specification that determines the weightings that will be given to each element. The specification is given below.

It is important to note that the numbers quoted may vary slightly from examination to examination as there is some flexibility to ensure that each examination has a consistent level of difficulty. However, the number of questions tested in each element should not change by more than plus or minus 2.

Element Number	Element	Questions
1	Asset Classes	28
2	Primary and Secondary Markets	10
3	Dealing	10
4	Offers and Capital Adjustments	19
5	Clearing and Settlement	6
6	Special Regulatory Requirements	6
7	Accounting Analysis	12
8	Risk and Reward	9
Total		**100**

CISI Associate (ACSI) Membership can work for you...

Studying for a CISI qualification is hard work and we're sure you're putting in plenty of hours, but don't lose sight of your goal!

This is just the first step in your career; there is much more to achieve!

The securities and investments industry attracts ambitious and driven individuals. You're probably one yourself and that's great, but on the other hand you're almost certainly surrounded by lots of other people with similar ambitions.

So how can you stay one step ahead during these uncertain times?

Entry Criteria:
Pass in either:
- Investment Operations Certificate (IOC), IFQ, ICWM, Capital Markets in, eg, Securities, Derivatives or Investment Management, Advanced Certificates; or
- one CISI Diploma/Masters in Wealth Management paper

Joining Fee: £25 or free if applying via prefilled application form   **Annual Subscription (pro rata):** £125

Using your new CISI qualification* to become an Associate (ACSI) member of the Chartered Institute for Securities & Investment could well be the next important career move you make this year, and help you maintain your competence.

Join our global network of over 40,000 financial services professionals and start enjoying both the professional and personal benefits that CISI membership offers. Once you become a member you can use the prestigious ACSI designation after your name and even work towards becoming personally chartered.

* ie, Investment Operations Certificate (IOC), IFQ, ICWM, Capital Markets

Benefits in Summary...
- Use of the CISI CPD Scheme
- Unlimited free CPD seminars, webcasts, podcasts and online training tools
- Highly recognised designatory letters
- Unlimited free attendance at CISI Professional Forums
- CISI publications including *S&I Review* and *Change – The Regulatory Update*
- 20% discount on all CISI conferences and training courses
- Invitation to CISI Annual Lecture
- Select Benefits – our exclusive personal benefits portfolio

The ACSI designation will provide you with access to a range of member benefits, including Professional Refresher where there are currently over 50 modules available on subjects including Behavioural Finance, Cybercrime and Conduct Risk. CISI TV is also available to members, allowing you to catch up on the latest CISI events, whilst earning valuable CPD hours.

Plus many other networking opportunities which could be invaluable for your career.

Professional Refresher

Self-testing elearning modules to refresh your knowledge, meet regulatory and firm requirements, and earn CPD hours.

Professional Refresher is a training solution to help you remain up-to-date with industry developments, maintain regulatory compliance and demonstrate continuing learning.

This popular online learning tool allows self-administered refresher testing on a variety of topics, including the latest regulatory changes.

There are currently over 50 modules available which address UK and international issues. Modules are reviewed by practitioners frequently and new topics are added to the suite on a regular basis.

Benefits to firms:
- Learning and tests can form part of business T&C programme
- Learning and tests kept up to date and accurate by the CISI
- Relevant and useful – devised by industry practitioners
- Access to individual results available as part of management overview facility, 'Super User'
- Records of staff training can be produced for internal use and external audits
- Cost-effective – no additional charge for CISI members
- Available to non-members

Benefits to individuals:
- Comprehensive selection of topics across industry sectors
- Modules are frequently reviewed and updated by industry experts
- New topics introduced regularly
- Free for members
- Successfully passed modules are recorded in your CPD log as Active Learning
- Counts as structured learning for RDR purposes
- On completion of a module, a certificate can be printed out for your own records

The full suite of Professional Refresher modules is free to CISI members or £150 for non-members. Modules are also available individually. To view a full list of Professional Refresher modules visit:

cisi.org/refresher

If you or your firm would like to find out more contact our Client Relationship Management team:
+ 44 20 7645 0670
crm@cisi.org

For more information on our elearning products, contact our Customer Support Centre on +44 20 7645 0777, or visit our website at cisi.org/study

Feedback to the CISI

Have you found this workbook to be a valuable aid to your studies? We would like your views, so please email us at learningresources@cisi.org with any thoughts, ideas or comments.

Accredited Training Providers

Support for examination students studying for the Chartered Institute for Securities & Investment (CISI) Qualifications is provided by several Accredited Training Providers (ATPs), including Fitch Learning and BPP. The CISI's ATPs offer a range of face-to-face training courses, distance learning programmes, their own learning resources and study packs which have been accredited by the CISI. The CISI works in close collaboration with its ATPs to ensure they are kept informed of changes to CISI examinations so they can build them into their own courses and study packs.

CISI Workbook Specialists Wanted

Workbook Authors

Experienced freelance authors with finance experience, and who have published work in their area of specialism, are sought. Responsibilities include:

- Updating workbooks in line with new syllabuses and any industry developments
- Ensuring that the syllabus is fully covered

Workbook Reviewers

Individuals with a high-level knowledge of the subject area are sought. Responsibilities include:

- Highlighting any inconsistencies against the syllabus
- Assessing the author's interpretation of the workbook

Workbook Technical Reviewers

Technical reviewers provide a detailed review of the workbook and bring the review comments to the panel. Responsibilities include:

- Cross-checking the workbook against the syllabus
- Ensuring sufficient coverage of each learning objective

Workbook Proofreaders

Proofreaders are needed to proof workbooks both grammatically and also in terms of the format and layout. Responsibilities include:

- Checking for spelling and grammar mistakes
- Checking for formatting inconsistencies

If you are interested in becoming a CISI external specialist call:
+44 20 7645 0609

or email:
iain.worman@cisi.org

For bookings, orders, membership and general enquiries please contact our Customer Support Centre on +44 20 7645 0777, or visit our website at cisi.org